AMERICA'S PUBLIC SCHOOLS IN TRANSITION

Future Trends and Issues

AMERICA'S PUBLIC SCHOOLS IN TRANSITION

Future Trends and Issues

T. M. STINNETT
Texas A. & M. University

KENNETH T. HENSON
Delta State University

Teachers College, Columbia University
New York and London, 1982

Published by Teachers College Press, 1234 Amsterdam
Avenue, New York, N.Y. 10027

Library of Congress Cataloging in Publication Data

Stinnett, T. M.
America's public schools in transition.

Bibliography: p.
Includes index.
1. Public schools—United States—History.
I. Henson, Kenneth T. II. Title.
LA212.S77   371′.01′0973   82-740
ISBN 0-8077-2684-2   AACR2

Manufactured in the United States of America

87 86 85 84 83 82 1 2 3 4 5 6

Contents

Acronyms

THIS is an alphabetical listing of educational organizations, associations, and agencies to which frequent references are made herein. These abbreviations are widely used in publications about education.

AACTE   American Association of Colleges for Teacher Education
AAHE   / American Association for Higher Education
AASA   American Association of School Administrators
AAU   Association of American Universities
AAUP   American Association of University Professors
ACE   American Council on Education
ACLS   American Council of Learned Societies
ACLU   American Civil Liberties Union
ACT   Association of Classroom Teachers (successor, in 1967, to
           DCI—Department of Classroom Teachers, NEA)
ADEA   Age Discrimination in Employment Act
AERA   American Educational Research Association
AFT   American Federation of Teachers
CCSSO   Council of Chief State School Officers (variously titled
           State Commissioners or State Superintendents of Education)
DOD   U.S. Department of Defense
EEOC   Equal Employment Opportunity Commission
FTA   Future Teachers of America
NAESP   National Association of Elementary School Principals
NASDTEC   National Association of State Directors of Teacher Education and Certification
NASSP   National Association of Secondary School Principals

NCA	National Commission on Accrediting
NCATE	National Council for Accreditation of Teacher Education
NCPT	National Council of Parents and Teachers
NCTEPS	National Commission on Teacher Education and Professional Standards
NEA	National Education Association
NRTA	National Retired Teachers Association
NSBA	National School Boards Association
PR&R	National Commission on Professional Rights and Responsibilities
RIF	Reduction in Force (usually in teaching resulting from decreasing enrollments)
SNEA	Student National Education Association
USDE	United States Department of Education (created, 1979)
USOE	formerly United States Office of Education, a division of the Department of Health, Education and Welfare. Replaced in 1979 by U.S. Department of Education

Introduction

IN a democratic country such as the United States, there are recurring periods of expressed malcontent. Often during these periods criticism is aimed at the public schools. There appears to be no off season for these attacks on the tax-supported bulwarks of a democratic society. When public anxiety is aroused by war, threat of war, inflation, depression—whatever shocks people into action—discontent and fault-finding are almost certain to follow. All too often the first suspected cause of these social, economic, and political problems is the tax-supported public schools. Almost as a reflex action, the populace focuses on the schools as a *cause célèbre* of the current irritant.

This reflex action is not only predictable, but also legitimate. Why? *Because, in a democracy, the one unfailing sign of a vital, healthy climate is the public's vigorous desire to participate in criticism—and to give suggestions for reforms or refinements—of public agencies such as the schools.* Between such public outbursts there is relative peace and quiet on the school front. The harassment of teachers by outsiders gradually diminishes. This diminution of outside interference has resulted, to some extent, from efforts of the organized teaching profession. Teachers' organizations have financed appeals to the courts, especially in cases involving alleged mistreatment of teachers and violation of existing laws or constitutional provisions. Since the early 1940s the courts (especially the federal courts) have rendered many decisions in favor of teachers, in order to protect them from mistreatment.

This book deals with some broad aspects of the attacks upon schools and teachers. The first two parts address the historical development of the schools and the current rising tide of dissatisfaction with their performance. Such dissatisfaction results in increased attempts to blame teachers for the real and imagined failures of the schools.

In Part I we see vigorous complaints about the prevalence of violence and about the alleged lack of effective discipline in the schools. Part II deals with actual physical attacks on teachers, and with the growing verbal abuse they receive from parents and citizens in general. Harassment also occurs, often resulting in cruel dismissals of the teachers involved. In Part III needed reforms in the schools are outlined, along with efforts to make teaching a respected and accepted profession.

In seeking to develop a series of better tomorrows, the public schools—with their periodic setbacks, the recurring gloomy verdicts of their patrons, and their popularly judged failures—tend to repeat their troubles and defeats. But they are destined to rise again. The public schools and their teachers can indeed gather from the harvest of their years the ingredients for a better future.

UNITY AND DIVERSITY IN EDUCATION

While preparing this book, we developed a steadily growing concept of education. A certain educational concept which sprang up on the soil of America became ingrained in the minds and hearts of its pioneers and grew into a giant, indestructible faith in the latent powers of ordinary human beings. People who hungered for freedom and self-direction found the germs of both in their own daring and their own yearning for knowledge. Of course, there has been throughout history—at least since man learned to write—great disagreement as to what constitutes the form and content of "proper education." Formal education has always been designed to reflect the prevailing notion of the good life. Since people disagree on what the good life is, they always have and always will disagree about education.

Existing alongside the public schools there have been (and should continue to be) parallel systems of private schools. There are widely differing opinions about the relative values and the effectiveness of these two systems. In addition, further variations in philosophy and direction can be found in schools operating outside this major public/private duality. Directed and financed by relatively small segments of our society, they often differ in educational philosophy from the state- and church-affiliated schools. Since a truly democratic society must not merely allow, but actually defend the right to diversity, that society must support the right to widely varying viewpoints and convictions about education. While there will never be a time when our public schools enjoy universal public acceptance and support, they must always have the devotion and support of the majority if they are to be sustained.

The proponents of the public schools must be prepared to expect and to answer as best they can—with facts and evidence—periodic attacks on or dissent concerning their effectiveness. They must be prepared to analyze criticisms, evaluate them, and acknowledge and seek to correct weaknesses. *They must never seek to stifle such discussions, but must always welcome them—as unfair and intemperate as the critics may often appear to be.* Those charged with the direct operation of schools—board members, teachers, supervisors, administrators, custodians—must never assume their own infallibility, but must always aggressively seek public involvement in the schools' operations.

In this book we discuss the recurring criticisms of the schools, and the processes that enable the public to become involved in the actual determination of policies, directions, and the content of educational programs. It is easy—and tempting—to assume an artificial posture of democracy. Such a posture will not work.

AMERICA'S PUBLIC SCHOOLS IN TRANSITION
Future Trends and Issues

I

AMERICA'S BATTERED SCHOOLS

1

The Schools Are in Trouble

PERHAPS the first sentence in this book should read: "The public schools of the United States—as the first quarter of the third century of its existence as a free, independent, and democratic nation continues—are in crisis again." This time the crisis center is focused directly and vigorously upon the nation's schools. To be sure, this is not the first crisis that the schools have faced—and it won't be the last. But the directness and intensity of the anger and the vehemence of the attacks by the general public seem to exceed any of the preceding ones.

In fairness, it should be said that the schools have their faults. They are not the perfect instruments that their proponents often claim they are and that many, of course, believe they are. They will always tend to fall short of being the perfect instrumentality for furthering the hopes and dreams of a free nation. This is so because they are dealing with people of all nationalities and tongues and mores and mind sets and economic and religious convictions. But they have advanced far enough along the road toward greatness to warrant vigorous defense of their accomplishments, and most certainly of their promises. Thus it should be stated at the outset that those who are eagerly looking at the schools and are astounded that there is so much violence in them should be admonished *to hold up a mirror to our society and to our homes.* There are to be found the primary bases for violence in our schools. Lack of discipline, too, can be attributed in large part to our society and our homes.

THE PUBLIC'S ATTITUDE TOWARD THE SCHOOLS

The public's assessment of the schools' biggest problem, according to the Gallup Poll in 1980, was as follows: lack of discipline, 26 percent; use of

3

drugs, 14 percent; poor curriculum and poor standards, 11 percent; lack of financial support, 10 percent; integration/bussing combined, 10 percent; large school/too many classes/overcrowding, 7 percent; and difficulty in getting good teachers, 6 percent.[1]

When citizens were asked to choose from a list of fourteen items the four that they felt would most likely improve education, their responses were:

1. Secure well-educated teachers and principals   50%
2. Emphasize the basics such as reading and writing   49%
3. Teachers and principals develop a personal interest in progress of students   44%
4. Establish good parent/teacher relationships   40%

Some interesting highlights of recent polls are as follows. Only one-third of the respondents knew the name of their local school superintendent. Better communications are cited as vital between parents and their schools. Only one in eight respondents knew the annual per capita cost of education in their districts. When asked, "Would you like to have a child of yours take up teaching in the public schools as a career?" in 1975 75 percent said yes; in 1980 only 48 percent said yes.

We do not intend to review the steps that have brought the American people to be so critical about their schools. Rather, the emphases of this book will be upon the factors that have produced the controversies, and upon some possible and reasonable approaches to solutions for the chief problems. Like the schools themselves, the solutions will come not overnight, but gradually.

For example, read the following as a prime example not of violence, but of lawlessness that makes people skeptical of what society stands for.

WASTE AND THEFT AT THE FEDERAL LEVEL

For many years now, there have been rumors and complaints about waste, theft, chicanery, and alleged bribery in the federal government. Congres-

[1] George H. Gallup, "The Twelfth Annual Gallup Poll of the Public's Attitudes toward Public Schools," *Phi Delta Kappan* 62 (1980), 33–34.

sional bribery (under the guise of contributions to campaign funds) and other gimmicks are so well hidden that the agencies and officials designated to police such illegal activities seem scarcely ever able to uncover sufficient evidence against the individuals and groups involved in these activities. Clever government employees seem to escape punishment that ordinary citizens incur.

Here is a front-page dispatch which appeared in many American newspapers on March 16, 1979:

CONGRESS TOLD UP TO 10 PERCENT OF TAX DOLLAR WASTED, STOLEN

WASHINGTON (AP)—The Justice Department estimates as much as 10 percent of the tax dollar is wasted or stolen, Congress was told Thursday.

Deputy Attorney General Benjamin R. Civiletti told the Senate Budget Committee that the Justice Department guesses between $1 and $10 of every $100 in federal expenditures is lost to fraud and abuse. That would mean a loss of at least $5 billion and up to $50 billion this year.

Fraud and abuse in the handling of federal programs and money are so widespread they can be found "wherever we look deeply," said Civiletti, the nation's No. 2 law enforcement officer.

Comptroller General Elmer B. Staats, who heads the General Accounting Office, told the commitee it is doubtful anyone will ever be able to estimate with any precision the total cost of waste and theft in federal programs.

But, he added, because there are so many government programs, so many complexities, so many transactions and so many opportunities, "indications are that waste, fraud and abuse are of mammoth proportions."

Sen. Edmund S. Muskie, D-Maine, chairman of the Budget Committee, and Sen. Henry P. Bellmon of Oklahoma, its senior Republican, expressed fear that Americans will become so disgusted with waste and mismanagement of their tax dollars that it will undermine the nation's tradition of providing for those in need.

Muskie cited a recent poll which he said showed most of those surveyed think at least 48 cents of every federal dollar is wasted.

But Staats, Civiletti and Inspector General Thomas D. Morris of the Department of Health, Education and Welfare noted significant progress in the battle against fraud and waste.

Staats reported on the first six weeks of operations of the GAO's toll-free "hot line," 800-424-5454, which citizens have used to give 3,000 tips on government waste and theft.

Of the 2,401 tips that have been received in an initial screening, Staats said, 1,488 appear to require investigation or audit, including 957 allegations of wrongdoing.

Nearly 44 percent of the 957 allegations involve federal employees, with accusations ranging from outright stealing to cheating on time cards. He said 19 percent point to individual recipients of federal aid, such as welfare.

"The allegations of wrongdoing that were received to date involve the funds of every one of the 12 Cabinet departments of the federal government and involve activity in Washington, D.C., and 48 of the 50 states," Staats said. No complaints came from Vermont or Wyoming.

One report came from the mother of a cult member. She complained that several persons receiving government disability payments had outside income and were living in the same house "in a cult-like society." The cause of their disability: They all had been certified as schizophrenic by the same doctor.[2]

Anyone who has spent time in Washington, D.C., will be aware of the constant mention of "monkey business" in the federal bureaucracy. The gossip is often directed at the General Services Administration (GSA), the agency established by Congress to watch over the proper expenditures of federal funds, appropriations mainly to erect public buildings and to purchase supplies, and to approve bills for payment of supplies and services.

Almost everywhere one turns in the nation's capital, there are rumors and loud talk about contractors' increasing bills for construction above the contract price; likewise on supplies and other purchases. Somebody has to approve these changes. There, it appears, is where much of the "monkey business" takes place. The firm which has been awarded the contract simply, through kickbacks to people in key places in the federal agency, gets them to approve illegal increases in contracted prices. This outright bribery is obscured by the ordinarily respectable term "kickback." This thievery allegedly has gone on for years; it has become a nationally known scandal, yet neither the Congress nor all the powers of the federal government can seem to bring an end to such stealing.

But the vise is beginning to tighten in this scandalous situation. In

---

[2] Associated Press, "Fraud, Waste Draining 10 Percent of Tax Dollars," *Dallas Morning News*, Mar. 16, 1979, p. 1-A. Used by permission.

March, 1979, the newspapers carried a story of the resignation of Jay Solomon, head of the scandal-plagued General Services Administration. President Carter had asked Solomon to take over the agency in 1977 because of his high reputation. When he began searching into the causes of the rumors, he ran into roadblocks at every turn. Also, Solomon appeared to anger a powerful congressional leader when he fired the No. 2 man in GSA. This probably indicates the imbedded forces which are at the root of the kickbacks and frauds. The moment an official begins digging to find those who are receiving kickbacks and bribes, there are immediate moves to stop the exposure, by appealing to the people who are serving the interests of untouched representatives of firms and individuals who have been fattened by theft and fraud.

COMPLAINTS ABOUT SCHOOLS

The above-cited examples parallel the quarreling that has led to unnecessary complaints about the costs and weaknesses of the public schools.

The case examples described in this book show (1) the prevalence of violence in the public schools, violence that adversely affects the quality of teaching; and (2) the recurring mistreatment of teachers, through either illegal or arbitrary actions of school authorities (and often by thoughtless cruelties of local citizens). Certainly these problems must be remedied, or this country will be in real crisis.

It should be pointed out, of course, that any nation has two alternatives here. The first—and perhaps easiest—is to abandon a notion which from the incipiency of the United States appears to have been not only its crowning glory, but one of its major hopes for preeminence among the nations of the world. That notion involves earnest dedication to the proposition that all human beings are (or ought to be) born free, and that they can become relatively equal by the free access to education—to the extent that each can profit from it.

The second alternative is, of course, to seek continuing refinement of the purposes and procedures of the public schools.

How does the existence of violence in society and in individual homes contribute to the widespread public belief that somehow the schools are the cause of it all? This is like charging the news media—TV and newspapers—with being the cause of violence because they report so much of it. It is true, of course, that schools are central meeting places where there is inevitably an exchange of conversation about what has happened in the community. But the public seems to believe that the schools are to be blamed because students hear and see so much violent behavior. The schools are an easy and powerful target for the accusations that they are the cause of violence, rather than an instrument for correcting it.

How easily any citizen, whether a genius or a near illiterate, can dismiss or forget the supreme importance of an educated population to our kind of society! This is sometimes said more eloquently by indirection. A case in point is the message of a cartoon by John Tinney McCutcheon in the *Chicago Tribune* many years ago. The cartoon was captioned "Hardin County, Kentucky, October 12, 1809." It depicted two men, one on a horse, and the other sitting on the front porch of a country store. The man sitting on the porch said to the man on the horse: "Haven't seen you lately, squire." "No," said the man on the horse, "I've been down to Washington to see a feller named Madison inaugurated."

Then the man on the horse posed a question: "What's happening here?" "Nothing," replied the store owner, "just another baby at Tom Lincoln's cabin. Nothing ever happens here."

This is the usual appraisal of a newborn. Yet, in this case, it was made by the recognized sages of the community. Of course, the store-keeper could not know that the new baby (Abraham Lincoln) was destined to lead one of the most fruitful lives in all human history. Lincoln's birth was heralded as of little or no importance.

This off-the-cuff evaluation of the future value of a newborn is not unlike the appraisal of too many citizens of the potentials of free schools maintained at public expense.

Presently, from almost all quarters, there are lamentations that our public schools and their two-and-a-half-million teachers have lost much of their potential for bringing adequate knowledge—and, still more important, the truth—to the fifty million students of America. This perfectly natural reaction of many among the taxpaying public can, of course, be refuted in major part. But even the warmest friends of the public schools must admit that these schools have come upon troubled times, the causes of which are not simple. Nor are they easily identified or explained or corrected.

Some Causes of Violence

Take the matter of violence, which has hit the schools in unprecedented volume and fervor in recent years. How is this new phenomenon to be explained? Among the complex of the causes of violence are factors in society itself which the personnel of the schools—teachers and administrators—cannot control or effectively alleviate. This is an old, old assertion—so old, in fact, that the public tends to shrug it off as a patent effort of school employees to evade responsibility. Whatever amount of truth may be contained in the typical reaction of parents and taxpayers to this explanation, the factors are there for all to see. But the identities and ramifications of influences on the behavior of children are not readily evident. The recent charge, rapidly gathering momentum by the futurists, that the schools and their employees tend to cling to outmoded beliefs and practices, ignoring the kaledioscopic nature of things and conditions already here or to come rapidly, needs reappraisal.

The mixed influences of television and the movies are pretty generally known, especially by parents, and to a great extent by the general public. In the first place, children are spending a great many more hours looking at TV than they have spent or will spend in school. Thus, besides the actual (though more or less unintentional) lessening of time normally used for formal study, the typical child is increasing the time spent listening. Of course, they learn a great deal this way but, good or bad, much of what they learn may not stay with them very long. Unfortunately, many of the things that remain are what parents had rather they had not heard and seen in the first place. Also, naturally enough, children learn much that is definitely harmful, fixing in their minds certain ideas that are bound to be harmful as they grow older.

What seems to stick the longest and to have the most harmful effects is the range of things they see on TV that definitely constitute violence of varying shades. How much this picturing of violence affects adults we do not know precisely, though the effect must be considerable. And with children there seems to be little doubt that the effects are very great indeed.

This thing of violence on TV is a two-way street. First, TV writers and producers probably pick up a large percentage of the bases for scenes which appear on TV from actual incidents which have taken place somewhere in our society, and from newspaper accounts of crimes. Also from magazines or books designed to sell to a clientele that relishes a particular kind of sadism, or behavior that is frowned upon by society.

How much of the vice existing in our society, which any knowledgeable person knows is considerable, may actually find its repercussions in the schools? It is simply naive in the extreme to assume that witnessing beatings, murders, and severe injuries with the use of common weapons does not have profound effects upon children. Sadly, students learn to imitate what they have seen in what they do, if they are aggravated or crossed in school.

One scene comes to mind as an unanswerable case of mimicry which resulted in the death of an intelligent and wholly innocent teacher. That is the case of the Austin, Texas, teacher who was shot because (in all probability) the classmates of the boy doing the shooting took advantage of the regular teacher's absence one day to try to make this brilliant boy (his classmates dubbed him "The Brain") look bad before his peers. It appears certain that the substitute teacher quite innocently asked the young boy to act as chairman of a round-table discussion by the entire class. Seeing an opportunity to poke fun at "The Brain," his classmates humiliated him in every way possible. Nobody knows, but the evidence seems to indicate that this lad brooded over his humiliation, and probably arrived at the false conclusion that his regular teacher (of whom it was reported that he was very fond) was involved in all this. Without checking his conclusion in any way, he appeared in class the next morning with a rifle. Without a word, and with one shot, he snuffed out the life of his teacher.

Television as Part of the Problem

TV is still in its infancy, as seen in both its programming and in deliberately seeking materials that will have a lasting effect upon the viewing student. Warnings to parents about the possible ill effects some TV programs may have upon young children—aided by edicts from national regulatory agencies—have been generally helpful, but much yet must be done to change TV programs for the benefit of stimulating learning. For example, the following are listed for the guidance of parents in determining fit programs for their children to view: PG (parental guidance), R (restricted), X (pornographic), and G (general audiences). The truth is that we (and this includes teachers and schools) have not studied deeply enough the means by which TV can be used—and used effectively—as a powerful teaching device.

Doubtless, school people will begin now to search intently for constructive ways to use TV to advance learning. If all the current furor over the problem results in stimulating learning and perception, the effort will pay off by removing many of the barricades to real learning.

There is no point in talking about barring TV from the schools, or in prohibiting children viewing TV during out-of-school hours. Energy spent in such an endeavor will prove to be wasted. The truth is, in TV, teachers have in their hands a compellingly powerful learning instrument. We need, as professionals, to search out every possible way of improving the learning of the fundamentals. We will then have at hand, and in schools, the instruments with which to become powerful teachers, the influences of which will revolutionize many phases of education.

Are Teachers to Blame?

Of course, there is no way for American teachers to escape the widespread blame for violence in the schools.

With the precipitate rise in the national cost of education in the elementary and secondary grades, quite naturally, the beleaguered taxpayer is turning to those who guide and work in the schools and asking, "How come?" The answer that *everything* presently costs a great deal more than it did only a handful of years ago is, in the public mind, only begging the question.

A deeply interested and involved onlooker agonizes over this period, which is resulting in a major share of the blame being attributed to teachers. And, as far off as this charge may be, the taxpayer deserves logical answers to it. Simple denials will not suffice. Below, we shall attempt to specify some common charges with reasonable and sensible answers. (A fuller treatment of the causes of increased cost of schools will be found in Chapter 19.)

Commonly, superintendents (or more precisely administrators) are accused of being the major cause of the prevalence of discipline problems in the public schools. Example after example of such allegations is given herein. Does it necessarily follow, therefore, that administrators are the major cause of the alarming growth of such problems in recent years? Is this confirmed by the facts?

In a relatively few cases, yes. But in general, the answer is no. As a general situation, the causes are much more broadly based than this. It is true, of course, that some—perhaps most—administrators are quite concerned about suppressing the news of severe disciplinary cases, on the assumption that any discussion about this will inevitably cause the patrons to suspect that the administrator of a given school (or school system) is weak and a poor disciplinarian. Of course, this is a very human trait, but only a minor cause. Those with broad experience in this area contend that only a relatively small number of administrators are so timid. Where some administrators acquire this reputation is probably in their decisions about what tactic would prove to be best, in a given disciplinary situation, for the student involved and for the school system. Naturally there will be—and there ought to be—dissent about the wisdom of such a decision. Thus, the administrator tends to be blamed.

Only a small number of observations will tend to convince one that the majority of parents may, in a given case where discipline is prescribed for a child, agree that the child deserved disciplinary action, but disagree vehemently with whatever punishment is decided upon, contending that another type should have been prescribed.

One of the situations which sometimes arises is the case of a female teacher confronted by a tough male student who appears to threaten physical harm to her. When she appeals to the principal for help with the boy, she is sometimes told to go back to her room; if she weren't so weak a teacher, there wouldn't be such incidents in that particular room. This is probably a prime case of a weak principal who wants the responsibility to be placed on someone else. Of course, in a few cases, the teacher might well be weak. But even so, it does not excuse him for washing his hands of any disciplinary action, or for leaving the teacher in danger of physical assault by the student.

Much of the reported violence in the schools involves vagrants or outsiders who wander into a school to see what they can steal or what trouble they can cause. This is, of course, largely a problem in cities where there are many schools and many unemployed. To provide at least one security guard in a given school (or to combine such a job with the janitor's work) would be feasible in some situations, but not in all.

While it has been indicated that many competent observers believe that administrators are too often blamed for the lack of discipline in the schools, they could be indirectly indicted for failure to find and institute changes, such as hiring security guards, or reducing the per-teacher load to a manageable level. (For additional suggestions on this point, see Chapter 15.)

A TELEVISION EVALUATION OF THE PROBLEM

One of the notable efforts to reveal to the public the plight of the public schools as a result of spreading violence and the lack of strict discipline of pupils, discipline which in earlier days was considered an integral part of a good educational climate, was a three-part CBS program aired on August 22, 23, and 24, 1978, and entitled: "Is Anyone Out There Learning?" This TV special, featuring Walter Cronkite and Charles Collingwood, impressed many teachers as attempting to be constructive and fair, except for one or two mild instances. It seemed obvious that this CBS feature strained at making a fair and unbiased presentation of the problems. These observations were not made from listening to the telecasts only, but from recordings which, when transcribed, gave a word-for-word rendering of the report.

But this feeling was by no means universal among teachers. Here is one teacher's reaction:

> If ever there was a television program designed to get teachers to talking back to their TV sets, it is the three hour, CBS news report "Is Anyone Out There Learning? A Report Card on Public Education" . . . due to the shallowness of the investigation—the program's findings can be capsulized as follows: students can't read, write, or figure; they're being passed through school via inflated grades and social promotion; they are not inspired or treated with a firm hand, so they are violent, absent, or take dope. The implication is that these conditions exist more often than not.[3]

This special TV report concentrated upon what's wrong with the American public schools.

---

[3] Fay Ford, "CBS Gave Only a Shallow Analysis of School Problems," *Kentucky Education News*, Aug. 24, 1978, p. 2. Used by permission.

Parents want their children at least as well educated as they [the parents] are—and the cost of education has quadrupled in the last fifty years. Functional illiteracy among seventeen-year-olds is running at 13 percent or higher. Students are passed to the next grade because they are physically big, but not necessarily grown in intelligence or emotions or anything else. This is known as social promotion.

There is a grass-roots demand for minimal competency testing before a diploma is awarded. The public demand is for "Back to the Basics."[4]

Denver was used in this broadcast, it was stated at the outset, because it is educationally a typical city in the United States. It mirrors the national situation. The telecast continues:

There is a "white flight" to the suburbs—the white population is moving out of the city leaving a predominantly black city.

Grade inflation—students are being given better grades than they deserve.

Many teachers are concerned about the balance between exotic electives and basic courses. Too many soft electives are chosen by students to get out of harder basic courses.

Seventy-six percent of the people polled favor back to the basics, while 19 percent of the people say keep education the way it is.

Social promotion compounds problems for students later on. Eighty-three percent of the people polled oppose this, and 11 percent of the people are in favor of social promotion.

Why are my children at a lower reading-writing level than their grade levels indicate? Why didn't the schools tell me this earlier? These are questions that parents ask. American teenagers come out of schools as functional illiterates and can't perform in the tasks expected of them today. Forty-two percent of the black seventeen-year-olds are functional illiterates. This is three times the national norm. There is also a 30 percent absentee rate among blacks in the inner-city schools. Absenteeism is a big problem all across the nation. How do you force children to come to school? There is no answer to meet the needs of the student. If parents can't force children to go to school, then teachers can't.

Attacks on persons and things—teachers' jobs are getting harder because of discipline problems. Some 70,000 teachers per year are victims of physical abuse. Part of the problem of discipline in schools is

---

4 Abstracted from "Is Anyone Out There Learning?" CBS special aired on August 22, 23, and 24, 1978.

the widespread use of drugs. About 80 percent of the children entering high school smoke marijuana regularly. Public view is very critical —84 percent say discipline isn't strict enough.

Literacy for entering college students means that it is assumed that students have had certain experiences when they enter college. For example, they are familiar with names such as Shakespeare and others. If they don't have it, they are partially illiterate. Also, 15 percent of the seventeen-year-olds can't read or write well enough in the everyday world.

How did elective courses contribute to this? Too many ways are available for students to avoid harder basic courses by taking easy electives.

Absenteeism is the first step toward dropping out of school.

Discipline is the number one problem and varies with district, school, and teacher. . . .

Some critics say that teachers are the only ones at fault. They say they are less dedicated, they don't work as hard as they used to, they don't give out as many written assignments.

Teachers are overwhelmed by demands put on them by society and the school administration. Too many teachers themselves are badly educated. They say that no professional training can get them ready for the stresses they face in the classroom.[5]

There are newfangled supplementary products ranging from card games to cassettes. Sales of these have dropped off since 1975 as the "Back to Basics" cry has grown louder. These are substitutes for reading and writing. Kiddie calculators seem to take away from learning the basics.

If teachers are not as dedicated as they once were, it is because they are concerned over the violence that is prevalent today. Vandalism costs $600 million a year, which is enough to supply the whole nation's children with schoolbooks.

The family has changed, and society ignores permissiveness. These are some reasons why discipline is lacking. What causes disorder? One cause is broken families. Another is "white flight" from cities to suburbs, which makes blacks feel inferior and react violently. Some say that violence in the schools is caused by racial integration, but violence is present in white schools, too.

Some parents say that other parents are to blame. They cite apathy, preoccupation with job or self, an inability to cope with children, or the changing society as reasons why parents are not as effective as they once

---

[5] Ibid.

were. "You can't touch my child or I'll sue you," some parents tell schools. However, some parents don't give teachers the primary blame for discipline in school. Teachers are caught in the middle between administrators and parents. Teachers won't discipline kids unless they feel they'll get backing from the administration. Where does the buck stop?

USE OF TELEVISION IN THE SCHOOLS

TV is a major factor affecting the lives and ways that time is spent for most people. About 40 percent say that TV has a bad effect; 23 percent say it has a good effect; the rest have said that it has a mixed effect, no effect, or that they have no opinion. Kids with lower reading levels usually watch too much TV. The way to learn to read is to read and read and read. TV is a thief of time; it may be detrimental to the learning process. By the time most students graduate from high school, they will have spent more hours in front of a TV than they will have spent in class.

Friends School, a Quaker school in Pennsylvania, experimented and had their students go for a full week without watching television. Students talked about the event as adults would talk about a diet: "If I can get through this first day, I can get through the whole week." The students were asked to make a list of alternatives to watching TV. Some listed such things as cleaning house, reading, and sewing; all of these alternatives brought about more family interaction. Would this bring about a lasting effect even after the week was up?

Many teachers and psychologists say that TV has shortened the attention span of school-age children, and that children who watch less TV have longer attention spans. Others say the reverse. Makers of the show "Sesame Street" say that there have been no studies to prove that TV hurts kids.

Often school reflects what the community is facing. Lack of influence of the home is a serious problem. Suggested remedies: turn off TV occasionally and encourage completion of homework before turning it back on.

Parental intervention can be beneficial at school, as well as at home. In the Hunt Valley School, parents visit in the classes and help the teachers with whatever needs to be done. In one year a total of 467 parents served for more than 4,000 hours as assistants, averaging about 8.6 hours per parent. The parents aid in situations such as reading labs. The parent-student ratio approximates 1 : 3. In this school, it is reported that there is a two-month gain in reading competencies for every month spent there by parents, with 90 percent of the children performing at or above expected reading levels. Some parents also help out in the library, cafeteria, and maintenance of grounds. It is not an accident that so many parents volunteer their services in the Hunt Valley School. The parents realize that they are an integral part of education. To them, it is a challenge, interesting, and they become keen observers of what is going on in education. These parents contend that their experience can be applied to other schools.

Parents and Use of TV

To return to the TV problem, 28 percent of the parents with children in school regularly limit the time their children can look at TV, and 35 percent regularly set rules as to the kind of programs their children can view. However, most parents restrict the time of TV viewing only now and then, or not at all. Two-thirds of the parents feel that TV should be used in the classroom. Also, psychologists, educators, and TV producers say that TV is a positive force in education. In Oceanside, New York, the elementary schools have the children view "Cover to Cover." This show stimulates the children to learn by giving them a summary of the first part of a book, and then asking them to read the book to find out how the story ends. This and similar shows are put on public broadcasting stations throughout the nation during the school year, reaching some 15 million children. The results are to expand reading variety, change reading habits greatly, and stimulate children to want to read more.

In Denver, "Prime Time School TV" aids teachers in getting the maximum benefit for students from their TV viewing. Emphasis is given to special programs and documentaries. Also, the schools have a grant which allows them to experiment with using everyday TV materials as classroom materials, with the children taking notes and participating in class discussion. The benefit is that this helps children to watch in more depth and to analyze what they are watching. "TV Reading Program" uses regular commercials. Children who watch it get scripts of favorite entertainment shows. In Philadelphia, children who started the year reading below grade level despised reading and liked TV, but they soon changed. TV can provide vocabulary lessons by using vocabulary lists from the script.

Most people in education agree that TV can be a valuable teaching tool, but they feel that there is too much TV viewing outside school. Moderation is the key measure to the value of TV viewing outside school.

Denver has the Metropolitan Youth Center, started ten years ago. It is a school for kids who cannot make it in regular schools. The program concentrates on basic skills: reading, writing, math, and language. Students and teachers work together closely. Students get along with the teachers and others at the center. No one "hassles" them; there are loose rules, but not many discipline problems. On the other hand, the absentee rate can be one-half the enrollment; 1:17 is the teacher-student ratio, and that makes the program expensive—more than $1,000,000 a year. The alternative to education is expensive, but the lack of this alternative is even more expensive. Without it, students would be full-time losers, and society pays for their loss in one way or another. A total of 22,000 students have qualified for diplomas through this program. Alternative education programs are geared to turn on students who would otherwise be turned off. There is a bonus to this concept; a number of educators say that when a school begins to "click," the number of discipline problems is reduced.

Wingate High School (New York) had all factors to handle discipline problems and worse eight years ago. Police were stationed in the halls to control violence. Many students couldn't read or even speak English. When a new principal came, he tried to use a microphone in the beginning to rally the students for education and its importance; the students merely said that they were not behind him. He decided to reevaluate his methods. Things began to change little by little, starting with the curriculum. For instance, a flight training course was taught that was originally designed to interest "high risk" students. It incorporated math, science, reading skills, and aerodynamics. It was taught by a former Eastern Airlines pilot. The students starting out didn't possess these skills, but as they got interested they became very enthusiastic and eagerly absorbed hard-to-read manuals. Not all the training took place in the classroom. Once a week they would go to the airport and have a chance to do some actual flying.

That was only one change in the classes at Wingate. Teachers began looking for additional ways to make the courses more relevant. They experimented in cooperative planning involving teachers, supervisors, parents, and students. In the medical science institute, many classes are related to medicine (English classes, for example, involve reading about medicine); these also helped markedly in improving reading skills and rates.

Most of Wingate's classes are designed to motivate students. But many students needed more than motivation: many couldn't even read. A priority of the school was to teach the students to read and to speak English. (Many came from Haiti and spoke only French.)

Today the students in Wingate consist mainly of minority groups. Ten years ago there was much violence between native American blacks and students from Haiti. Today, on the surface at least, Wingate seems comparatively peaceful, although those problems have not entirely disappeared. Some say the discipline problem has solved itself because the students are now more interested in education. They treat the building as if it were their own home—graffiti is gone; vandalism has been greatly reduced. "No Smoking," however, is not entirely in effect.

The Haitians said, while this report was being made, that they wanted more language courses, especially at the higher academic levels. One Haitian (second in his class) plans to attend Yale University. The students commented that many, though not all, of the problems at the school have been cleared up. It has taken a combination of leadership, hard work, common sense, and cooperation.

Teachers say problems still exist, but that it's much better than it used to be. Adaptation of school curriculum to the community it serves could work almost everywhere. "How can we meet the needs of our students?" The students will learn because they want to learn, and because they *can* learn.

THE CITADEL OF THE SELECT

An article in *Time* magazine reflects a thesis set forth in this book, to the effect that the schools tend to be a mirror for what goes on in society. The article comments on a book entitled *Campus Shock*. The surprising thing about the book is that it purports to describe some of the things that go on, not in the much-berated public schools, but in our most prestigious colleges and universities. Indeed, the article says:

Here at last is the book for parents who have been bemused by the way their college-age children treat what was once regarded as academic arcadia, the U.S. Liberal Arts College, as if it were a cross between a snake pit and a marine boot camp. [The book] is a reporter's notebook of horrors—gleaned from 675 interviews in the eight Ivy League schools, plus the University of Michigan, the University of Chicago, Stanford, and Berkeley. . . .

As Lamont sees it, life . . . in the $7,000 a year Halls of Ivy was a round of rape and robbery and rising racial distrust, of crowding and cheating and grade grubbing and sexual anxiety and fear of future unemployment (for history and English majors particularly).

The causes: heavy enrollment due to greed plus the need to admit more women and blacks, sometimes led to tenement-like conditions in dorms.

"Taking a girl on is like taking a fifth subject," said a Harvard sophomore.

"Cheating is a way of life here," one Penn student told him. By 1976, only half the undergraduates at Stanford would say that they thought cheating was unjustifiable. In one year 4,500 books were stolen from the Berkeley library.

As a University of Chicago professor confided, "We lack the language to teach right and wrong."[6]

In this chapter we have sketched some of the major problems and criticisms of the public schools. What's to follow will seek to analyze these problems and suggest some possible approaches to new solutions.

---

[6] "Poisoned Ivy?" *Time,* July 2, 1979, p. 62. Copyright 1979 Time Inc. All rights reserved. Reprinted by permission from TIME.

2

Effects of Violence on the Schools

THE extent of violence in the United States has long been a puzzle to Americans, and especially to curious onlookers from other nations. The reaction among the latter tends to be one of puzzlement that could be characterized thus: "Why, in the richest nation on earth, would there be any reason for the use of so much violence? Here is a nation with a plentitude of everything for its population: where there is little or no starvation, because there is food enough not only to feed the people of the nation itself, but to help feed some other nations besides. Why should there be want of any kind?" Well, of course, such reasoning skips many points, such as private ownership—the food belongs not to the government, but to individuals who will sell it. The hungry, the unemployed, and the poor often are unable to buy.

Is it possible that violence in America is the surface reflection or manifestation of its deeply rooted social problems? And, instead of correcting our problems of unemployment, poor housing, lack of health care, and an often unjust legal system, could we be responding by increasing the penalties for offenders? Is this gross misplacement of corrective measures not evidenced by the fact that we have 465,000 people in protective custody while Japan, with half our population, has only 75,000 people in prison?[1] Is it ever logical to respond to violence with punishment, in lieu of seeking out and eliminating the underlying causes of the violence?

CHILDREN AND VIOLENCE

Child Abuse and Murder in the Home

In our society violence is taught early in life. Each year over three hundred thousand children are abused in their own homes and by their own

---

[1] United States figure from 1980 *Source Book of Criminal Justice*; Japanese figure quoted by Ramsey Clark, former attorney general.

parents and guardians. Every two minutes a child is being attacked by one of its parents. Every day children are running away from home because of emotional, physical, and even sexual abuse.

The Los Angeles Press reports the case of a young girl who appeared in court when she was eleven years old, but who was only eight when she was first molested by her own father. This child was a witness for the prosecution against her father, who was charged with having sold her into prostitution. When asked who was the first man to molest her, her answer was, "My dad . . . I don't know. I think it was my dad." Her father, age 35, is divorced from her mother. He was among nine men indicted by a Los Angeles County grand jury on charges of molesting children and selling photographs of them to pornographic magazines.

According to Marvin E. Wolfgang, director of the Center for Studies in Criminology and Criminal Law at the University of Pennsylvania, one-fourth of the murders in the United States occur among family members. He says: "People commit violence against those with whom they are most intimate. If a person doesn't care about some poor slob, he or she isn't likely to hurt them. . . . Americans tend to legitimize violence by glorifying war, buying guns, and supporting the use of physical punishment. . . . *Even the routine act of spanking children can teach them that superior force is power.*"[2]

Crimes Involving the Young

The illegal selling of drugs to schoolchildren, even to the very young in some places, has become so widespread that extraordinary efforts are being taken in some schools to stop this vicious racket. For example, in Madison, Wisconsin, school officials have ordered the shortening of the lunch break for junior and senior high school students. In addition, students are not allowed to leave the school grounds during their lunch break. These actions have been forced by the growing number of children who have been coming back from their lunch period under the influence of drugs.

Teenage shoplifting has become a billion-dollar ripoff, according to some experts studying the field. And strangely enough, hunger, poverty, or need does not motivate these teenagers in their thievery. Here are some of the reasons kids give for their actions: "for kicks," "I didn't know it was a crime," "I know they won't do anything to me if caught—

---

[2] Marvin E. Wolfgang. Used by permission.

I'm underage." The majority of these juvenile shoplifters come from middle-class families, not from poverty-stricken ones.

The TV and Exploitation of Sex

There has been in recent years an increasing outcry against the prevalence of sex-related stories and scenes in the movies and on TV. Through TV, such scenes have their impact upon the behavior of children in the public schools. And, in general, the public tends to place all blame for such behavior upon the lack of discipline in the schools.

This is unfair, and it is at best an escapist kind of tactic on the part of parents. Of course, many commercial interests which produce such shows engage in this type of thing solely for the sake of profit. And their proponents, by some clever nuance of hypocrisy, are among the first to denounce the schools as failing to enforce rigorous discipline.

Whatever the precise degree of influence that television may have on the behavior of children or adults, all hard evidence is that it is great.

Violence Is a Cancer

In Dallas in April, 1978, a fifty-six-year-old grandmother pulled a .38-caliber pistol from her purse and shot and killed the school janitor for spanking her grandson, age nine. This tragedy occurred at the Dunbar Elementary School.

The grandmother came to the principal's office one day about three o'clock and asked to speak to Woodrow Porter, Jr., the janitor. Porter admitted to the woman that he had spanked the boy because he caught him bending his (Porter's) car antenna, outside his home that morning. School officials thought the argument was settled. But as Porter and the grandmother left the office, the grandmother shot the janitor in the chest and neck.[3]

In a panel discussion on school violence at the 1978 annual NEA national convention, a Dallas teacher reported: "When I looked up and saw her, I only got to say 'You must be Kevin's mother. Let's sit down and talk.' Then she jumped me, beat me, choked me, and knocked me down the stairs." This is only one of more than 60,000 assaults on teachers in the United States in the 1977–78 school year. Another teacher on the panel—from Los Angeles—said, "I can't begin to tell you how rough

---

[3] "Grandmother Jailed in Custodian's Death," *Dallas Morning News*, Apr. 29, 1978.

it is. Violence is a cancer." She had two teeth knocked out by a gang of three high school students and suffered a hearing impairment.

Teachers also cited the inaction of administrators in dealing with student violence. A boy sent to the principal's office in an elementary school returned to his classroom in ten minutes. Of course, he resumed his bravado display for the entertainment of his fellow students. "Parents," said some of the teachers, "are all for discipline, until it happens to their child; then they want to punish the teacher."

The situation involving attacks by parents on teachers who have disciplined their children has become shockingly prevalent. One editorial writer suggests that if the constituted authorities refuse to allow teachers to give publicity to attacks on them "because this would be bad publicity, the teachers will have to act on their own interests. Let them sue the pants off their assailants if that is what it takes to protect them and keep the peace."[4]

Violence Against Teachers and Discipline

The following is a syndicated columnist's view of the discipline problems in inner city schools:

> For real urban adventure, I'm not sure if anything can top teaching in some of the city's schools. Especially if the teacher is a little white-haired lady.
> That would be Mrs. June Snell, who is 60 and 5-2. . . .
> One recent day, Mrs. Snell noticed that one of her students, a kid named Derrick, walked a little wobbly when he got to class.
> Mrs. Snell thought to herself: "Derrick is drunk." That didn't surprise her, since Derrick, 16, had come to class half or fully loaded several other times. But this time she was sure Derrick was drunk because he had a drink in his hand. . . .
> Mrs. Snell doesn't permit drinking in her class. . . . So she said: "Derrick, put the drink on my desk." [After an extended argument,] Derrick, who had Mrs. Snell by about five inches in height, . . . let her have a right cross to the jaw. . . .
> They went to the school disciplinary office and Mrs. Snell was told that if she wanted to pursue the matter, she'd have to go to the nearest police station and bring charges. . . . But then came the first problem. She has no car and she couldn't find anyone at the school who would drive her to the police station. You would think that when a

---

[4] William Murchison, "Battle of the Classroom," *Dallas Morning News*, July 11, 1978, editorial page.

teacher takes booze from a student and gets punched in the face, the school system would find a way to get her to the police station. But they didn't. So she had to . . . mooch a lift from one of the security guards.

At the police station she told her story to a juvenile officer. He tried to talk her out of bringing charges because it would be a lot of bother. . . .

A few days later, . . . she called downtown to the school system's legal office. She wanted to get their advice. . . . [It was] 2:30 p.m. A secretary told her everyone was at lunch. . . . nobody returned her call. . . .

[After calling the next day and the next,] Mrs. Snell went to her principal and the principal himself called the legal office. The principal was told that nobody was available to talk to him, either. So much for clout. . . .

[Finally, after additional attempts to get help,] Mrs. Snell gave up asking for legal advice and decided to take her chances in court. Fortunately, Derrick gave up easily. . . . He admitted having been drunk and punching Mrs. Snell in the chops. The judge told him to go on the wagon and gave him probation.

Mrs. Snell won, but after the kind of nonsupport she received from the school administrators, she isn't sure if she'll ever go through that much trouble again. The next time a kid comes to class that way, she might ask him for a snort.[5]

According to a study released in 1978 by the National Institute of Education, 5,200 junior and senior high school teachers are attacked each month (or 52,000 per ten-month period). This total compares to 49,079 assaults on policemen during the same period. Why, then, you might ask, aren't teachers leaving the profession? The answer is that thousands of highly qualified teachers are doing just that. A report by the National Education Association in 1971 found that, given a chance to choose again, only 45 percent would choose teaching. A repeat of this survey in 1977 found that the number who would still choose teaching as a career had declined to 38 percent.[6]

SOME PLANS TO REDUCE VIOLENCE IN SCHOOLS

The escalation of violence in the public schools has grown so rapidly in recent years that school districts are experimenting with many ways to

---

[5] Mike Royko, "Teacher Gets a Lesson in the Lack of Clout," *Chicago Daily News*, Feb. 8, 1978. © Field Enterprises, 1978. Reprinted with permission.

[6] Reported in "School Violence," *Today's Education*, Feb.–Mar., 1978, p. 16.

curb it. Here are some examples, with names of the school districts deleted.

1. In a small school system, violators of school rules are given one day of solitary confinement in a relatively small room, devoid of all equipment except a desk and a chair, with no choices for the student except to study or to sit and stare at the walls.

2. Parents in an Illinois town take turns patrolling the school grounds for vandals.

3. Grades seven through twelve (in a police-student project) learn about and gain understanding of law enforcement, through role-playing and problem-solving, in a surburban area.

Several Texas towns have developed the following plans:[7]

1. In Austin, the Crockett High School's Alternative Basic Curriculum (ABC) is a last chance for ninth and tenth graders having persisting behavioral and academic problems. This is called the ABC Program, and applicants have to be admitted through approval of their applications by a committee of teachers and administrators. The involved student must sign an agreement to abide by the guidelines of the program. The heart of this effort is regimentation. Parents bring the involved students to school and turn them over to a monitor who sticks with them throughout the day. Those students cannot leave their instruction group; they are marched to physical education classes in the gym and back. They must finish their homework or be subject to expulsion. Classes are limited to fifteen students.

2. In Dallas, in twenty-two high schools, Youth Action Centers are operated. As a general rule these centers have five staff members, as follows: a teacher in charge, a paraprofessional youth advisor, an officer from the Dallas Police Department, an assignee from the Juvenile Department, and a clerk. Attendance is the chief focus. This means locating students who are out of school and working with them, as well as their parents, to get them back in class. In this connection, there is a twenty-four-hour communication center connecting the centers with the Dallas school district's security department and school buses.

3. In Houston, special efforts are being made to deal quickly with

---

[7] As reported in *Texas Outlook*, July, 1978, p. 10.

cases of violence and disruption. Where once complaints were filed with police substations (which took far too much time to get action), now the security department investigates and gathers evidence required for conviction. Offenses are reported directly to the municipal court, which is specifically designated to expedite prosecution. Also, a specially equipped alarm system is being installed in all schools to aid in fire detection. This system has been developed because of an unprecedented year of school fires—fifteen in all—at a cost to the district of about $470,000.

4. San Antonio schools have reduced their vandalism costs, contrary to what is happening almost everywhere else. They do this by turning out all lights in school buildings, in disregard of the old belief that a well-lighted area discourages crime. Vandalism costs have been reduced from $160,000 to $40,000 annually—not counting the reduced lighting bill.

Honor Student Shoots Teacher

Here is a case that makes even the most understanding and sympathetic friend of the public schools wonder where the cause of violence lies, and how such behavior can be ameliorated. Generally, one suspects that only the inept or the intellectually subnormal, the products of impossibly disorganized homes, are involved in such extreme behavior. But the boy in the incident described in Chapter 1 involving the shooting of an unsuspecting substitute teacher was certainly not the product of a deprived home life. On the contrary, that boy was the son of a former White House press secretary. And, while one may tend to associate violence in the schools with poor performers, that boy had been a straight "A" student. Such a tragedy ought to cause both teachers and the general public to ponder seriously the difficulties and the hazards, as well as the creative happiness, that teaching in the public schools can bring forth.

Ordinarily, if a child with an unfortunate background or a trend toward enjoying misbehavior commits a crime or runs away from school, the public dismisses the case as due to incompetent teachers who can't or won't enforce discipline. But what are we to say about a case like this? There is not much one can say, except that whoever is dealing with the monumental job of somehow inducing good behavior in a child who by his age and inclinations deliberately seeks to follow the wrong ways must be alert to every nuance of thought, feeling, and action. Teachers must invent ways to steer gently but unobtrusively.

New York City Tightens Penalties for Violence

The New York City Council, prodded by the fact that a number of city teachers are suffering from "battle fatigue" resulting from student violence and abuse, has attempted to get at the causes. A panel appointed to study the situation recommended criminal prosecution for assaults on teachers, more expulsions, and longer suspensions. In the school year 1976–77, there were 2,420 assaults, 617 robberies, 2,420 larcenies, 828 bomb threats and arson-related fires, 83 sex crimes, and 682 narcotics-related offenses in the New York City schools.

Some Unusual Types of Violence against Teachers

Clara Klinjer, a ten-year veteran remedial reading teacher in a Brooklyn vocational high school, was hit by a piece of iron wrapped in a rolled newspaper held together by a rubber band. The thrown object hit her in the neck and knocked her down. She was able to get up and reach her home, but was never able to work at her job again because of persisting headaches and dizziness—and because of fright which she cannot throw off. She has only to complete her dissertation to receive a doctoral degree. In commenting on her situation, she said: "I know I'm not handling this very well. I cry easily when I am reminded of this. It's been two years and I am getting worse. I'm really very bitter." To add to her fear and bitterness, Mrs. Klinjer was told by other teachers that the boy who hit her bragged about it, saying, "I hit and I hit her hard and when she comes back, my mother and I are going to put her in a wheelchair." The teacher never learned what provoked the attack. The boy was never disciplined, and the teacher never learned why not.[8]

This is a disgraceful situation, and society is going to be compelled to find remedies for it. Between 60,000 and 70,000 teachers are attacked by students each year in the United States. Since 1972, murders in the classrooms have increased by 18 percent; rapes have increased by 48 percent, and assaults have increased by 77 percent. Today's teachers are much like combat troops who have served at the front too long. They come down with ailments like migraine headaches, ulcers, and hypertension; they are unable to sleep. Teachers ought to be trained to handle explo-

---

[8] June White, "Battered Teachers React with Combat Fatigue," *Atlanta Constitution*, Dec. 26, 1978, p. 20A. Used by permission.

sive situations if they arise, and to deal with confrontations and violent outbursts; they ought to share their experiences in faculty meetings. In addition, school administrators should be prepared to deal with such violence, and must avoid placing wholesale blame on teachers involved.

DIMENSIONS OF VIOLENCE IN SCHOOLS

In a survey released by the NEA at its 1978 annual convention, it was estimated that 3 percent of public school teachers were attacked by students in the preceding year (1977–78). This would total about 61,000 teachers for the nation. Most of this violence occurs in junior and senior high schools. Teachers at the convention seemed to feel that principals and superintendents downplay the problem because reporting the precise facts would enhance the convictions of some school boards that administrators cannot handle the situation. For example, a teacher from Orlando, Florida, reported that the school board rejected the teachers' report showing that the number of cases of violence for that year was three times as high as that reported by the board. Many teachers are quitting or taking early retirement. *For example, in the nation the number of teachers with twenty years or more of experience has been cut in half since 1961.* A recent federal government report has indicated that in excess of 6,700 schools have serious crime problems; more than 5,000 teachers are attacked monthly; and one-fourth of all schools are plagued with vandalism each month. This vandalism diverts an estimated $600,000,000 each year from the education budgets. This is equivalent to the cost of hiring 50,000 additional teachers, without additional taxation. Parents come in for their share of blame for this worsening situation. Those parents who howl the loudest are likely to be the first to complain or to file a lawsuit if their own children are disciplined for misbehavior. *Lack of discipline at home is given by teachers as the major factor in this outbreak of violence in the schools. Others indict TV viewing of violent programs, prolonged periods of nonsupervision of children in the home, and overcrowded classrooms.*

There appears to be little real agreement concerning the causes of this outbreak of youthful rebellion. Of course, two groups will feel the cutting edge and squirm under the criticisms of the public. Principals, presiding (as they generally do) over one school, tend to get the bulk of the criticism. But school superintendents are being increasingly criticized for not finding some workable answers to the problem. Teachers themselves are widely (and, all too often, viciously) denounced for failure to maintain order in their classrooms.

All of this inevitably directs the attention of knowledgeable critics to the early years of the public schools, especially to the one-room school in the rural or semi-rural setting. As a general rule, these schools were run by the "school masters" and not "school marms." This was not a pro-or-con argument about the virtues of either sex. But, basically, it was evidence that the public believed that the situation required men, and muscular men at that. Women were believed to lack the strength to control boys intent on rowdyism. Thus the story of Ichabod Crane had some basis in reality.

A study by the U.S. Department of Health, Education, and Welfare has reported that 6,000 junior and senior high school teachers are robbed at school each month, and over 5,000 are physically attacked in that period of time. The U.S. Senate appointed a subcommittee which reported in 1977 that in the preceding three years the attacks on teachers were up by 80 percent, and assaults on students had increased by 85 percent. This subcommittee was so horrified by what it found in school behavior that its chairman said: "For a growing number of students and teachers, the primary task is no longer education, but preservation."

SOME KEYS TO EFFECTIVE SCHOOL DISCIPLINE

Throughout the history of the public schools in the United States, discipline has been a problem in varying degrees. However, in the last decade the severity of the problem and the number of pupils involved have ballooned to unprecedented proportions. Discipline has now become perhaps the number one problem facing the schools.

William Glasser, in discussing this problem, proposes a program based upon what he calls "Reality Therapy":

1. Be personal. Use personal pronouns, "I care enough about you to be involved, to be your friend."
2. Refer to present behavior. "What are you doing right now?" Avoid references to the past. Emphasize behavior, not feelings.
3. Stress value judgments. Ask students to evaluate their own behavior.

4. Plan . . . keep the plan simple with short spans of time.
5. Be committed. Build in a way to check back, follow up. Give positive reinforcement.
6. Don't accept excuses. Eliminate discussion of excuses to show you really know students can succeed. Re-plan with them. . . . Don't give up.
7. Don't punish. Punishment lifts responsibility from students. Set rules and sanctions with them. They have to understand that they are responsible for themselves.
8. Never give up . . . a good basic rule of thumb is to hang in there longer than the student thinks you will . . . minimum of one month, two months often are needed.[9]

State Passes New School Discipline Laws

The Texas legislature may have set a new trend toward tougher legal provisions to enforce discipline in the public schools. In 1979, it enacted three major laws devised for this purpose, and these laws became effective with the 1979–80 school term. A teacher can now oust an "incorrigible" from the classroom for the duration of a school term; a student can be sent to jail for a physical assault upon a teacher; and it is a Class C misdemeanor to bring alcoholic beverages onto school campuses, with violators subject to a fine of up to $200. The legislators found that, because of existing laws setting the minimum legal drinking age at eighteen, a lot of alcohol was being brought onto the campuses. Previously, there has been no legislation prohibiting alcoholic beverages on school grounds. This was found to be a major problem in high schools in large cities. It is now a Class B misdemeanor to threaten or do bodily harm to a teacher. The maximum punishment carries a fine of $1,000 and six months in jail.

SUMMARY

Recent studies have consistently found a distressing number of cases of violence in the public schools. What are the causes? That is not an easy question to answer. Some blame the Supreme Court decision outlawing separate schools for the races. Others point to the growing employment

---

[9] William Glasser, "Ten Steps to Good Discipline," *Today's Education*, Nov.–Dec., 1977, p. 61. Used by permission.

of both parents outside the home. Still others feel that the growing violence in our society, on TV, in the movies, and in what children read is to blame.

When this trend first became evident, many dismissed the serious nature of the violence. They attributed it to the age-old shibboleth that "boys will be boys," implying that the violence is not more than usual boyish pranks; here and there, a fistfight erupts. But now the matter has gone far beyond misbehavior. There have been assaults, rapes, extortions, thefts, burglaries, and vandalism in the schools.

The U.S. Senate subcommittee appointed to study the problem reported that in the large cities there was an increase in serious assaults on teachers of over 600 percent in a four-year period (1965–68). The NEA estimated that nearly 70,000 teachers annually suffered physical attacks by students, and more than 150,000 teachers suffer serious damage to their property. Another committee studying the problem has reported that some 75,000 teachers each year suffer injuries serious enough to require medical treatment.

School Violence Declining

By the end of 1979, a survey revealed that a drastic decline in the extent and nature of violence in the public schools was clearly evident. The following cities report evidence of a downward trend in violence: Chicago, Miami, Memphis, Detroit, Little Rock, Portland (Oregon), and Birmingham. To be sure, some cities reported a worsening of the situation: Newark and San Francisco, for example. Some cities report a leveling off in acts of violence; among these are Boston, New York, Albuquerque, and Los Angeles.

The major causes of this decline appear to be an increase in the number of security officers in the hallways, and a much tougher attitude of school officials toward student violence. Also, a number of cities report the use of training programs for both teachers and students in the psychology of violence, to enable the prevention of unwanted behavior before it can start.

3

The Schools Mirror Society

WHEN one seeks an analysis of the causes of violence and the alleged breakdown of discipline in the schools, realistic and definitive answers are hard to come by. Inevitably, there must be a critical look both at the schools and at the society which establishes and supports them.

To focus first upon society: It is only a truism that schools will invariably reflect to some degree, as a mirror, the impact of what is going on in society. This is basic in a democracy.

Of course, it can be (and should be) asked, properly and with good reason: Is not society also a mirror inevitably reflecting the inflow of mores and goals of the students which the schools constantly return to it? And the answer, of course, has to be yes. Likewise, then, the schools must share some measure of responsibility, along with other social, religious, civic, economic, and government agencies.

But, again in fairness, it must be added that the impact of the schools on the unseemly behavior that is continually present in our society is not so powerfully and quickly reflected in behavioral patterns as that of society upon the schools. The schools strain to pour a steady stream of students and graduates, whose education has prepared them for fruitful and productive citizenship, into society. This always has been and always will be a disturbingly slow, tedious process. Society will tend always to have greater influence—especially in those periods when the flow of children into the schools far exceeds the normal output of the schools into society by graduation or other withdrawals. This imbalance occurs especially during times of prosperity or economic depression, in peace and in war, in recurring periods of increasing or falling birthrates and, thus, in increasing or falling school enrollments.

What are the elements pictured in society's imaginary mirror? All one has to do to discover the answer is to read the daily newspapers and see these events magnified beyond life size and often distorted by regular viewing of TV and the movies. One will find stories of murder, robbery, rape, arson, gangland crimes, the domination of whole communities by the Mafia, the kidnapping and sale of young boys, presumably for homosexual rape. Also, some personnel of our governments—local, state, and national—will be depicted as unbelievably corrupt.

Stories of alleged payoffs to police officers appear almost daily in papers somewhere in the United States. Selling dope is a flourishing business in virtually every city in the United States; this is too often accompanied by kickbacks to local police to blind them to this nasty business. And the smuggling of drugs into this country, which goes on at an alarming extent, goes on largely undetected and is apparently unstoppable. An investigation of the GSA (General Services Administration), which supervises federal payments, especially for buildings and furnishings, has estimated that the annual total of bribes, payoffs, and kickbacks involving employees of the federal government, which will eventually be reported in detail, will reach a staggering total in the vicinity of $25 billion annually. This, coupled with recent exposures of widespread bribing of members of Congress by foreign agents, specifically by a representative of South Korea, have tended to give the public a frightening image of corruption in our government.

The mirror, which is being held up so that all those involved in the public schools (children as well as adults) can observe society, must include the proliferating practice of child abuse in the home. This often involves brutal beatings of young children by their own parents for some minor irritations. Day by day this is becoming a national scandal. It includes kidnapping young children and selling them for prostitution or sexual abuse. Appalling reports tell of the extent of abuse of young children by their own parents.

Moreover, the prevalence of pornography in national publications is widespread. When hauled into court for violation of state or local laws, the offenders generally cite the First Amendment, which guarantees the freedoms of speech and press. This pornography racket is now spreading to include very young school-age children.

In the face of all these mirrored images—brutality, corruption, and savagery—it would be preposterous to assume that these conditions do not have profound effects upon children in the public schools.

If one should seek a simplistic answer to the problem of violence, and the closely related one of the alleged lack of discipline in the schools, *it would be wise to hold up a mirror to our society and our homes.* In that glass one will see the vast majority of the twin problem areas of the schools.

RACKETS REINCARNATED

The old gangland "pay-off for protection" came to light in a small New Jersey town in the fall of 1978. The facts reported seem to indicate that the tactic of shaking down younger and weaker children to obtain lunch money, an old one in many metropolitan school districts, was beginning to invade the smaller communities in some areas. It seems that thirteen boys threatened a much smaller, weaker boy with repeated beatings if he did not "kick in" funds daily as lunch money for the gang. Over several months the boy provided the gang with over a thousand dollars "protection money," which he took from his parents' secret hiding place. There was no report of the prospects of a trial and punishment.

WHAT IS CHARISMA?

During the autumn of 1979, there broke over the puzzled American people the bizarre story of the murder and/or suicide of over nine hundred American citizens, in a far away, almost unheard-of place called Guyana. This—of all things—was the fruit of an American evangelist, religionist, cultist, or probably just a sick man. The reader may make his own choice of nomenclatures for such shocking, unbelievable shenanigans.

The story is included here because, of all the evidence and instances gathered to demonstrate the failings (or at least the weaknesses) of the system of American education, it seems to win the prize as evidence that something is wrong with an educational system which exists alongside such absurd cultism. How could a cult that had developed thousands of miles away, in California, in so-called enlightened America, be led to migrate to the northern jungles of South America at the behest of this cult leader, there to take their own lives or help to administer to their children a deadly poison? Probably not since the wholesale suicide incidents of the Japanese, when they became aware that they were losing the war with the United States and jumped to their deaths from the cliffs of Saipan, has the world seen such a hypnotic charade of self-destruction.

The sad, closing episode on this strange aberration of the human mind and spirit seemed to have a respectable beginning with a well-thought-of cultist by the name of the Reverend James Jones. First, the colonists of Jonestown, Guyana, killed a congressman from California, Leo Ryan, who had come to observe them and to find out the realities of such weird behavior after having received complaints from many of them. Three newsmen and a defector from Jonestown also died, after which there ensued one of the most bizarre actions ever performed by human beings: self-destruction, mostly by the voluntary drinking of a poisonous potion, under the appealing urging of their leader, the Reverend Jim Jones. Why? No one seems to know—except that apparently their leader "went off his rocker." Every conceivable kind of rumor was circulated about the event, but nobody seems to have any kind of rational explanation for it. The United States government sent many planes and rescue squads to fly the bodies of the dead back to their native country. Hundreds were buried in unmarked graves. This whole episode still remains shrouded in deep mystery. How could an obviously deeply idealistic group of people, in search of a better, kinder, more understanding world, spend all the energy, time, and money to build a colony dedicated to these higher, finer ideals—and then turn it, almost as if at a signal from some higher power, into a hideous and unbelievable holocaust of slaughter and suicide?

Congressman Ryan was the leader in the exposure of the cult idea. His son had been a member of the cult, but had quit in disgust. The next day his body was found. This led to the rumor that Jones had threatened death to any deserter from the colony. Congressman Ryan then organized a group to visit Jonestown. But newsmen, invited by Ryan to go along on the investigative trip, began to question Jones about rumors that the colony was heavily armed. Jones "blew his top," so to speak. Also, several men in the camp began to transmit messages to the eight newsmen accompanying Ryan. The messages indicated the deep desire of many to depart from the life which they had entrusted to one man. A total of fourteen people wanted to flee the colony with Congressman Ryan. This knowledge "blew the cork" on Jones' mind. The death of the congressman set off the wholesale slaughter and suicide plan. Nurses and mothers were ordered to give cyanide to the babies. Many mothers first gave the poison to their babies and then took a dose themselves. Cups were filled with poison from a large vessel until the entire colony of 912 was wiped out. What is the explanation for such aberrations? One can't help wondering if education has any answer to such a tragic fiasco.

Those seeking an answer to the strange power of an obvious societal deviate such as Jim Jones (the so-called Reverend) will find many leads but few definitive answers. Other than an unquenchable appetite for power, there were few hints as to what made the man and his cult tick. Toward the press, he used two major weapons: flattery, and subsidies or grants. He also went off into a number of sidelines that tended to be profitable. For example, he had music written and published for the use of his youth choirs. Then he established a record-producing company with the same clientele. Meanwhile, he bought a spacious auditorium in San Francisco which became the center for his widely varied activities. He began publishing a newspaper, the *Peoples Forum*. Also, he bought an old synagogue in which he opened another church. The temple also bought thirty minutes for a program on a San Francisco radio station. "Operation Bread Basket" was organized, with the ostensible purpose of feeding and clothing the poor in Guyana. Jones also took his group into active politics and was instrumental in electing George Moscone mayor of San Francisco. In return, Moscone appointed Jones to a city Housing Authority Commission; Jones later became chairman of that body. (Incidentally, Moscone and another associate were later shot and killed by a disgruntled former city employee.) Jones also organized support for the election of President Jimmy Carter.

Then the growing power his movement was developing began to raise questions and, later, suspicions. One group of his followers accused Jones of being an out-and-out fraud and a cynical politician. Strange as it may seem, this charlatan held unbelievable power over his followers. He could order marriages ended and arrange new ones. He exhibited evidence of being a sexist, often preaching long sermons on sexism. But for himself, he reserved the right to indulge as he pleased, under no restraints.

THE GALLUP POLLS—THE RATINGS
OF THE PUBLIC SCHOOLS

The Gallup Poll sought a poll on the ratings of the public schools by sampling opinions of Americans eighteen years of age or older. Ratings were based upon the usual grading scale used in the public schools: A, B, C, D, and F. The results are shown in Table 3.1.

It is clear that the A ratings declined considerably from 1974 to 1981; B ratings dropped from 30 to 27 percent. Those from C and D steadily rose, C from 21 to 34 percent, D from 6 to 13 percent. The ratings for "Fail" and "Don't Know" changed two and ten percentage points respectively.

What does the public see as the major problems confronting the public schools (which would seem to be the causes for these steady decreases in the ratings of the public schools)? In the Gallup Poll parents with children in public schools listed the following problems most frequently: lack of discipline, 26 percent; lack of proper financial support, 16 percent; poor curriculum/poor standards, 14 percent; difficulty in getting good teachers, 14 percent; use of drugs, 13 percent; integration/busing (combined), 9 percent. Other causes listed with lower percentage ratings included large schools/overcrowding, parents' and teachers' lack of interest,

TABLE 3.1.
Public Opinion of American Schools

	Response in Percentages							
	1981	*1980*	*1979*	*1978*	*1977*	*1976*	*1975*	*1974*
A Rating	9	10	8	9	11	13	13	18
B Rating	27	25	26	27	26	29	30	30
C Rating	34	29	30	30	28	28	28	21
D Rating	13	12	11	11	11	10	9	6
Fail	7	6	7	8	5	6	7	5
Don't Know	10	18	18	15	19	14	13	20

NOTE: From George H. Gallup, "The 13th Annual Gallup Poll of the Public's Attitudes Toward the Public Schools," *Phi Delta Kappan* 63 (1982): 35. © 1981, Phi Delta Kappan, Inc. Used by permission.

pupils' lack of respect for other students and teachers, pupils' lack of interest/truancy, crime/vandalism, and management of funds. "Don't Know" was listed by 5 percent.[1]

DISCIPLINE RELATED TO LAW ENFORCEMENT

The growing and heated criticism directed at the schools finds its counterpart in the shameful record of law enforcement throughout the United States. It is a widely recognized fact that only a small percentage of crime committed in the United States is punished by the application of existing law to the guilty criminals. A staggering proportion of those committing crimes are never arrested, and of those who are arrested, a still smaller percentage are ever brought to trial. And it must be remembered that the rash of plea bargainings is attributable to the laxness of crime detection and enforcement.

Whether this sorry record is the cause of a seeming revolt against the police is, of course, not known precisely. But doubtless the suspicion (and known fact, in many instances) of police corruption and the collusion of some courts have had a disastrous effect upon the rising tide of law violations. Almost daily the press wire services report the arrest or conviction of police officers somewhere in the United States, charged with accepting bribes to allow drug peddling to go on unhindered by the law. And the charge of police brutality throughout the nation (if true) is simply a disgrace in a so-called free society.

One result of this corruption and suspicion of corruption has been the rapid diminution of respect for the police. Contrast this with the deep respect of the public in England for the unarmed "bobby," who seems to stand out as a beacon of respect.

At the same time, widespread evidence is coming to light of the rapidly waning respect for the police in the United States. For example, here is a newspaper report from a university city:

> Respect—it's something most members of a community have toward policemen. But—police are beginning to wonder as the number of assaults on officers has risen 42 percent this year. Officers have been

---

[1] George H. Gallup, "The 13th Annual Gallup Poll of the Public's Attitudes Toward the Public Schools," *Phi Delta Kappan* 63 (1981): 34.

assaulted 34 times through September 1, 1978. The number was 24 in the same period in 1977. One officer said he could not tell what the reasons for the increase in assaults are. "It usually happens when we arrest someone or pick up somebody on an arrest. When we start to put the handcuffs on, the person being arrested often starts swinging at the officer. It's getting worse," he said. Every officer on the force has been assaulted at least once, many of these assaults have occurred with the offender snatching the policeman's pistol from its holder. The number of arrests for intoxication, use of drugs, and family disturbances have increased. Family fights are extremely serious, and the officer must in such cases be a psychologist. One officer, answering a summons to stop a fight between a man and wife, was turned on by both and beaten seriously by the two.[2]

What is startling about this report is the fact that it comes from a small city, dominated by a state university. One would assume that in such a setting the level of intelligence would be higher; and that antisocial or anti-law enforcement would be expected to be rare.

Another (and much worse) collusion is that of the criminal who has an influential politician as his sponsor. All too often the officials charged with enforcing the law are mere actors pretending to enforce it by postponements, plea bargaining, or sentences so inconsequential as to make the law a sort of grotesque and laughable gesture in the general direction of "justice."

Generally, this exertion of political influence is scantily veiled. But it is growing so common that the public is becoming cynical when a wealthy suspect or the friend of a powerful politician is arrested. Some observers, regardless of the weight of evidence, can predict the sentence in advance.

The point here is that such turbulence in society is bound to have its impact on the schools in the community. And the evidence at hand would tend to indicate that such attitudes are widespread in the nation as a whole.

REVOLT AGAINST SCHOOLS AND TAXES

The reluctance of people to pay taxes to support essential institutions, such as police and fire departments, is still with us, and perhaps always will be. This is in all probability a universal, perfectly natural sentiment,

---

[2] *Bryan College Station Eagle*, mid-Sept., 1976. Used by permission.

but it has its limits. The Boston Tea Party was not so much a revolt in the interests of freedom as it was a violent reaction to the taxes the Crown assessed on tea imported from the Far East.

Because public education—the great dynamo of the nation's progress through the years—is supported by public taxation voted by the taxpayers themselves, it is in almost constant turmoil, partly because of resentment against the taxes that must be paid to support it.

Norman Cousins, veteran editor of *Saturday Review*, has written that education is the first casualty in the second act of the taxpayers' revolt:

> Pent-up prejudices against teachers and teaching are popping out all over. The arts are being derided as secondary to what is to be the genuine purpose of education: namely, to teach people to do things for which they will be paid. . . . The concept of a teacher who doesn't have a full teaching load but is given time to think and read . . . this concept is being gunned down in some places by know-nothings with the zeal and mirthful vindictiveness of a posse closing in on its quarry. . . . At a time like this, the real failure of education becomes apparent. *Education has failed to educate about education . . . schools have somehow failed to get across the biggest truth of all about learning: that its purpose is to unlock the human mind and to develop it into an organ capable of thought . . . purely in long range educational terms, a well rounded education is the best investment a society can make in its own future.*[3]

Is it any wonder that we have California's Proposition 13? The miracle is that we have not had many more. Perhaps we will.

One of the great puzzles of our educational history is that we have never, as a nation, taken the time . . . or we didn't pause long enough to think about it . . . or it was conceived to be a matter of no importance. Why in Heaven's name haven't we long since offered, as a required course in high school, a comprehensive full-year course in "Education—Its Purposes and Its Fruits"?

MIRROR, MIRROR ON THE WALL

In this century the following national crises caused vehement and unreasoning charges that our public schools were to blame, in large mea-

---

[3] Norman Cousins, "The Taxpayer's Revolt: Act Two," *Saturday Review*, Sept. 16, 1978, p. 56.

sure: World War I (1914–18; America's participation, 1917–18), the
Great Depression (1929–33), World War II (1939–45; America's participation, 1941–45); and world threat of Communism resulting in the
arms race between the United States and Russia, the Sputnik scare
(1957–60). These were bitter and dangerous events. The horrendous cost
of arming for war, the drafting of millions of youths, and the inevitable
death of thousands of our young men by these wars caused such agony
of suffering that our people, quite naturally, sought some sectors of our
national life to lay the blame upon. The public schools received a considerable share of the blame. Even the most sensible people find it inviting to have someone or some organization to blame. The so-called Mc-
Carthy Era in the early 1950s also resulted in vehement criticism of the
public schools.

Being at heart and purpose a peaceful nation that tends to shun the
constant preparation for war, these two world wars caught the United
States almost totally off guard. A scapegoat had to be found for the guilty
feelings of the whole people. The public schools offered an easy target
that could not fight back.

In the late 1930s, when the drift toward World War II became in-
exorable, the apprehensions about the upcoming war became so intense
that the NEA felt forced to establish the National Commission for the
Defense of Democracy through Education, to defend the public schools
and teachers against unjust attacks. This commission became the Defense Commission and later, under the name of the DuShane Defense
Fund, money was provided to defend teachers in court cases. In this era
of national blight, so great was the public anxiety that many states passed
laws requiring all teachers in the public schools and publicly supported
colleges and universities to make public record of all organizations to
which they belonged. Of course, this was a specific violation of the First
Amendment, and was so ruled by the federal courts. But at the time
there was no teachers' association with the funds to take these cases to
the courts. Eventually all such laws were found unconstitutional. And in
the 1970s, the NEA voted to maintain an account of at least $1,000,000
at all times to come to the aid of teachers unjustly dismissed from their
jobs. The Defense Fund resulted in hundreds of court cases involving
mistreated teachers. With financial help from this fund and often with
additional help from the National Association for the Advancement of
Colored People (NAACP) and the American Civil Liberties Union

(ACLU), teachers have won the vast majority of cases. The result has been a totally new status for teachers in the United States. Rarely now are teachers mistreated for petty causes.

Yes—it is inevitable that the public schools mirror much of what transpires in society. And, in turn, society will reflect the impact of the schools.

4

Social Promotion
and the Rise of Examinations

FOR some years now, the degree of public interest in various kinds of tests to be used in the schools has varied from indifference to near hysteria. The variation has generally been influenced by the nation's general condition—prosperity, depression, war. During periods of prosperity, the public generally has tended to be satisfied with the products of the schools. But with depression, inflation, war, or burdensome taxes, the public with knee-jerk regularity turns upon the schools and blames them and their teachers for the current ills of our society.

If some aggressive nation produces a new, awesome weapon, our schools are blamed for failure to teach science and math.[1] If some nation approaches the United States in the number of Nobel Prizes awarded in a given year—which has rarely, if ever, happened—this happenstance is immediately cited as evidence that our schools have failed. Eventually there follows a cry for testing all children in the public schools. Such clamor is usually closely followed by demands for the testing of teachers. Slogans like "Back to Basics" become fervent. Moreover, many taxpayers see a chance for the lowering of taxes, so the clamor gets louder and louder. The famous Proposition 13, adopted in California in 1978, influenced efforts elsewhere to sponsor legislation to cut school taxes.

Of course, there are two broad purposes served by rigid examination systems: (1) to admit individuals to some institution, group, or class; or (2) to deny individuals admission to some institution, group, or class. The winners are exultant; the losers are downcast. In fairness, it should

---

[1] In this connection, see T. M. Stinnett, "Check That Statistic," *Educational Record*, Apr., 1957, pp. 83–92.

be added that examinations also serve (1) to evaluate the efficiency of schools, and (2) to evaluate the ability of teachers.

In England, until recently, the Eleventh-Year Examination determined whether a student would be permitted to go further with his education or admitted to higher education. In France, there is a similar pattern of admission to or rejection from the university. However, the pattern has been altered there to some extent in recent years. Also, in Germany, a national examination system determines the kind of schools a student may attend.

In all three nations there are points at which students in public schools must demonstrate, by passing examinations, that they are capable of entering higher education.

As a matter of fact, this frenzy over examinations actually developed in the United States in the late 1950s. Such a ballyhoo was raised by the Soviet Union's launching of Sputnik that the American people were led to believe that our schools were falling dangerously far behind, particularly in science and math. The National Defense Education Act was passed in 1958 by Congress, appropriating hundreds of millions of dollars in federal funds to aid schools in improving their programs in math and science.

In France, compulsory school attendance begins at age six in the 80,000 elementary schools. Nearly half of the children were formerly enrolled in these schools until age 14. In 1967 the compulsory attendance age was raised to 16, and two additional grades were added to the eight-grade elementary school. Children with a strong bent toward academic subjects enter an academic secondary school (lycée) at the approximate age of 15. Only about 15 percent of these children, prior to World War II, gained entrance to the lycée. These schools have great prestige because they are the virtually exclusive route into the universities. Since World War II, the percentage of the 12–16 age group admitted has risen to about 25 percent of the age group at the secondary school level. This increase has resulted from the pressures of children of working-class families.

A second group, also about 25 percent of the total, leaves the elementary school at the end of the fifth grade to enter a lower secondary school which offers grades 6–10 inclusive. Until recent years, most of the children of France have not had access to the lycée because they had no family tradition for the step. Also, in many rural counties in France, there were no schools of this kind for children to attend. Beginning in the 1960s, the French government began building lycées in these areas.

To cite evidence that the French are at long last beginning to give all children a better chance at a university education: in 1960, only about 11 percent were eligible; by 1970, nearly 20 percent qualified. France, in 1967, expanded its vocational schools and offerings, which now tend to absorb those rejected by university schools. In 1967 France had almost 20 percent of its university-age group enrolled. However, the failure rate is extremely high—about 60 percent of those admitted.

COMPETENCY TESTING IN EUROPEAN COUNTRIES

When one visits these countries, especially France and Germany, he will be made conscious (by talk and newspaper accounts) of student suicides. The following quotation of September 30, 1978, provided by the *London Daily Telegraph* service, is illustrative:

> BONN—Despair among German children over their failure to get good grades in an old fashioned teaching system is causing an increasing number of pupils to attempt suicide this year. Two citizen groups have reported that an estimated 14,000 German school children, aged 10 to 19, tried to kill themselves last year and 800 are expected to commit suicide this year (1979). The problem is worsening. Ten years ago, there were 363 suicides in the same age group, and two years ago the figure was 517 of whom 103 were between 10 and 15 years of age. One of the leaders of this campaign to lessen the impact of grades is Wilhelm Ebert, a Bavarian teacher who is currently chairman of the six million member World Teachers Federation. [This probably refers to the WCOTP—World Confederation of Organizations of the Teaching Professions.] He said that the present German school system is producing a race of pupils with competitive "elbow tactics" thinking in which only grades mattered.[2]

SPREAD OF THE COMPETENCY TESTING MOVEMENT

"Back to Basics" in education has become almost a nationwide shibboleth in the United States. Like almost every other fad that has inundated public education, this, too, will pass. But only after much straining and groaning.

---

[2] As quoted by *Houston Chronicle*, Sept. 30, 1978.

There are, of course, many motivations involved in this drive for competency scores. Periodically one nostrum after another, one sure-fire remedy after another, arises in a welter of denunciations, then recedes when no miraculous results appear. But, fortunately, each successive campaign "to save our schools" does add some new approaches which tend to be constructive and helpful. Thus (as ought to be true in a democracy) debates, argumentation, and a variety of proposed cures for obviously faltering practices arise.

By the beginning of the 1978–79 school year, thirty-three states had adopted some sort of statewide minimum competency testing plan, either by the state board of education or by legislative enactment. A new total of thirty-seven states had adopted some type of statewide plan to enforce minimum mastery of the "basics" for students to be able to graduate from high school. Now, with the well-known Proposition 13 adopted in California, in all probability we shall see intense efforts to lower the level of tax monies for the schools, with stepped-up charges against the schools of gross failure to perform the essential functions for which they were established.

Of course, much of the loud beating of the breast for such a cut in school taxes will be by "big" taxpayers, many of whom have no children in school. Or if they do, they are able to send them to private schools. Something like 60 percent of all adults in the United States are not parents of school-age children, and this percentage is increasing each year. This fact is important when tax-voting time comes around.

Of course, legislative action or state board of education action to develop tests to measure these essentials is quite sincere. Unfortunately, that task is not as simple as it may appear to the voters. Virtually every kind of test is handicapped by content that is obviously biased in favor of some groups or against others. The states presently seem bent upon the use of minimum competency standards, and the trend seems to be toward different approaches in each state.

Testing Teacher Competency

The critical questions here are: (1) Do tests adequately measure teaching ability? (2) Do they indicate that higher education institutions need to improve the quality of their preparation of teachers for the public schools? Probably improvement is needed in both areas.

Americans seem to have almost a genius for devising or proposing or embracing easy solutions for the problems of the public schools. Several years ago, a speaker for the giant industries suggested that there was an easy solution to the problem of educating the 45–50 million American children of school age. The suggested solution was to contract with private business, specify the results to be accomplished, and pay industry in proportion to the portion of the contract achieved.

Competency Testing for High School Seniors

The newspapers reported in July, 1978, that some 260,000 high school seniors in New York State would be required to pass competency tests in the "three R's" (or the so-called basics) in June, 1979, to receive diplomas. The article reported that 15 percent of the 1977–78 school-year eleventh graders, statewide, and 37 percent of New York City eleventh graders had already failed comparable sample tests. The New York Board of Regents had required the passing of a test for many years, but the new plan apparently calls for much stiffer exams.

There appears to be a trend toward the use of such tests nationwide. Already eleven states—including New York, Florida, and California—have adopted such tests as a requirement for graduation. Some twenty-four other states have adopted minimal competency education tests but do not, as yet, require this as a prerequisite to graduation from high school.

Minimum competency testing is used in thirty-four states. Tests must be passed before a high school diploma can be issued. A total of 82 percent of the people polled say this is a good idea. In Denver, proficiency and review tests in arithmetic, grammar, reading, and spelling are used. Students must pass all four tests to get their diplomas; if not, they can graduate, but only with a certificate. Some dislike this testing as it tests at about a sixth-grade level and ensures minimal competencies only. Almost all who take it eventually pass; they start in the ninth grade, with 40 percent failing it the first time around, and 2–4 percent still not passing it by the time of graduation. It is a multiple choice exam and is graded by computer.

Some questions: Does it measure true competencies? Who decides what competencies to test? What do you do with those who fail? When should the tests be given? Some say start giving the tests earlier, to measure progress so that changes can be made before it is too late. The trend in the nation now is toward earlier testing.

How is the testing to be used? Are the students who fail to be held back? No; social promotion from grade to grade is prevalent. Some districts don't do this, however. In Greensville, Virginia, the motto is, "If students don't learn they don't pass." The test is a national standardized one that is given twice a year, and a diploma means something. In four years the achievement levels have risen from the bottom one-third to above the national norm. Those who fail the tests don't go back to the same classes; they are given new classes with new teachers and get remedial work. There is some controversy—some blacks are at a disadvantage when taking the national standardized tests. However, not all blacks disagree with this system. One mother said that she was glad that her son was kept back after taking the tests because he was able to get the help needed to put him on a level that would allow him to compete with the other children in the classroom. Other critics contend that there is too much emphasis on standardized national tests and that teachers should have more say in who will pass.

In Hempstead, New York, there is a black district with a black school board. One out of four children failed this year. Their philosophy is, "Parents have a right to get their money's worth."

In Chicago, a mastery learning technique is used. Testing is used every week, and deficiencies are diagnosed. Benjamin Bloom of the University of Chicago developed this, and it is based on what the student has learned as well as what he needs to learn. They use formative tests and the failers are tutored and given the tests again without penalty. Bloom says that almost any student can master almost any subject, given these four conditions: (1) every student is expected to perform at A or B levels; (2) testing provides frequent feedback; (3) immediate corrections can take place outside normal classroom hours; (4) each student can get an A or B because there is no curve used. Grades are based on performance.[3]

However, some teachers say that too much testing is required in such a system, and that the remedial work needed is beyond the resources of the school.

---

[3] Benjamin Bloom, J. Thomas Hastings, and George F. Madaus, *Handbook on Formative and Summative Evaluation of Student Learning* (New York: McGraw-Hill, 1971), pp. 44–57.

Some people say that quality of teachers must also be improved. "Have teachers teach teachers how to teach. Master teachers show other teachers techniques and do a better job than professors could."

In Berkeley, California, the Bay Area Writing Project stresses writing and holds that there is no one correct way of teaching it. Teachers who write are better teachers of writing, they say. Other similar projects are being set up across the nation.

Multiple Nationalities and Test Scores

Test scores of pupils in a school system where there are several mother tongues represented among the families of the children enrolled are bound to vary widely. This, and the matter of attempts at common fairness to all citizens influenced Congress to pass legislation in 1974 providing financial aid to school districts with prescribed proportions of children speaking a foreign language. The Bilingual Education Act assists school districts with children who cannot speak English to employ teachers who speak both English and the child's native tongue. This is a great ideal, and an evidence of the fairness that this country has attempted to exhibit to all people who come to its shores. Incidentally, this compassionate effort by the Congress has not met with universal approval among Americans. Many vehemently denounce this effort as a "waste of the public's money."

But imagine what a dilemma would be forced on a school district like that of Houston, Texas, without such legislation. Threatened by a cutoff of federal funds for not meeting the requirements of providing instruction in the mother tongues of its minority children, it had a thorough survey made of the nationalities and mother tongues of its pupils.

The survey revealed a total of about 200,000 children of school age in the district; 98 different languages were spoken in the homes of these children. Included were languages that most Americans scarcely knew existed: Urdu, Arabic, Swahili, Czech, Gujarati, Farsi, Kurdish, and Telugu. The largest number of tongues spoken were: Spanish (42,192); Vietnamese (1,032); French (871); Chinese (563); and Greek (224).

But consider the absurdity of judging the quality of instruction in the huge school district by the mean scores of the pupils on the competency tests. No standardized test in the world can measure the success or failure of a school district with unfailing accuracy; yet the public tends to go for any substandard criterion as evidence of an inefficient school district and of incompetent teachers.

MALPRACTICE SUITS AGAINST TEACHERS

Another possible cross for teachers to bear is being projected by some experts. That probability is the malpractice suit against a teacher who fails to teach Johnny to read, or write, or spell, or cipher. This latest nightmare for teachers has been anticipated by Dr. Robert Spillane, superintendent of schools in New Rochelle, New York. Of course, this kind of court action has in recent years been a nightmare for physicians and a few other professional practitioners. Teachers, says Spillane, are likely to be next. Only one or two such cases have been filed as yet, and these were lost by the parents. But, say the experts, let one parent win such a suit—then will come the deluge.

The most likely specific complaint (and the experts seem to believe that the parents may win on this) involves graduating high school students who can read only at the elementary level. In such cases, the parents would have a strong case for indicting teachers for neglect by passing the child from grade to grade, knowing his or her reading level was substandard.

Of course, the alternative is to flunk children who cannot read at grade level. In such a case, the poor teacher is in worse trouble from the anger and bitterness of the involved parents. Either way, it appears difficult for the teacher to win.

HIGH SCHOOL CURRICULA AND COLLEGE ADMISSION

As early as 1842 George B. Emerson, the first principal of the Boston Latin High School (established in 1821), recognized that there was a need for some standard to measure progress toward the preparation for college entrance. In his book with Alonzo Potter, *The School and the Schoolmaster* (1842), it was proposed that some yardstick was needed to raise the standards of the secondary schools.[4] At the time it was proposed

---

[4] For a thorough critique of standards, see "Down and Out in the Classroom: Surviving Minimum Competency," a symposium, in *National Elementary Principal*, Jan., 1979, pp. 11–42.

that if all colleges in the northern and middle states could be persuaded to unite, they could raise the standards of all preparatory schools.

This proposal was implemented a half-century later, by the beginning of the formation of the regional accrediting associations, of which there are now a total of six. The New England Association of Colleges and Preparatory Schools was founded in 1880; the Association of Colleges and Preparatory Schools of the Middle States and Maryland, in 1892. Out of these two associations emerged the beginnings of the College Entrance Examination Board, which in time disassociated itself from the regional associations, becoming nationwide in scope and concentrating upon college admission examinations. The North Central Association of Colleges and Secondary Schools was established in 1894. As a guide to college, this association through its Commission on Accredited Schools (1901) defined the standard for approved secondary schools. The Southern States Association of Colleges and Preparatory Schools (changed to Secondary Schools in 1912 and still later to the Southern Association of Colleges and Schools) began to accredit elementary schools also. The Northwest Association of Secondary and Higher Schools was founded in 1918. The College Entrance Examination Board evolved about 1900 from the Association of Colleges and Preparatory Schools of the Middle States and Maryland. The scope of this new board began expanding until it served all schools in the United States, including private academies, the major function of which was preparation for the select colleges and universities of the East.

The curricula of the prestigious schools tended to dictate those of the high schools. In a meeting with the president of Harvard and others, many principals complained that the admission requirements of the colleges differed so widely that the principals were unsure of all the preparatory courses they should offer. They were advised to sponsor an organization to bring about some unity in the requirements. This resulted in the founding of the College Entrance Examination Board.

Beginning in the decade 1910–20, the principals of the public high schools in other parts of the United States began to complain that they were under great pressure to offer vocational and other practical courses which were unacceptable toward meeting the requirements of the college entrance examinations for admission to the prestigious colleges. These principals set up their own association in 1917, called the National Association of Secondary School Principals (NASSP), so that they could have an influence in determining the contents of high school curricula. (Involved here was the old, old clash between the advocates of the classical subjects and those of the so-called practical courses.)

In 1890, the Committee of Ten was appointed by the National Education Association to study the proper relationships between secondary schools and colleges, with special reference to college entrance requirements. This committee believed that the high schools had a broader function than that of preparing high school students for admission to college. They knew that many high school students would not or could not (and perhaps some should not) attend college. High schools, in their view, should prepare students for life, as well as for admission to college. In other words, the public high schools should have, in addition to preparation for college admission, a terminal function. This report in 1892, combined with the Kalamazoo decision in 1874 (in which the court held that "common schools," for which taxes had been levied for many years in most states, also included high schools), transformed the high schools from exclusive institutions into "people's schools." Public high schools proliferated all over the United States, to the extent that eventually they were available virtually to all American boys and girls, even to those living in remote rural areas.

THE COMPETENCY TESTING DRIVE

Concern—at times almost hysteria—about education has in recent years reached unprecedented proportions. This concern has given birth to the newest uproar over fears that pupils can graduate from high school and still be woefully inadequate in certain areas such as math or science; that is, inadequate as determined by a testing program that might itself be inadequate.

High school seniors fail to measure up on the Scholastic Aptitude Tests (SATs). Do these tests measure with accuracy? They are developed by the Educational Testing Service, a highly reputable agency. For the past fourteen years, SAT scores of high school seniors have dropped steadily. Why is this? Many factors, both in society and in the schools, help to explain the primary causes for the decline. Ironically, the primary cause was extension and expansion of educational opportunity in the United States. One case example here pinpoints the notable increase in the number of students taking the tests who came from groups that have consistently made lower-than-average scores. These are students from lower socioeconomic groups, minorities, and women.

There is no one cause, but a variety of causes; and these vary from year to year.

Although ETS varies the specific test items from year to year, the exams tend to remain basically the same, despite the drastic changes in society since 1963. Some critics of the "critics of the schools" believe that the composition foci of the tests need changing. Of course, from 1963 to 1970, there were mammoth changes in demographics. In the period after 1970, the study commission suggested several factors that may have had adverse effects upon student scores. Briefly stated, these items are as follows.

1. The period 1972–75 is characterized as the period of sharpest decline. These years, often named the period of "Revolt of Youth in the United States," were marked by several negative, stimulating factors: the effects of the Vietnam war, riots, political assassinations, burning cities, unprecedented corruption among government officials, and changing roles of the family educational leadership. These factors were bound to have great effect upon the motivation of students. This period was marked especially by the changing family structure and a change in its role of educational leadership. Particularly noticeable was the increase in the number of children in homes where only one parent was present. While it was unable to cite specific proof, the committee felt that this situation was reasonably certain to have had a negative effect.

2. The time spent by schoolchildren in watching television (10,000 to 15,000 hours by age 16—more hours than they had spent in school in those years) must affect school achievements and contribute significantly to the decline in test scores.

Origin and Development of Statewide Testing

Beginning about 1960, there developed in the United States a drive for statewide testing of the products of the public school system. Actually, the origin of the statewide testing idea was with inauguration of the Regents Examination in New York State, which occurred in 1865. This movement began to spread by the 1920s, when new forms of objective tests were developed; the development of intelligence and aptitude tests gave added interest to this movement. The National Defense Education Act of 1958 (NDEA) contributed to the growing testing and guidance programs, as well as stimulating development of scholarship programs. By about 1960, some twenty-six states had mandated testing in some form. This total later grew to forty-two states. In twenty-six states, state departments of education conduct statewide examinations. Responsibilities are shared with state colleges and universities in nine states; in seven states a single state college or university has the sole responsibility; in five states the state program is voluntary.

Florida seems to have been the first state to introduce a statewide student competency testing program, in the school year 1977–78. The program was designated Florida's educational "accountability system." This program included standardized testing of basic skills in the third, fourth, and eighth grades. In the eleventh grade there was a test of functional literacy required for graduation from high school.

The executive director of the NEA dubbed the program a politically inspired one; using the results in Florida, he said that such programs rarely result in actual improvement in education.

A report (or evaluation) of this effort was sponsored by NEA and its state affiliate, the Florida Teaching Profession. An outstanding scholar of education, Dr. Ralph Tyler, was engaged to direct the program. Tyler praised the Florida State Department of Education for the effort, but as an effort to improve education it did not pan out. He charged undue haste by educators in putting the state's Educational Accountability Act of 1976 into effect.[5]

One serious aspect of the tests, Tyler said, was the performance of poor black students on the functional literacy exam. The president of the Florida Teaching Profession said, "When 77 percent of the black children failed the test as compared with 17 percent of the white children, this indicates that there is something wrong with the test. Such a test must take into account the special problems of minority children and should have created a procedure for helping them learn more adequately, but not humiliating them by labelling them as 'functional illiterates.' "[6] Moreover, some experts in the field pointed out that the effects of these tests will tend to persuade the failing eleventh graders to give up the idea

---

[5] "Impact of Minimum Competency Testing in Florida," *Today's Education*, Sept.–Oct., 1978, pp. 20–38.

[6] Ibid.

of graduating from high school. Also, many leaders fear that these scores will be used to evaluate negatively the effectiveness of many teachers.

Some pointed out the danger of efforts to water down the public school curriculum. Others criticized the tests for almost total emphasis upon reading, writing, and arithmetic, and for neglecting such essentials as science, history, literature, and the arts.

The leading Florida educators reported that, despite its problems, the testing program had the positive effect of stimulating great interest on the part of many parents; in addition, members of the legislature were willing to appropriate more money to help the schools.[7]

A total of thirty-three states had (by 1978) adopted some form of competency testing for admission to teacher education programs in their colleges.[8]

After the second annual competency testing, the Florida State Commissioner of Education reported that the results throughout the state were gratifying.[9] In fairness, this favorable report should be included in this discussion to represent the viewpoint or interpretation of the sponsors of the periodic use of competency testing. As stated elsewhere, this testing program was mandated by the Florida legislature in 1976, influenced, as have been such developments elsewhere, by repeated reports of so-called social promotion of children (that is, automatic promotion of children at the end of each year spent in school) regardless of whether the children could demonstrate mastery of certain basic skills by scores on competency examinations.

In the law, the state legislature mandated proof of accountability by extending the statewide program to include grades three, five, eight, and eleven. Tests were built around performance standards adopted by the State Board of Education. In addition, the grade eleven students were required to take a functional literacy test, which was based on the application of basic skills to functioning in everyday situations.

Commissioner Turlington reported that "the results support the belief that Florida was right in implementing a state-wide system of performance standards. . . . By being first we have had to face the wrath of

7 Ibid.

8 J. T. Sandefur, "Future Scenarios for TESCU" (Paper delivered to representatives of the Teacher Education Council of State Colleges and Universities, Cleveland, Ohio, October 29, 1981), p. 8.

9 Ralph D. Turlington, "Good News from Florida, Our Minimum Competency Program Is Working," *Phi Delta Kappan*, May 1979, pp. 649–51.

those who think it is somehow unfair to insist that future high school graduates know how to read with understanding and to do functional arithmetic."[10]

The results of the first testing, conducted in October, 1977, revealed an 8 percent failure in communication and a 36 percent failure in mathematics on the functional literacy test, for eleventh-grade students statewide. This information influenced funding of a $26.5 million program by the legislature for the school year 1978–79. The State Board of Education set up a task force to gather information and expert testimony and report to the board in January, 1979. The 1978 tests were revised and refined. The State Department of Student Assessment Education stated, subsequent to comprehensive review and to refinement by selected public school personnel of the state, that final scores of the 1978 school year resulted in increases in achievement at all grade levels. The results were evaluated as demonstrating that the program is sound and should be continued. Some 97 percent of elementary grade students scored five points higher in communications than in 1977; in mathematics, the scores were 10 points higher. About 89 percent of black eleventh graders passed the communication parts of the 1978 tests, an increase of 15 percent from 1977. The percentages of black eleventh graders in mathematics increased so that 40 percent (rather than 17 percent) of blacks met the requirements for receiving diplomas. A gain of 23 percent should dismiss the suggestion that the tests are culturally or racially biased.

Of the twelfth graders taking the examinations in October, 1978, 78 percent of blacks passed the communications portion, as did 95 percent of whites. In the mathematics portion, 55 percent of the blacks and 80 percent of the white students passed. Total passing scores for all ethnic groups were 88 percent on communications and 69 percent on mathematics. "The statistics speak for themselves," Commissioner Turlington writes. "We are finding those students who need help and providing them the help they need. The program works."[11]

Of course, because it is such a radical departure from past practices, there will be great dissent among both laymen and teachers concerning the validity of such testing.

The Chicago school system is one of the large city systems which has chosen to give an examination at the end of grade eight, for promotion to

---

[10] Ibid.
[11] Ibid.

high school. Failing this exam, students have two choices: (1) repeat the eighth grade, or (2) face the probable failure to be graduated from high school. The exam in reading requires that the student read at the eighth-grade level. About 15,000 of Chicago's 40,000 eighth graders did not receive their diplomas the first spring. Students who fail are required to attend a summer reading course—a daily one and one-half hour course for seven weeks. Chicago's schoolchildren have been consistently below the national average in reading in recent years.

A Miracle Football Coach Is Defrocked by a Competency Test

Lou Holtz, in his first year as coach of the University of Arkansas football team (1977–78), swept the Southwest Conference with only one loss, a three-point loss to the conference champion. Ranked second in the conference and fourth nationally, Holtz was hailed as a miracle worker, a title which he clinched with his team's unexpected and overwhelming victory over the University of Oklahoma in the Orange Bowl on January 1, 1978. But when tested against a computer which presents situations from actual football games and then gives a choice of several possible plays, Holtz tried five situations and made the wrong call each time. The computer graded each participant as a coach, player, fan, and so forth. Holtz qualified as a "cheerleader."

The foregoing serves to remind the most critical of laymen that it is so tempting to embrace an easy answer to the difficult task of selecting qualified teachers. Of course, competent teachers must be prepared with a broad grasp of knowledge and understanding of general education, and a deep love of their teaching field or fields. But that is not enough. Most anyone who has pursued the treadmill of securing an education could identify teachers whose mastery of these two areas was superb, but whose understanding of human personality, drives, and ambitions was less than sensitive, to say the least. Where do these latter talents come from? Nobody knows. They are not taught, at least not directly. By indirection? Yes, perhaps.

THE STAMPEDE TO COMPETENCY TESTING

In the midst of the current furor over the existence of violence and the alleged lack of discipline in the public schools, the public has embraced a new and disturbing nostrum as a sure-fire cure for both. That cure-all is competency testing of students. So heady is this alleged remedy that now there is insistence that it be applied to teachers as well.

So enamored have large portions of the public become with this new gimmick that the resulting pressures have resulted in legislation requiring competency testing in thirty-three states for admission to teacher education programs; still other states require competency testing for retention in their programs.[12] Such testing programs are mandated either by law or by the designated legal education agencies. This is, of course, in pursuit of that highly valued characteristic called "accountability." What a delightful word. All dedicated citizens must salute such a pursuit. If they could but ascertain what it means precisely, and how it is to be accomplished precisely, all would be well. (Or would it?)

---

[12] Sandefur, "Future Scenarios for TESCU," p. 8.

II
AMERICA'S BATTERED TEACHERS

5

Teachers and a Critical Public

IN actual court cases teachers have sought to secure the constitutional rights that other citizens of the United States exercise quite freely. These rights, which are rarely denied citizens by arbitrary, unjust, or harsh treatment, are clearly set forth in the Bill of Rights (the first ten amendments to the Constitution) and in certain other amendments, particularly the Fourteenth.

To be sure, blacks were denied many of these rights until relatively recent years. And in some areas they are still denied to some extent, by arbitrary treatment. But when cases are brought into federal courts, generally these rights are affirmed. Also, women were long denied many of the rights which are now common to citizenship, such as the right to vote and to hold office, and the right to full and free education. Only since the second decade of this century have women had the right to vote; and not until about the end of the last century was the right to full and free education gradually extended to them.

Today we find these denials hard to believe, having so recently celebrated the bicentennial of this country's independence. But they were true, cruelly so. It is a reflection, perhaps, of that old adage that we tend not to be concerned about things that don't affect us personally. We tend only to become concerned when events or trends threaten our own personal rights.

Recently, four newspapermen were jailed, upon the order of a judge, for refusing to reveal the sources of information for a published news story. The threat to "freedom of the press" in this action, and several similar threats by congressional committees, seems to be of little concern to the people. In fact, it appears to many that "freedom of the press" is just another example of favoritism granted by the Constitution for the exclusive benefit of a special group—in this case, newsmen.

Of course, the authors of this provision were not thinking about special privileges for the press, or the profitability of the press. They were thinking of the welfare of the people; of the indispensable need of the people to know what is happening and to be free to talk about it. Most of those in the newspaper business could probably survive without the constitutionally guaranteed privilege of freedom. They could probably survive even if the press were licensed and what was printed was limited to handouts from the government. Newsmen have managed to survive in nations where all news media are in fact branches of the government, and/or the newsmen are paid by the government.

But it should be constantly brought to the attention of the American people that democratic government, free government, cannot and does not survive under such conditions. Although newspeople who publish facts about a trial are sometimes denounced by judges who are sincerely trying to protect the constitutional rights of the person on trial, such denunciations may appeal to the average layman as just and for the general welfare. Yet there is a thin partition here between that and actually being in the direction of furthering tyranny. One step in this direction under the best of intentions can influence other steps which may unwittingly lead in the direction of suppression. It can be assumed that no people, especially no free people, would ever intentionally condone steps that may lead to tyranny. But silence can unwittingly indicate assent or further tolerance toward tyranny or to that eventuality. Court orders which unduly prohibit free press coverage of trials, or editorials critical of the courts' rulings, may lean dangerously toward court orders banning the expression of opinion about a given trial or the behavior of a given judge.

Public indifference to the constant abuse of the rights of any group of people is also dangerous. Teachers are a case in point. Throughout our history they have often been underprivileged in terms of public respect. Why this is so is not easy to discern and to describe.

THE DEVELOPING PICTURE

A still popular but very old bit of folklore from our early schools reflects the taboos of communities to which teachers were often compelled to adhere. An applicant for teaching the three-month term of a one-room school was, according to existing law, required to be examined by the local authorities (usually a three-member school board) for the purposes of issuing a legal certificate. The spokesman of the board asked the applicant: "What do you hold is the shape of the world?" Sensing the seriousness of the belief of the community, the applicant, after some thought, replied: "Some say it is round and some say it is flat. But I can teach it either way."

Among the hardest fights that teachers have encountered over the years has been to break the tradition of conformity in religion. This began, of course, with the notion that the teacher should be an adherent of the same faith or denomination to which a majority of the people in the employing community belonged. This petty imposition stemmed from the early practice of the school being supported by popular subscription and the old, old notion that those who paid for a service had the God-given right to specify the beliefs of those furnishing the service. This had been one of the hardest of all public prohibitions to throw off, partly because of the idea of religion as a sacred thing and not subject to question. It is well known that earlier, even in this century, in small communities, the hiring of teachers depended upon their church affiliation. Even in the larger towns and small cities, school superintendents went to great lengths to search out and recommend the employment of a rough balance of teachers according to the share of the people belonging to each of the major churches.

And of course the imposition of the mores of a given community upon the teacher was as acceptable by the citizenry as that of the imposition of religious beliefs. It is interesting to note that the revolution of teachers that resulted in their winning legal rights to which they were entitled as American citizens had, like so many great happenings in history, its aegis in small beginnings. Among these were the Kate Frank case in Oklahoma in 1943, and the Fern Bruner case in California in the mid 1950s. These were not the first, of course, but they did mark the real beginnings of concerted actions by the teachers' representatives—their professional organizations, in these cases; the NEA in the first, and the California Teachers Association in the second. These cases were, in a real sense, among the first emergings of the concept that women should have the full rights of citizenship. Until these two cases, although teachers constituted the bulk of the membership of these associations and therefore their membership dues constituted the bulk of the operating funds, they still were treated to some extent as members only because of the sufferance and tolerance of the males and the administrators. Elsewhere in this book we have pointed out that no woman was elected president of the NEA (organized in 1857) until 1910, and this one was the superintendent of schools in one of our largest cities (Chicago). The voice of the women members began to be considered to be of some importance in that national organization by 1920. By that time, in part because of the inevitable passage of time and in part impelled by the new militancy of the American Federation of Teachers, women teachers already made up by far the majority of the total teaching staffs in the elementary and secondary schools. They organized the NEA Department of Classroom Teachers in 1920 and became more aggressive participants. Thus was brought to an end the exclusive and dominating regime of men as school administrators and presidents of prestigious colleges and universities.

Between 1857 and about 1870, women, who provided the bulk of the financial support for the new organization, were not permitted to appear on the floor of its convention. They could not even address the annual meetings. Instead, they had to secure a male member to read their remarks.

In 1920, the upsurge of classroom teachers in the NEA was a large factor in a small revolution resulting in a representative assembly based on proportionate representation, establishment of the NEA *Journal* (presently *Today's Education*), establishment of the Committee on Federal Aid to Education, founding of the Research Division and of committees to study tenure and salary provisions, as well as a legislative commission. In 1941 the Department of Classroom Teachers (DCT) became a department of NEA; in 1967 its name was changed to Association of Classroom Teachers. In 1942, a full-time staff was provided that department. Somewhere along the line, either by resolution or common agreement, the practice of electing a man teacher to be president of NEA one year and a woman teacher the next became operative. Until the early 1970s, when a new constitution was adopted providing two-year terms for NEA presidents, male and female presidents were alternated from year to year.

"Teachers Now May Act Just Like People"

Thus read the headline of an article in the *New York Times* of July 4, 1976, as it began to chronicle what happened or what could have happened to a beginning teacher in a small town in Oklahoma twenty years ago. She was told by her school bosses where to live, not to smoke or drink, not to become involved in politics, and to be sure to attend church services whenever they were held.

Things are changed now.

The NEA at its annual convention in the summer of 1976, for the first time in its history, voted to endorse a candidate for president after the conventions of the two political parties. (It endorsed the Democratic candidate, Jimmy Carter, in part because he had pledged major support for education. Particularly he supported the creation of a Department of Education, which became a reality in 1979.) Now, it is a regular occurrence for NEA in its monthly newspaper not only to endorse candidates for national office, but periodically to publish box scores on members of Congress, giving the dates on educational bills in Congress and labeling them "right" or "wrong," in accordance with the NEA's position on the bill. With about two million members, their families, and influences, this can be a telling sign.

It is clear that teachers, who have throughout the history of the public schools in the United States been under the weight of a bundle of "do's" and "don'ts," have at long last achieved the status of first-class citizens. Teachers have long felt that they should be able to engage in activities that other people who work to support themselves can.

Of course, the proliferation of tenure legislation and court decisions has gone a long way toward securing these gains for teachers. But the chief motivator has been the changes the years have brought in the mores of the American people. Also, the steady growth in the number of men in teaching has had a decidedly positive influence upon the achievement of these rights. Finally, the size and aggressiveness of teachers' professional organizations have been strong factors in achieving these results.

While the trend is unquestionably toward freeing teachers to live their own lives, the traditional mind set of the people toward expecting circumspect conduct from teachers, as has always been the case with ministers, cannot be completely discarded in one generation. There will continue to be, here and there, reversions to old forms, customs, and expectations. But the trend toward letting teachers live their own lives is too strong to be reversed. Of course, teachers should continue to realize—as do ministers—that the public is going to expect conduct far above the norm for the usual workers, since they have such unique opportunity to influence the lives of children. And teachers should cherish this attitude, because it is intended as a high compliment. Especially is this now true, since teachers have the resources to appeal for their lawful rights in the courts, and are winning case after case.

Abuse of Loyalty Oaths

In 1950 John Beecher was fired from his position at San Francisco State College for refusing to sign a loyalty oath during the hysterical McCarthy era, when the imagination of the American people had been fired up to look for and to expect to find a Communist under almost every rock. So hysterical had the inflamed imaginations of the people become that such a refusal was *prima facie* evidence of guilt. It took twenty-seven years for Mr. Beecher to be vindicated. In 1977, the California legislature unanimously voted to reinstate those who had refused to sign such an oath. In the meantime, Mr. Beecher became a living legend. He strode across the campus with his head still held high, and his snow-white hair and long white beard became a trademark of integrity. Today, he is teaching children of those who were his students when he was cruelly dismissed as the result of the rantings of a long-discredited demagogue. Although he never doubted that he would be vindicated, it is to the discredit of freedom-loving Americans that he had to wait so long.

Dismissal of a Black Teacher

The 1963 case of a black teacher in North Carolina created repercussions throughout the United States. It was not the first, but one of the most dramatic examples of the federal law against discrimination being upheld and the teacher being returned to her position, a case in which the local school board was defeated at every turn. Also, it was a dramatic, precedent-setting case in which the NEA, for the first time so far as we can determine, was asked by a federal court to serve as an expert witness in certifying to a teacher's competence. Mrs. Wilma Johnson and her husband became involved in a civil rights march in their community at a time when that state was rocked with anxiety and outrage by the drive of the blacks and their civil rights organizations for full citizenship rights. The teacher had been employed by her district in an all-black school for several years.

Only a few weeks before participating in the civil rights march, she had received a letter from her principal (also a black) praising highly her competence as a teacher. At the time for renewing teacher contracts in the spring, she received a letter from her principal advising her that the board had decided not to renew her contract. Immediately she inquired as to the reason for the board's decision. Again by letter, she was informed by the principal that she was being released because of "incompetence as a teacher." She protested that only a few weeks earlier the principal had sent her a letter praising her competence. Not getting any action on her protest, she sued in a state court for reinstatement to her position. The state court upheld the school board in its action.

Finally, she and her state education association appealed to the NEA for help in appealing the case to the federal courts. Funds were granted from the DuShane Defense Fund to underwrite attorneys' fees. When the case came before the appropriate federal district court, her letter from the principal was introduced to rebut the charges of incompetence. The court requested the NEA to examine the teacher as to her qualifications and competence for the position she had held, and to present testimony in the court as to its findings. The NEA Professional Rights and Responsibilities Commission assembled a committee of seven members, all outside the NEA staff, including a school board member, two college professors, and several teachers, to examine Mrs. Johnson. For two days this committee subjected the teacher to searching questions, examined the records of her college preparation for teaching, and found her exceptionally well qualified for the job she held. The chairman of the committee appeared in the federal court and testified that the committee had found the teacher well qualified. This is believed to be a precedent-setting case in that it was the first in which a court had called upon a national professional teachers' association to give expert testimony regarding a practitioner's competence, although that has been the practice of courts with respect to other professions, such as medicine. The federal court ruled in favor of Mrs. Johnson. It ordered the offending school board to reinstate her to her job, and to pay her back pay for the time she had missed because of the firing. Also, in another unusual step, the court ordered the lower court to assess a heavy fine against the members of the board, to be paid by them personally and not from school funds, for illegal discrimination against the teacher.

Nepotism and Maternity Issues

Another prominent form of mistreatment of teachers has been practiced in varying degrees since the earliest schools were established and extends to recent years. That policy prohibited married teachers from being employed. In many cases working women were prohibited from marrying; those who did marry were usually fired from their jobs. During the Great Depression it was a common practice to bar the employment of two members of a family in a given school district. This was, of course, due in large part to the scarcity of jobs. It was common practice until a decade or so ago for school boards to have a regulation against employment of a man and his wife. If both were employed by the school district during the same school term, one spouse (usually the woman) lost her job.

There was also the practice of firing a married teacher if she became pregnant during a school term. The idea seems to have been that childbearing was an indecent sort of business and that students had to be spared visible evidence of it. An offshoot of this practice was that of requiring a pregnant teacher to give up her teaching job within a prescribed number of months (usually four) before the expected birth and for a limited period after the birth. In recent years federal courts have overthrown this rule as interfering with the constitutional rights of the teacher. The four-month limitation seems to have been a common practice not based on medical evidence, or so the courts have generally held.

THE KATE FRANK CASE

In 1941, the NEA established the National Commission for the Defense of Democracy through Education primarily to defend the schools and teachers against charges of subversive activities and lack of patriotism. Such charges were often fabricated by zealots or persons who sought to gain favor from the unrest caused by the approach of World War II. With the approach of the war, prices were skyrocketing and people were apprehensive and distraught. Such a climate is made to order for those who would seek to capitalize upon unrest. In creating the Defense Commission, the NEA had as its motive the protecting of schools and teachers in the service of youth.

One of the earliest (1942) cases of teachers to come to the attention of this newly formed Defense Commission was that of Kate Frank and one of her colleagues in the Muskogee, Oklahoma, schools. This was probably the first case in which teachers' court costs and subsistence were supported by NEA. Miss Frank had taught in Muskogee for twenty-three years. She taught commercial subjects in the high school and had previously taught science and math elsewhere in Missouri. She held a bachelor's degree from Southwest Missouri State Teachers College, and a master's degree from the University of Missouri. In the spring of the 1942–43 school year, the school board suddenly announced that, because of shortness of funds, it was having to cut the school term to eight and one-half months. Miss Frank and two colleagues, doubting that this was true, led a protest movement which resulted in the payment of the two weeks' salary due teachers under their contracts. Miss Frank and her colleagues, Mrs. Mabel Runyon and Mrs. R. P. Chandler, spent most of the ensuing summer researching the facts about the school district and its financing, using the official records in the county courthouse. As they suspected, there were ample funds on hand to have completed the scheduled nine-month term. They published the facts as they had discovered them, demonstrating to parents that their children had been denied a full school term by a stingy school board. At the time nothing was said, because the terms of two of the board members who had voted for shortening the school term were expiring the following spring. In the school board election these two members were reelected. Almost immediately thereafter the three teachers were advised that they would no longer be employed by the board. There was an uproar in the community at this cruel treatment of the teachers.[1]

The National Education Association sent a representative to look into the situation in the Muskogee schools. On June 27, 1943, at the NEA annual convention in Indianapolis, the Department of Classroom Teachers unanimously adopted a resolution protesting the discharge of the three teachers without a statement of reason or right to a hearing. Because these discharges were caused by the board's opposition to the right of teachers to maintain effective classroom teachers' organizations and to exercise their political rights as citizens, the Department of Classroom Teachers urged that the NEA Committee on Tenure make a thorough investiga-

---

[1] *You Are Fired* (Washington, D.C.: National Commission on the Defense of Children Through Education, 1942). Personal interviews with author, Dec. 16, 1976; July 18 and Oct. 5, 1977.

tion of the underlying causes of the dismissals, and that the Defense Commission take such action as they deemed appropriate to defend these teachers.

On June 29, 1943, the NEA Representative Assembly voted to refer the case to the NEA Executive Committee, with directions that every resource of the association be used to obtain justice for the dismissed teachers. On July 1 the NEA Executive Committee voted to commend the prompt action on the case by the Tenure Committee and the National Commission for the Defense of Democracy through Education. The secretary of the latter visited Muskogee and conducted a vigorous investigation. He secured a meeting of the board and the dismissed teachers, but he was unable to get the board to rescind the dismissals.

At a meeting with the superintendent of the schools, the superintendent denied that he had recommended the dismissals, but the board contended that he did. But none of the teachers had been consulted or advised prior to their firing; nor were there statements of any kind regarding the causes of their firing. Each learned of the action from newspaper stories of the board meeting.

Another factor influencing the board in its antagonism toward the teachers was the number of civic organizations that had been aroused by the facts revealed by the teachers, about needlessly reducing the school term. They had run an independent slate to oppose the three regular Democrats backed by the "political boss" of the board. The platform for which the civic groups fought was to work for better schools and a nine-month school term. The Muskogee Classroom Teachers Association, which Kate Frank headed as president, participated in various activities of the citizens committee but not in the committee's selection of candidates for the school board.

Still another factor irritated the board. One of the members of the board, several days preceding the election, was instrumental in having a special meeting of the teachers in the district. One of the school board members who was running for reelection was present at the meeting. Since the meeting had been called ostensibly to get the teachers to approve a resolution commending the school board, two members of which were running for reelection, Kate Frank spoke in opposition to putting the teachers in the posture of endorsing any ticket. Another teacher presented a motion that the vote be taken by a secret ballot, but this motion was defeated and a voice vote was taken, in which endorsement of the resolution was given. Naturally, the position of Miss Frank was resented by the board members. The resulting election was a hotly contested one. Two Democratic candidates and one independent candidate were elected on April 6, 1943; on May 19, a special meeting of the board voted not to reappoint Miss Frank and her two colleagues who had aroused the ire of the board.

This is the first case to be highly publicized in which the NEA entered the field of supporting a fired teacher to the extent of underwriting the cost of court cases and providing subsistence for the fired teacher during unemployment.

While it may have been coincidental, the reader cannot help wondering if the prominent stature of Kate Frank in the profession did not have great influence in impelling NEA to project itself so vigorously into her defense. When one looks at the list of her influential positions, one can hardly avoid the consideration of that possibility. Here is a list of some of her activities by the time of her firing: (1) helped organize the Muskogee Classroom Teachers Association in 1934; (2) gave vigorous support to securing the single-salary schedule, sick leave with pay, group health and accident and hospitalization insurance; (3) worked for a teachers' retirement law and a tenure law; and (4) served as president of the Muskogee Classroom Teachers Association. At the state and national levels Miss Frank was, or had been, (1) first president of the Northeastern District of the Oklahoma Classroom Teachers Association; (2) first president of the Oklahoma Education Association in 1937–38 (the second woman ever to serve in this position); (3) an attendant at every NEA convention since 1933; (4) Oklahoma State Director for NEA, 1937–43; (5) member of NEA Budget Committee, 1941–43; (6) NEA Vice-President, 1942–44; and (7) member of the Executive Board of the NEA Defense Commission, 1941–44.

Whatever influence the professional status of Kate Frank may have had in prompting the NEA to act vigorously in her defense is of little consequence. The important thing is that the NEA had demonstrated to itself, and to the teaching profession, that it acted effectively to secure justice for mistreated teachers. And, in time, it revealed to the people of the United States that teachers were worthy of being treated as first-class citizens.

It probably is true that the two colleagues of Miss Frank suffered at the hands of the board because they were too closely associated with her.

The man who was designated by many as the political boss of the board indicated that the dismissals were reprisals, that Miss Frank had fought the board too hard and had to be dismissed.

Probably the basic factor motivating the board was its vehement opposition to an active classroom teachers' organization. Apparently the board looked upon such a group as some sort of indentured servants, who were presumptuous in assuming that they had the full rights of first-class citizens. To bring down Kate Frank, president of the Muskogee Classroom Teachers Association, would clearly warn classroom teachers that there were strict limits to their rights and activities. Also, it was known that Miss Frank had been frequently consulted by citizens' groups which supported the independent candidates in the election.

The Defense Commission persuaded Miss Frank to become executive secretary of the Muskogee Teachers Association until the court suit was settled, promising to pay her salary. The money was raised by voluntary donations of the members of the NEA Department of Classroom Teachers. With constant agitation in the community, the members responsible for her firing were defeated in the next election, and Miss Frank was restored to her position.

The voluntary fund was continued with donations until the NEA decreed that this would become the Donald DuShane Memorial Defense Fund in honor of the former secretary of the Defense Commission. Donations and funds from NEA sources were used to keep the level of the fund at a minimum of $100,000; in 1968, NEA enlarged this amount to $1,000,000. Presently, funds to support teachers in court cases to regain their positions come from appropriations from general NEA funds provided by membership dues.

The Consequences of the Kate Frank Case

The importance of this case to the well-being of the teaching profession cannot be exaggerated. While there may have been other incidents of teacher mistreatment preceding this precedent-setting one, little or nothing is known about them. They received scarcely any attention beyond the narrow confines of the local setting.

Thus the year 1943 has become a red-letter date in the development of the profession of teaching in the United States. It laid the foundation and gained increasing public support for the National Education Association's contention that Kate Frank, like every teacher, has the right to belong to a teachers' organization of her own choice. Moreover, teachers have the right to participate in activities to improve education, to secure better teaching conditions, and to secure adequate financial support for the schools. They must be free to exercise full citizenship rights, including the right to express views on political issues and to work and vote for candidates to public office. Teachers, as servants of all the public, have the right to tenure.

The response of the people of Muskogee was quick and effective.

The NEA now had a public platform of action and reform, which has to a great extent dominated its work since 1943. And down through the years, the support of the public increases with the growing concept and extension of human rights. It is no secret that prior to 1943 public understanding, and the scope of its concepts in regard to the rights and freedoms of teachers, had not widened much from the early days of the Republic. But from here on the public concepts of teachers and their work have expanded rapidly. Today there is hardly a place isolated enough from reality to attempt to deny teachers the free rights of all citizens.

Of course, in all fairness, it must be added that NEA has had valiant moral support all along the path of this great development. The American Federation of Teachers, the American Civil Liberties Union, the National Association for the Advancement of Colored People, and many other sympathetic groups have helped tremendously.

6

Enforcing Teacher Competency Examinations

THE current agitation for more reliance upon examinations to measure pupil achievement and teacher competency is not a new thing in education. Almost throughout the history of general education in the world there has been some reliance upon examinations for admission to higher schools and to most professions. In comparatively recent years this emphasis has grown to the extent that the demand is for standardized, research-oriented, professionally developed examinations. Above all, these examinations are presumed to have great reliability in the measuring of effectiveness of schools and teachers.

How did this come about? There is no easy answer to this question. The probability is that originally this was one means of setting apart as superior those who by birth or wealth or influence, or by the vagaries of orientation to the fields of study, did well on the typical exams purporting to measure ability. The types of curricula completed by these groups tended—and still tend, to a significant extent—to be the bases for measuring both the intelligence and scholastic achievement of people in general. Although this practice has in varying degrees prevailed for centuries, there still remain many unanswered questions and some lack of proof of these theses.

COMPETENCY-BASED EDUCATION—ANOTHER FAD?

Among all the gaudily dressed fads that the public persistently and insistently embraces, none seems to be as promising as that currently parading under the fetching nomenclature of "Competency-Based Education." So enraptured is the public with this new gimmick that it graciously annexes the preceding modifier "Minimum." And with this generous qualifier, the conviction is cinched that herein lies the road to the promised land of education. In the last half-dozen years or so, this promise has become so appealing that most of the states have zestfully set forth to put it to work to improve education.

Some are holding back reluctantly because, simple enough, this promised miracle instrument has not convinced them as yet. And among the seeming minority are some who look with a measure of foreboding upon this great promise.

COMPETENCY TESTING NOT A CURE-ALL

The idea of compelling teachers to measure up by demonstrating their capacity through the medium of so-called competency tests has much to commend itself to the public. Unfortunately, such tests tend to have pronounced weaknesses when used as absolutes, or even for near accuracy. First of all, it is extremely difficult to devise a test that is not biased toward some group, or especially some individual who has pursued an education that covered certain prescribed subjects and not other subjects. The term "biased" is not meant to imply a deep-seated or emotional dislike of an individual or class. A test becomes biased against an individual who has not pursued (or did pursue, but many years ago) a given subject or subjects on which test items may be based. For example, one teacher may have completed a college curriculum which especially emphasized the cognitive, classical liberal arts fields; another may have pursued a more general education. Standardized tests tend to be deeply biased against black teachers because their race had little or no access to schooling of any kind prior to the early years of this century, or even later in many cases. Almost all conceivable standardized tests based upon the long-standing, superior curricula pursued by whites are likely to be strongly biased against blacks in general, and against black teachers in particular, in the sense that the latter may not have studied the information contained in the questions.

There are, of course, other valid reasons for looking askance at test scores and evaluating the competency of teachers on this basis. Ernest L. Boyer, a former chancellor of the State University of New York and a U.S. Commissioner of Education, has spent all of his adult life in the field of education. Speaking to the Council of Chief State School Officers in 1978, he said: "I'm uncomfortable with simple measures of teacher or student evaluation. . . . Obviously teachers have to know the material they teach. But the skill of teaching is profoundly more complicated. Of course, there's no way to defend sloppiness, but there are important skills of teaching we can't measure."[1] Commissioner Boyer favors periodic evaluation of an instructor's performance. While at SUNY he instituted school and faculty review of the presidents at each campus. The presidents were appointed for five-year terms; at the end of a term, the review was completed.

Wesman Personnel Classification Test

In one major city, the superintendent recommended that the Wesman Personnel Classification Test (which half of a sample group of first-year teachers failed) be adopted by the school board as a teacher-hiring standard, replacing the National Teachers Examination. The reason was that teachers who scored above the 50th percentile on the Wesman test tended to have better ratings by students. Also, the Wesman—a sixty-question test—takes about thirty minutes to complete, and can be administered by district personnel and graded quickly.

Teachers' organizations were reported to oppose the test as too simplistic to measure the competence of teachers. The administration contended the examination was only one of eleven criteria used to evaluate applicants for teaching positions.

Teacher Testing—An Arbitrary Method
of Measuring Performance

In June, 1973, NEA filed an *amicus curiae* brief in the Eighth U.S. Circuit Court of Appeals, asking the court to sustain an Iowa federal court ruling that a teacher cannot be fired solely because his or her students have scored low on standardized tests.

Norma Scheelhouse, an elementary teacher in the Woodbury Central Community District who had been dismissed after ten years in the district, was ordered by the court to be reinstated and awarded more than

---

[1] Associated Press dispatch from 1978 convention of Chief State School Officers. Used by permission.

$13,000 in back pay. The school board appealed the court's verdict. The NEA argued that a set of scores on tests is an arbitrary method of measuring teacher performance; also, the NEA argued that the teacher was entitled to due process although she was not under tenure.

NATIONAL TEACHERS EXAMINATION

In September, 1973, a federal appellate court decreed that nine black teachers be reinstated and receive back pay from the Chesterfield County Schools in South Carolina for the 1970–71 school year. They had been fired because of low scores on the NTE (National Teachers Examination). The NEA and the South Carolina Education Association had submitted a brief urging reversal of the ruling of a lower court.

The brief stressed the fact that the county's number of black teachers decreased by one-third in the preceding three-year period. In 1968–69, the county board had adopted the requirement that every teacher have a "B" or higher certificate, or an NTE score of at least 425. The brief pointed out that the "B" certificate score had changed frequently; as a result, the brief asserted that dismissed "C" teachers had, in several cases, scored as high as or higher than "B" teachers who were retained. The plaintiffs charged that this policy was discriminatory, and that it was adopted despite that knowledge. The court ordered reinstatement and back pay for the nine teachers, as set forth above.

Fights on Teacher Exams

The General Assembly of North Carolina, in the summer of 1975, amended its statute governing teacher certification to permit teachers who had previously been denied a certificate for failing to meet the minimum composite score of 950 on the NTE, but who met all other requirements, to be issued probationary certificates valid for two years. Such teachers may be employed on the same terms as persons with regular certificates if they have good performance ratings and demonstrate academic competence, including knowledge of subject matter, methods, and principles of education. This certificate, however, is valid only for a temporary period.

Subsequent to this legislation, an NEA suit sought invalidation of North Carolina's required NTE scores as a condition for certification. In

August, 1975, a federal court struck down the statute as being invalid and unconstitutional to the extent that it requires refusal of certification to otherwise qualified applicants. The court found that North Carolina had selected a cutoff score designed to eliminate a certain percentage of applicants without demonstrating a correlation between the score and competence in teaching. A court injunction now requires the certification of about 15,000 applicants denied certification under the 1964 regulation.

In September 1975, the NEA joined the South Carolina Education Association and nine black teachers joined the U.S. Department of Justice in a suit charging racial bias in South Carolina's NTE cut-off scores as the requirement for an "A" class certificate. (A composite score of 975 was required, with 450 on the weighted common examination.)

An April, 1977, decision of the U.S. Supreme Court upheld South Carolina's use of the National Teacher Examination to make decisions about certifying and paying its teachers. By a 5-2 vote, the court sustained the decision of a lower federal court which had concluded that South Carolina did not adopt the test requirements with a discriminatory purpose, and that the test had been validated in a manner consistent with Title VII of the Civil Rights Act of 1964. The Department of Justice brought suit, alleging that use of the examination discriminates against black applicants. NEA and the South Carolina Education Association also participated as intervening plaintiffs. In a state where more than 95 percent of the teachers are white, the test disqualified 83 percent of black applicants and 17.5 percent of white applicants. South Carolina is the only state that uses the NTE to set salary levels in spite of criticism from the Educational Testing Service, which developed the controversial examination.[2]

A United States District Court Reverses
Previous Decision on NTE

In April, 1977, the United States District Court of South Carolina (Columbia Division) rendered judgment in favor of the State of South Carolina and several appropriate state divisions (or departments), against the United States, the National Education Association, and others. The plaintiffs sought relief with respect to the use of minimum score requirements in certifying and determining the pay levels of teachers.

---

[2] "Trends," *Today's Education*, Apr.–May, 1978, p. 7.

One issue was to determine whether the use of the examination and the use by the state and its board of education of a minimum score on the examination violated the equal protection clause of the Fourteenth Amendment, or the Eleventh Amendment. The court held that neither amendment was violated. The decision states that the data on population each year since 1954 show that the proportion of white teachers vs. black teachers closely paralleled that of the population from 1945 through 1978. The state issued four grades of certificates—A, B, C, and D. Classes of certificates and percentages receiving them according to their grades on the NTE were: Class A certificates to the top 25 percent; B certificates to the middle 50 percent; C certificates to the next 15 percent; and D certificates to the lowest 10 percent.

In 1957, a new system of certification had been instituted. The NTE is composed of three batteries of tests: (1) the common examinations include tests in professional education, and in methods and principles of teaching; (2) general education—English, social studies, literature, fine arts, science and mathematics; (3) the area examinations contain tests in the subjects the teacher expects to teach. To secure an A certificate the applicant had to make a score of 500 or more on the common examinations; for a B certificate, a score of 425 to 499 was required. To get a C certificate, the applicant needed a score of 375 to 424; for a D certificate, a score of 332 to 374. Scores below 332 did not earn a certificate.

Again in 1969 the state changed its certification program, providing for only the professional certificate and the warrant. For the professional certificate, a minimum score of 975 was required, with a score on the common examination of at least 450, and the same minimum on the area examination. For the warrant, a minimum score of 450 on the common exam and 400 on the area examination, or a total of not less than 850 on the two exams, was needed.

The decision of the U.S. District Court was that the involved South Carolina officials were concerned with improving the quality of public school teaching, certifying only those applicants who possessed the minimum knowledge necessary to teach effectively, utilizing an objective measure of applicants coming from widely disparate teacher-training programs, and providing appropriate financial incentives for teachers to improve their academic qualifications—and thereby their ability to teach. The court supported *the conclusion that the NTE is professionally and carefully prepared to measure the critical mass of knowledge in academic sub-*

ject matter. The NTE does not measure teaching skills, but does measure the content of the academic preparation of prospective teachers.

Thus, the way is cleared for the licensing authorities to use tests as a measure of the extent of knowledge an applicant will need to teach a given subject or field.

In fairness, it should be pointed out that South Carolina had to change its program several times, as delineated above, to obtain a plan that (1) was not ruled discriminatory and (2) does not seek to measure teaching skills.

The above described decision of April, 1977, was challenged by the U.S. Department of Justice in a suit entered on June 18, 1977, as in violation of the Civil Rights Act of 1964, as amended in 1972. The district court sustained the decision of the first court.

Decision of U.S. District Court on the South Carolina Use of NTE

Since the 1954 decision of the U.S. Supreme Court in *Brown v. Board of Education,* which overturned the "separate but equal" decision of the Supreme Court in *Plessy v. Ferguson* in 1898, it has been quite natural to suspect that the states of the Deep South would search for means by which the traditional racial and salary bias against black teachers could be continued. There has been since 1954 suspicion of and vigorous efforts to ferret out illegal tactics toward blacks by which existing racial differentials could be continued. It so happens that this search has been especially focused upon South Carolina.

In September, 1975, a suit against the State of South Carolina, the South Carolina Board of Education, the South Carolina State Retirement System, and others by the U.S. Attorney General charged a violation of the Fourteenth Amendment and of Title VII of the Civil Rights Act of 1964. Minimum score requirements on the NTE were being used to certify and to determine the pay level of teachers within the state. The NEA and the South Carolina Education Association joined in the suit as plaintiffs.

For over thirty years South Carolina and its agencies have used NTE scores to make decisions with respect to the certification of teachers and the amount of state aid payable to local school districts. Local school boards use scores on the NTE for selection and compensation of teachers. From 1969 to 1976, a minimum score of 975 was required by the state for its certification and state-aid decisions. In June, 1976, after an exhaustive validation study by Educational Testing Service (ETS), and after a critical review and evaluation of this study by the South Carolina Board of Education's Committee on Teacher Recruitment, Training and Compensation, and the Department Staff, the state established new certification requirements involving different minimum scores in various areas of teaching specialization that range from 940 to 1198. The court holds that these regulations are properly before it, since the plaintiffs were undoubtedly aware that the validity study by ETS, upon which these regulations were based, was well under way when the suits were filed.

The local boards are required by the state to hire only certified teachers (S.C. Code 21-45, 21-371, 21-375), but there are no uniform standards with respect to test scores used by the local school boards in selecting from among the pool of certified applicants.

Plaintiffs challenged each of the uses of the NTE. They contended that more blacks than whites historically have failed to achieve the required minimum score, and that this result creates a racial classification in violation of the constitutional and statutory provisions cited in their complaints. Each complaint seeks declaratory and injunctive relief with respect to the use of the minimum score requirement in certifying and determining the pay levels of teachers adversely affected by the minimum score requirement, and monetary relief for alleged financial losses of teachers, together with costs. Plaintiffs also asked for attorneys' fees.

South Carolina requires persons who teach in the public schools to hold a certificate issued by the State Board of Education. From 1945 to 1975 the state has had four certification systems, each requiring prospective teachers to take the NTE. Candidates are able to take the NTE an unlimited number of times. (The tests are given by the state three or four times each year.)

The record before the court indicates that during this period the racial composition of the South Carolina teacher force has closely paralleled the racial composition of the state's population. The 1950 census reported that 61.1 percent of the population was white and 38.8 percent was black. In 1953–54, the state employed a teacher force that was 58 percent white and 42 percent black. The 1960 census showed a population that was 67.1 percent white and 34.9 percent black. In 1966–67, the teacher force was 65.6 percent white and 34.4 percent black. The 1970 census showed a population that was 69.5 percent white, and 30.5 percent black. In 1975–76 the teacher force was 70.1 percent white and 29.3 percent black.

Supreme Court Upholds Teacher Exams

As previously reported, the Supreme Court of the United States in 1977 upheld the decision of a lower court which had concluded that South Carolina did not adopt the test requirement with the purpose of discriminating against black teachers, and that the test had been validated in a manner consistent with Title VII of the Civil Rights Act of 1964. The suit had been brought by the Department of Justice, alleging that use of the examination discriminated against black applicants. NEA and the South Carolina Education Association also participated as plaintiffs.

Thus, the court held that the evolutionary process of the licensing plans did not eventuate into a process that discriminates. But it took several years, and several adverse federal court decisions to achieve this new status.

In the process of trying to clear the way for acceptance by the federal courts of NTE, the Educational Testing Service had in 1974 notified South Carolina that its contract with the state would be terminated at the conclusion of the existing contract in August 1975, because of the state's use of the scores for determining teachers' salaries. South Carolina was denied use of NTE for three months, at which time it agreed that (1) a validity study of NTE would be conducted; (2) test scores would no longer be used to classify teachers for salary purposes; and (3) a simple classification system would be applied to all teachers. Agreeing to these principles, the state was again authorized to use NTE by ETS, and the federal court soon after approved the use of these examinations as being nondiscriminatory.

The Impact of Teacher Surplus

One of the major (and obvious) reasons for the increasing use of the NTE is the prevailing surplus of qualified teachers seeking employment. Our colleges and universities are now producing something like 100,000 teachers each year who cannot find jobs. This means there are several applicants for every job opening, often many times more. Thus the larger school districts need some definitive and reliable means of appraising several aspects of the qualities required of good teachers. This is a major reason for the prevalence of the use of the National Teachers Examination.

According to the Educational Testing Service, approximately one-half of the 140,000 graduates of teacher education institutions took the examination in 1976–77.

States Using National Teachers Examinations

The Educational Testing Service, in a survey made in the fall of 1977, reported a total of thirty-eight states make some use of the NTE examinations; a total of 238 school systems use the NTE scores. Sixty-one systems require the scores, and seventy-seven encourage their use.

The following seven purposes were listed as the ones used by the states:

1. Certification: Mississippi, North Carolina, South Carolina, and Virginia.
2. Additional teaching area endorsements to regular certificates: California, Delaware, Nebraska, South Carolina, West Virginia.
3. Validation of credits earned at non-accredited institutions: California, Delaware.
4. Alternative to certain approved program requirements for regular certification: California, Colorado, Nebraska.
5. Obtaining data for statewide teacher examinations of educational studies: Alabama.
6. The scores are encouraged but not required in Alabama, Maine, New Hampshire, and Virginia.
7. Licensure for speech pathologists and audiologists: California, Connecticut, Delaware, Hawaii, Iowa, Kentucky, Montana, New York, Ohio, Oregon, Rhode Island, Tennessee, and Utah.

THE APPEAL OF TESTING

The present craze to test everybody and everything that has to do with the schools has several motivations. One, of course, is the cluster of firms which make up the group commonly designated as the "testing industry."

This has grown to be a multi-million-dollar business. And, although as a general rule these are nonprofit organizations, the profits can be large, and the prestige and sense of power yielded are huge indeed. As would be expected, the testing industry would engender a number of "spinoff" businesses that are beginning to inhale the enticing aroma of profits ahead. Some of these are unrestrained by nonprofit status. Indeed, some not only are accepting profits, but are actually (and gleefully, one may surmise) pursuing the outer limits of the glorious promises of profits. Especially evident in this process are the "private" test-coaching schools. These are not schools in the basic sense of the word, but are purveyors of the irresistible idea that dreaded barriers to passage through the gates of academic respectability, prestige, and scholarship can be overcome through cram sessions.

Then, there is perhaps the most impelling magnet of all to many members of "the public." When teachers are pictured as woefully inept ignoramuses, such reports are irresistible tidbits for that segment of the public whose members never were able to master the multiplication tables or parse even the simplest sentence. These people can then boast, in a comparative sense, (1) of the powers of their own imagined scholarship, or (2) of the "terrible tempered" schoolmasters they had as children. Said teacher flew into a rage at the pupil who made the most minuscule error, and in the vastly enlarged memory of that time, his rage has multiplied a thousand-fold. This huge multiplication of memory is exceeded only by the enlargement of the alleged punishment of the "scholars" so unfortunate as to have had such "hell-bent-for-perfection" teachers. Listening to the aberrant memory enlargements gives one the notion, without the reminiscent and gleeful teller saying so specifically, that he and most of his colleagues had real scholarship beaten into them. That is, as broadly implied, they did not have the superb mentality to acquire these things easily and quickly. What a wonderfully easy attainment of a certain mental eminence would eventuate in the enlarging vista of a half-century or more hence! And what a glorious opportunity to denounce, with outraged dignity, the depths of ignorance and fallibility to which currently existing school teachers and "scholars" have descended! Especially, since he (the reciter) had endured the very depths of hell itself to acquire a respectable education. Thus it is that an older generation rises to the pinnacle of intellectual responsibility (greatly aided, of course, by the testers) on the shoulders of an inept generation of teachers and scholars. Indeed, who among his now out-of-school-for-a-generation-or-so colleagues can resist such a chance of attaining a pleasing promontory of gratuitous superiority?

The steady escalation of criticism of the public schools finds ammunition in the constant yelping of the devotees of testing of children at the various grade levels, in the firm devotion to the concept that these scores are a magic open-sesame to the measuring of progress in education.

Of course, there is merit—great merit—in such testing insofar as it attempts to measure the grasp of the fundamentals of learning. But as to the full measurement of a child's developing potential, tests can be at the same time disturbingly inaccurate regarding the depth, breadth, and height of a given child's grasping for the best that is within him.

7

Dismissals of Teachers from Jobs

THIS chapter will detail several cases of dismissals of teachers, reemphasizing the need for tenure legislation in every state, and will show the progress that has been made toward this end.

As would be expected, there is strenuous opposition among some influential groups to tenure for teachers. Perhaps most opposition comes from some school board members and associations, some state education officials, and some school administrators. Citizens, in general, tend to dismiss tenure as impractical. Each of these groups has its own arguments and reasons. The chief point in favor of tenure for teachers is that teachers should be free to present the facts and not be deterred by fear of being fired. College teachers have largely won this right to academic freedom.

Despite some unfavorable reactions, the notion of tenure has gained much ground in recent years. Forty-six states and the District of Columbia have tenure laws of some type, or have passed continuing contract laws for teachers. As a general rule, states with such legislation require hard evidence of charges against teachers before they can be dismissed from their jobs. Also, as a general rule, state laws specify as causes for dismissal incompetency, insubordination, inefficiency, and failure to observe school board rules. State laws tend to require that teachers receive advance notice if their services are unsatisfactory: the board must provide a statement of charges, and the right to a hearing, before a teacher can be dismissed.

We hope the time is past when teachers can be dismissed on petty charges. Federal courts in recent years have been most considerate in seeking justice for teachers because of failure of the respective employing boards to accord teachers "due process," as defined by the Fourteenth Amendment. This would include the right to a hearing—to be faced with the charges against them. This amendment specifies the right to counsel, the right to examine witnesses, and the right to present witnesses to testify favorably for the accused. Under some forms of tenure legislation, teachers are helpless to defend themselves against false charges, or against outright dismissal in order to create a job for a member of an influential family or for a political crony. The federal courts have tended to overrule the firing of teachers for having exercised their constitutional rights. In addition, courts are increasingly requiring boards to meet rigorous standards for selection and supervision procedures. In this connection, it should be mentioned that about twenty-five states have passed collective bargaining or negotiation legislation which applies to teachers. As a result, teacher organizations in some of these states have negotiated provisions for a grievance procedure where a dismissal may be threatened. While it may appear that the attainment of tenure for teachers has been a long, drawn-out process, the fact is that rapid progress has come to pass in the last decade or so. It must be remembered that as long ago as 1919, the NEA established its first committee to study the need for and probability of securing tenure legislation. Thus it has taken more than a half-century to bring this problem to the edge of universal acceptance, and most of this progress has been made in the last two decades.

CAUSES FOR DISMISSAL

Tenure, of course, cannot be a one-way street which disregards the inherent rights of children and parents while it protects teachers. Thus we will find several kinds of provisions which tend to assure tenure. Laws dealing with rules for fair dismissal practices demand (1) specification of causes, and (2) the presentation of substantial evidence in support of the stated causes. Some of the causes for dismissal specified in such laws are incompetency, insubordination, gross inefficiency, and repeated violation of school board rules. Generally, these laws specify that a teacher must receive advance notice or warning of deficiences, and must be given a chance to correct them before charges are made.

AID FROM PROFESSIONAL ORGANIZATIONS[1]

Since the Kate Frank case marks the beginning of financial support for mistreated teachers by the organized teaching profession, as represented by NEA, it should be further discussed in this chapter. At the time of her firing, Kate Frank had served on the executive committee of the NEA, had been vice-president, and was a member of the National Commission for the Defense of Democracy through Education. Dr. Donald DuShane, then executive secretary of that commission, came to Muskogee, as did the chairman of the NEA Tenure Committee. In conversations with the school board, Dr. DuShane could secure no reasons for Miss Frank's firing. He persuaded Miss Frank to accept the position of executive secretary of the Muskogee Education Association, pledging to raise the money to pay her salary from donations of teachers throughout the United States. Miss Frank at first declined, because she knew she could get a teaching position elsewhere, but DuShane persuaded her to stay as a service to the teaching profession. This she did—and was within a couple of years reinstated to her position.

Supreme Court Strikes Down Forced Maternity Leave Case

On January 21, 1974, the U.S. Supreme Court, by a 7–2 vote, struck down mandatory maternity leave provisions as violating the Fourteenth Amendment's due process clause. Although school boards had asserted that some teachers became incapable of performing certain duties during the latter part of pregnancy, the courts held that this did not justify sweeping mandatory leaves. This ruling means that a pregnant teacher will no longer be compelled to leave her job at a specified number of months before the expected birth.

As a result of this ruling, two teachers in Cleveland were granted back pay and court expenses amounting to more than $30,000. The NEA spent more than $25,000 on the cases, and the Women's Law Fund largely financed these two.

---

[1] The NEA case examples are excerpted from "DuShane Defense Fund Report," issued periodically each year by the National Education Association.

Examination Scores, Certification, and Salaries

The NEA and the North Carolina Education Association joined the U.S. Department of Justice in February, 1974, challenging a North Carolina law requiring teachers seeking certification to achieve specified minimum scores on the National Teachers Examination. The case involved twenty-four black teachers who were barred from employment, higher pay, or promotion because they had not achieved the prescribed minimum scores. The teachers had to be employed on a nonstandard basis and were paid less than teachers with certificates who performed the same work. Some were employed as teacher aides or substitutes. The Justice Department contended that the law was racially discriminatory and violated the Civil Rights Act of 1964 and the Fourteenth Amendment. Evidence presented in the court hearing indicated a marked decline in the number and percentage of black teachers and principals employed in the state. The department asked the special three-judge court to enjoin defendants, including the state of North Carolina, from using minimum NTE scores as a basis for certification of teachers; to require defendants to issue certificates to the twenty-four aggrieved teachers; and to provide them with back pay. It was further contended that there is little or no correlation between scores on NTE and teaching competence. (The Educational Testing Service, which develops and publishes the NTE tests, has never made claims for any such correlation.)

In Nansesmond County, Virginia, thirteen black teachers were restored to their positions on the same grounds. They had been dismissed because they did not achieve the cut-off score of 500 on the National Teachers Examination. The court held that NTE does not purport to measure the teachers' actual knowledge of the subject matter assigned to be taught or his performance in the classroom, but places primary emphasis upon general and professional education. It is arbitrary to apply a general knowledge test to teachers of different subjects, because their jobs are substantially different.

Teachers Refuse to Sign Pledge

A federal district court declared unconstitutional an Alabama act which required teachers to sign a pledge that they had not participated in, encouraged, or condoned any mass truancy or any extra-curricular demonstration not approved by the city or state board of education. A number of teachers in Thomasville, Alabama, had refused to sign the pledge, and did not receive scheduled pay raises.

The Bizarre Case of Three College Professors

When a professor at a Virginia college had a letter under the title "Why I Believe in Sex Before Marriage" published in a popular magazine, he was denied an expected $1,200 pay raise and his academic and extracurricular responsibilities were diminished. Two other teachers at the college who had expressed support for him were fired.

The writer, a tenured professor and an ordained Methodist minister, said that he believed the magazine article would be useful in his course "The New Morality." His letter also said that from his work with students, he was convinced that if more parents would teach their children that the body is sacred and beautiful, and that sex is not dirty and vulgar, there would then be less of a generation gap and a resurgence of the vitality of married life and the home. The professor testified that he did not approve of premarital sex, but that he thought his course in social and intellectual history should acquaint students with every conceivable viewpoint they might run into after college. The professor's suit alleged that the college president had arbitrarily and maliciously intimidated him by giving him the worst possible schedule, ordering the removal of his name from the approved chaperone list, refusing to allow him to serve as sponsor of the juniors (although he had unanimously been elected), refusing him summer employment (despite the favorable recommendation of his department head), and intimidating students to prevent them from accepting invitations to his home.

The court suit was withdrawn following an out-of-court settlement as follows. The professor was given a salary raise to $16,000, retroactive to the beginning of the school year; he was awarded $9,000 damages, and all academic and extracurricular restraints which had been imposed were removed. One of the two instructors who supported the professor agreed to resign at the end of the school year with the action being recorded as leave without pay, and the college agreed to refrain from giving adverse recommendations in case of applications for employment to other institutions. The other instructor was granted leave for the current year at half-pay, and was promised the first open position in his department if he wished to accept it.

Indiana Teacher Accused of Insubordination Reinstated by Courts

The Lafayette, Indiana, school corporation denied a history teacher renewal of contract for the 1969–70 school year on the grounds of insubordination. The teacher won a $15,000 settlement. The school corporation also agreed to expunge from the record the nonrenewal action, showing that he left the system voluntarily.

The teacher charged in his court case that the board hearing did not follow procedures of due process guaranteed under the Fourteenth Amendment.

Teacher of Japanese Ancestry Denied Promotion

In April, 1974, the NEA filed a brief urging the U.S. Civil Service Commission to grant Fred I. Nakagawa, a teacher in the Overseas Dependent Schools in Japan, a retroactive promotion and back pay, and to take steps to prevent future racial discrimination in accordance with civil rights laws, presidential orders, and its own regulations. The Civil Service Commission notified the Air Force that its December, 1973, decision rejecting Nakagawa's contention that its decision constituted race discrimination was in error. Nakagawa is an American teacher of Japanese ancestry; he was denied promotion to an administrative position in an American (Department of Defense) school in Japan, where he had served for nine years, because of that ancestry.

Arbitrary Action of Board

A Missouri teacher, John Gilvinjer, was fired by the Center School District No. 58 in 1970–71 because he presented a report to his teachers' association about the district's ability to raise teachers' salaries. In January, 1974, a federal district court ordered the district to restore the teacher to his position and to pay him $34,577.54 in back pay. He also received thirty-two days accumulated sick leave, retirement fund interest, tenure and other contractual benefits as if he had been employed since the 1970–71 school year.

Secret Changes in Personnel File

A junior college teacher in Minnesota, dismissed on the basis of alleged racist allegations in his personnel file, won reinstatement in a suit in a federal district court. He was first employed in 1969–70 as a physical education instructor. The next year, when he protested an excessive workload, the dean of students decided not to reappoint him. To support his case the dean solicited and placed in the teacher's personnel file documents containing racist charges. Despite a favorable recommendation from a faculty review committee, the college president notified the teacher of his termination, denying him a hearing or other means of appeal. The federal judge found the racist allegations to have no basis in fact. Also, the judge held that failure to reappoint the teacher violated his procedural due process rights.

8

Organizational Memberships
of Teachers

THE Bill of Rights, consisting of the first ten amendments, in the Constitution of the United States, spells out the rights of all Americans. The First Amendment states the rights of free speech and assembly, and the Fourteenth Amendment confirms these rights, with its "due process" provisions.

Here is the exact wording of the First Amendment: "Congress shall make no law respecting the establishment of religion, or prohibiting the free exercise thereof; or abridging the freedom of speech, or of the press; or the right of the people peaceably to assemble, and petition the Government for a redress of grievances." Thus, teachers—like all other Americans—are assured the legal right to associate with people or join organizations of their choice, so long as they are not involved in efforts to overthrow the government of the United States.

A classic case of the attempted violation both of academic freedom and freedom of association is that of Fern Bruner, of California.

In September, 1951, Jimmy Tarantino, a news commentator on a San Francisco radio station, unleashed a tirade against Fern Bruner, a teacher in the San Lorenzo High School, saying that she had been accused many times of being a Communist or a Communist sympathizer and recommending her dismissal.[1]

This broadcast occurred on a Sunday night. The next morning the superintendent of the school district that included the San Lorenzo High School had many telephone calls asking whether Miss Bruner had been

---

[1] Account from "Spotlight Reversed," report of California Teachers Association Ethics Commission, Bay Section, California. See Harry A. Fosdick, "A Victory for Every Teacher," *National Education Association Journal*, 42 (Oct., 1953): 397–398.

dismissed or whether such action was planned. None of the callers inquired if the charges were true.

The superintendent immediately called on the California Teachers Association to investigate the matter. After a conference with Miss Bruner, the CTA investigating committee sent a letter[2] to the manager of radio station KYA, where the broadcasts were originating, expressing a desire to help in the removal of Communists from the profession and also expressing a desire to protect their members from false and reckless charges.

But Tarantino, instead of muting his attack, became more vituperative. He did, however, agree to meet with a CTA field representative and provide information which might assist CTA investigation of the charges. At a meeting held on September 18, he revealed that all of his information had come from individuals in Benicia, where Miss Bruner had taught for nearly four years. He named H. D. Frane (editor of the *Benician*), Mrs. Olivia O'Grady, and Mrs. Elizabeth McKay as likely interview subjects. *Tarantino had not checked his information with any authorities, despite his broadcasts.*

CTA personnel checked with Mr. Frane, Mrs. O'Grady, and Mrs. McKay, as well as with teachers, board members, students, and community leaders. They found that Fern Bruner was born in Oklahoma in 1924. Her father, a garage owner, moved the family to San Francisco, where he was employed by the John Deere Company. Miss Bruner graduated from Mission High School in San Francisco, after which she attended Anderson College in Anderson, Indiana, receiving a B.A. degree in 1945. She then earned a master's degree in religion from Oberlin College. She was active in extracurricular activities on both campuses. In October, 1947, she accepted a position as English and social science teacher at Benicia (California) High School and taught there for four years. She was offered a contract for a fifth year, but resigned to accept a position in the San Lorenzo High School.

In the summer of 1949, the California legislature adopted a resolution requesting Congress to call a constitutional convention which would consider amendments enabling the United States to participate in a stronger world government. Miss Bruner assisted in raising funds for a

---

[2] Signed by Harry A. Fosdick, field representative of California Teachers Association, and sent to manager of KYA Radio. See Fosdick, "A Victory for Every Teacher."

group of Benician young people to join a caravan of students to Washington in support of the movement. Funds were contributed by many outstanding citizens, and Miss Bruner became the escort for the group.

Following this experience, students sought and received permission from the administration to form a local unit of the United World Federalists as an extracurricular club in the high school. Miss Bruner was selected faculty adviser.

The CTA report of their investigation found all of Tarantino's charges false. Here are some of the charges (in italics).

1. *Miss Bruner was reported many times as being a Communist or one of its sympathizers.* The only reference to such a connection appeared in the minutes of Benicia school board for June 13, 1950, when a Mrs. O'Grady was found to say, "I would like to know if the board is going to continue to employ Miss Fern Bruner, who believes in and has taught this Communistic World Federalist scheme."

2. *Miss Bruner was a leader in the phony World Federalists' organization . . . who put her in that job?* This question is a clear implication that Fern Bruner was sent to the World Federalists by the Communists, to pervert that organization. The CTA Ethics Commission found no evidence to support this hypothesis. Nor did the commission find any evidence that she had a Communist background.

3. *A rumor went around to the effect that there had been a public mass meeting in 1950 demanding Fern Bruner's dismissal from her position in Benicia High School.* Of all the people who attended the meeting, only Mrs. Olivia O'Grady, who had organized it, demanded her dismissal. All others attending the meeting denied that its purpose was to recommend the firing of Miss Bruner.

4. *Another statement which implied Miss Bruner had quit under fire was "She resigned early this year."* Her principal and all five members of the school board testified that she was an excellent teacher and that she had already accepted a position elsewhere. She had planned to change positions the year before, but the board suggested that she stay and fight the charges being made against her.

6. *During the CTA investigation it was asserted that a certain letter proved that Miss Bruner praised Red Chinese leader, General Mao, to her school children.* Mrs. O'Grady testified that Miss Bruner read to her class quotations from Paul Hoffman, once the distinguished president of

the Studebaker Corporation and subsequently a federal government official, in which he explained why America and Americans could never embrace Communism.

The CTA Ethics Commission completely exonerated Miss Bruner of all charges made by Tarantino and Mrs. O'Grady. Also, the commission recommended that the California Teachers Association finance whatever legal representation Miss Bruner might need in order to secure justice in the case.

Following publication of its Ethics Commission report ("Spotlight Reversed"), Tarantino continued to broadcast his unproven charges. He denounced the CTA's report as "whitewash."

The CTA then instituted legal steps to secure justice for Miss Bruner and the association. On February 27, 1952, Gardiner Johnson, CTA legal counsel, demanded retraction of all charges. KYA retracted the statements made about the CTA, but neither the station nor Tarantino withdrew charges against Miss Bruner. Shortly thereafter a slander suit was filed, naming Tarantino and station manager H. G. Fearnhead as defendants. After more than a year, a four-week trial was conducted, concluding on August 7, 1953. The jury awarded Miss Bruner $25,000 from Jimmy Tarantino, also $25,000 from Station KYA, and $5,000 from station manager H. G. Fearnhead. All paid except Tarantino, who had no funds. The verdict against him remains unpaid.

RIGHT TO ORGANIZATIONAL MEMBERSHIP

The provisions of the First and Fourteenth Amendments assure teachers of their legal right (as American citizens) to form and join local, state, or national associations to guarantee their job rights and interests.

An Arkansas law in 1960, compelling teachers to file each year an affidavit listing every organization to which they had belonged or made contributions during the past five years, was considered by the Supreme Court. The court held that teachers have the right of free association. It further found that unjustified interference with that right violated the due-process clause of the Fourteenth Amendment. This decision nullified, of course, all such existing laws. A number of states had passed a law requiring teachers, as public employees, to file such declarations.

The court ruling implies that teachers have the right to form and to promote membership in their associations, to express freely their concerns to the community and to school officials, and to represent their organization in negotiations with the school board.

In areas where right-to-work laws exist (and in rural areas where labor-management relations are not common), some school boards feel free to interfere with teachers' associations; they seek to influence teachers to conform to older practices in employee-employer relationships. Means of interference include interrogation, closer supervision and domination of the association, and refusing dues-withholding provisions (aimed at adversely affecting membership recruitment).

Teachers subjected to such pressures have several avenues of recourse. First are constitutional safeguards. The First Amendment can be used to defend against harassment, to petition public officials, and to permit the answering of student questions on issues concerning the association. For example, in a California school district, teachers were prohibited from circulating a petition on school property, where they had been seeking signatures of teachers during duty-free lunch periods. The petition they were circulating was addressed to public officials and pertained to the financing of public schools. The California Supreme Court ruled that such an activity should not be thwarted unless those who opposed it could show evidence of a threat to order and efficiency in the schools.

In New Jersey, a teachers' association exercising collective bargaining rights for its members sought to enjoin the school district from enforcing its policy barring teachers from answering students' questions about negotiations between the teachers and the board. The state court held that this prohibition placed prior restraint on freedom of discussion, unless such discussion would materially affect discipline.

Some school boards have set up policies denying UniServe directors the right to represent teachers at administrative hearings or to visit teachers during school hours on school premises. (UniServe officials are trained negotiators, paid jointly by the NEA and by state education associations, who represent teachers, especially in negotiations regarding teachers' salaries and working conditions.) In one state a school board has adopted a policy that permits teachers to be represented in grievance procedures. Under this policy, teachers can be represented by a person who is mutually agreeable to them and to the board. In a case which has recently reached the appellate court, a teacher seeking a board review of the principal's recommendation was denied representation at the hearing by any one of seven UniServe directors whose names were submitted to the board. In refusing, the board gave the teacher the choice of another teacher as an attorney. The district court upheld the board; the teacher has appealed. The case would appear to violate the First Amendment rights of both the teacher and the UniServe director by depriving them of free speech and free association. It may also pose an equal-protection problem by denying teachers access to their colleagues while that right is granted to others.

Another obvious violation of teachers' First Amendment rights involves the dismissal of those who are leaders of their association. An Oregon teacher testified that his teaching contract was not renewed because he had participated in negotiations for his local association. The court found in his favor on the grounds that the board's decision involved retaliation against him for the negotiation activities. The teacher was ordered reinstated and awarded back pay. A Missouri teacher was dismissed after he reported to his local association on the board's ability to raise teachers' salaries. The Eighth U.S. Circuit Court of Appeals held that he was dismissed for constitutionally impermissible grounds, ordered him reinstated, and awarded him back pay of about $38,000.[3]

In New York, the president of a local association challenged portions of the administrative manual, charging that it restricted the right of free speech by prohibiting placement of unstamped mail in faculty mailboxes. A federal court held this to be a violation of teachers' rights and enjoined the school district from preventing the distribution of association publications on school property.

Florida Law on Organizational Membership Invalidated

A federal court declared a Florida statute unconstitutional in 1969. This law had excluded administrators from becoming members of professional education associations. The NEA and two of its affiliates, the Florida Education Association and the Palm Beach County Classroom Teachers' Association, joined in challenging the constitutionality of the law. The judge held that it violated the guarantees of free association in the First and Fourteenth Amendments.

---

[3] See Betty Sinowitz, "The Teacher and the Law," *Today's Education*, Apr.–May, 1978, pp. 20–21.

The law had applied only to Palm Beach County. It prohibited supervisory and administrative personnel from membership or participation in organizations whose activities included the collective representation of teachers in regard to terms, tenure, or conditions of employment. The penalty prescribed was dismissal. The law, which was enacted without the governor's signature, resulted from one county's hostility toward such officials. A group of principals there had walked out with their teachers as part of a statewide protest in 1968.

Impact of the McCarthy Era upon the Rights of Teachers

The McCarthy Era, from the late 1940s until mid-1950s, was made to order for the proliferation of gross mistreatment of public school teachers. The excesses of this period made it possible for arrogant, cruel, and biased men to point accusing fingers at a teacher, and often to get the teacher fired by simply referring to him or her as "that commie." Without one shred of evidence, and only with this phrase, a teacher could have a life's work and reputation ruined. The story of Fern Bruner of California revealed how helpless teachers were. Only the cruelty of her treatment attracted the attention of the California Teachers Association, which financed an appeal to the courts for justice. This step by the CTA, and its successful outcome, became an example which influenced other state associations. Finally, virtually every state professional organization of teachers and the National Education Association created special funds to defend teachers against similar flagrant injustices. In recent years these associations have won a big majority of such court cases, by proving that the rights of teachers as American citizens, as set forth in the Constitution (especially in the Bill of Rights), have been violated. Many of these cases have gone to the Supreme Court for decision.

HARASSMENT OF TEACHERS

But McCarthyism was *just one* gimmick that some elements of the public seized upon to get rid of teachers they did not like. There were many others, dating back to the beginning of public support, by taxation, of the schools. Many citizens tended to feel that paying taxes to support schools conferred upon them the right to criticize or condemn the personal qualities, the dress, the conduct, and often the religion of the teacher whose salary was being paid in part by them. This appeals to the dictatorial attitude that exists in some degree in many an American. While one may be the first to complain about oppression of any type, yet he may display the most bitter and vindictive sense of unfairness toward anyone who is weaker, or who is in some measure economically dependent upon him.

One of the clichés that teachers in almost every generation hear repeatedly is that teachers have been compelled by inflation to cease pleading with outstretched arms for any pittance the public is willing to grant. On the contrary, teachers have been compelled, in the last two decades, to become increasingly militant to obtain reasonable and fair adjustments in their salaries. Such militance has eventuated in demands for professional negotiation—and, later, for collective bargaining—to obtain satisfactory contract adjustments, in salaries and working conditions, and the right to strike.

Chapter 18 presents detailed data on the growth of teacher strikes and the bargaining process. Thus when teachers hear the well-worn charge, "Teachers are not as dedicated as they used to be," they tend to interpret it not in terms of lessened devotion to children and their growth. Rather, they are inclined to interpret it as "Teachers are not willing to be satisfied with treatment as economically deprived, second- and third-rate citizens." Using almost any pertinent criteria for measuring the quality of teachers, today's are the most highly qualified ever, in terms of preparation and public responsibility. Before this cliché is accepted some key terms have to be clarified. This is especially true in terms of the wholly new conditions teachers now face.

The growth of violence in the schools has been shocking and puzzling. A national meeting of several hundred school security officers and supervisors reported violence of a type never before experienced and property losses in the public schools of more than $600 million in the year 1975 alone.[4] A survey in two schools of two counties reported that 25 percent of the students feared bodily harm during school hours.

Of course, many in our general population tend to attribute this alarming increase in violence to laxity of teacher discipline or to teacher incompetence. Surely that is too simple an answer. The complex causes of this wave of violence include the influence of movies and television,

---

[4] Report of the Subcommittee to Investigate Juvenile Delinquency, U.S. Senate, Feb., 1977, p. 84.

with their tendencies to picture violence as a seeming virtue; the example of growing violence and lawlessness among the American people as a whole; and the inefficiency of courts in meting out justice. And there is, of course, the awesome growth in our population, the development of huge cities, and the prevalence of automobiles and other forms of transportation which enable a criminal to cross dozens of different jurisdictions in a day's time.

All of these factors are having an inevitable impact upon the schools. A recent article in the NEA journal, *Today's Education*, reports the shocking effects on teachers themselves.[5] This article contains excerpts from a report by UCLA psychiatrist Alfred Bloch, who studied 250 Los Angeles teachers who had been "assaulted, harassed, or threatened with violence by students, parents, or vagrants between 1971 and 1976." These teachers exhibit psychological symptoms similar to those of survivors of war disasters and sufferers of "combat neurosis." Unlike military personnel, teachers are driven to a state of final collapse because their transfer requests are often denied, leaving them no avenue of escape from an intolerable situation, and their fears are ignored. Dr. Bloch found symptoms of physical trauma and/or psychiatric stress, ranging from headaches and skin disorders to peptic ulcers, hypertension, and respiratory problems. Psychological symptoms included anxiety, fear, depression, insecurity, emotional tension, nightmares, phobias, blurred vision, dizziness, fatigue, and irritability.

It is estimated by the Department of Health, Education, and Welfare that each month no fewer than 6,000 junior and senior high school teachers are robbed at school and 500 suffer serious physical attacks. A teacher has said, "We are no longer talking about teaching, we are talking about survival." Since 1971, Dr. Bloch has treated more than six hundred teachers for this form of combat neurosis. There is a limit to how long teachers can endure the violent treatment they are receiving from students. A new term has been coined for the three R's: "Rotation, Rest, and Recuperation," which should be given teachers in each two- or three-year period.

The sad reality of this whole situation is often attributed to the lack of cooperation between teachers and administrators. One Los Angeles teacher who was attacked ran to the principal's office for help. Instead,

---

[5] Sinowitz, "The Teacher and the Law."

she was criticized for leaving her classroom. In addition, she was ordered not to converse with her colleagues about this attack. The failure to get any help from any source produced major depression in the teacher, leading her to attempt to take her own life when she could no longer bear the failure and humiliation. She has not been able to return to her teaching job.

In one county system of schools, administrators publicly dismissed discipline as not a problem. The teachers, who knew this wasn't so, conducted their own survey over a period of two school years. More than 100 teachers reported that they had been assaulted by students, three times as many as school officials had reported. In addition, 200 of the teachers reported that students had damaged their personal property in retaliation for disciplinary action.

The NEA reports that only about 10 percent of incidents of violence are ever reported. Teachers simply remain silent to protect their jobs; principals do the same thing, for fear of being accused of being unable to gain control of students.

Any way one looks at the problem, it is serious. As a result, our system of public schools, which has to a great degree carried the hopes of the largest and oldest democracy in the world for a brighter, happier, healthier nation, may fail because we have abdicated our responsibilities as citizens.

THE AMERICAN FEDERATION OF TEACHERS

The teaching profession—at the national level and, to a lesser degree, in many local school districts—has entertained the idea of joining with organized labor to bring about more effective pressure for improved salary scales and working conditions. This ideological flirtation has gone on since the early years of this century, but the compulsive urge to make teaching a profession has persisted among teachers since the very founding of public schools in the United States. Although this compulsion for professionalism continues, the continuing disdain of a sizable portion of the public for this goal of teachers, and the failure yet to underwrite the cost of well-prepared teachers for the schools, are beginning to cause inroads on this hope of teachers for making a respected profession of teaching. Like laborers before 1935, many teachers have come to feel that not merit, not superb service, not the providing of indispensable and high-quality education for their children would ever convince the public to provide better working conditions. Only the sheer power of force could do so.

The inevitable legislation providing the machinery for recognizing the full power of laborers came into being in 1935. For teachers, however, this is a problem still awaiting a definitive solution. To be sure, the overwhelming majority of teachers still strive to implement, and still desire, the professional approach, but in some degree it is a touch-and-go situation.

Presently, 80–90 percent of America's public school teachers still have membership in the respective state education associations and the National Education Association, but the issue of professionalism or unionism still is unsettled. Such has been the demonstrated effectiveness of the labor organizations that the NEA has been compelled to adopt a compromise position, approving the use by association members of collective bargaining and the strike, under certain specified conditions. In 1971 the NEA Representative Assembly pledged support to affiliated associations which felt compelled to use the strike after all other means had been exhausted.

The American Federation of Teachers (AFT) was formed in 1916. This came about when a sizable group of local teachers' associations, despairing of the effectiveness of their local, state, and national associations in bringing about improvements in their working conditions and salaries, withdrew from those local associations and formed the AFT in affiliation with the AFL-CIO.

A case in point—of the intolerable conditions faced by some local associations—was the situation in Chicago. By 1899 the teachers had not received a raise in twenty years. The pay of beginning elementary teachers was $500 per year; annual increments were so small that at the end of eleven years these teachers reached the maximum of $800. Repeated pleas from the teachers were ignored. The situation became so desperate that a meeting of the disgruntled teachers was held and the Chicago Teachers Federation was organized to study the reason for this low pay scale. This study of the situation revealed that the only organization with any real power to help remedy the situation was the American Federation of Labor, so the teachers' federation became an affiliate of this group.

The teachers' study of the situation revealed some disgraceful facts. They found that several utility firms, as well as some other businesses, were avoiding taxation via non-assessment of their property. Also, it was revealed that some land given to the city for use of the schools had large buildings on it, buildings which were in the name of business firms and were not even listed on the tax rolls; this situation had existed for many years. In 1901 the teachers collected money from their members to press a writ of mandamus ordering an assessment of such property. This action alone produced an increase of property taxes in the city of several million dollars, and of school funds by about a quarter-million dollars, but it did not result in any increase in the teachers' pay. In 1902 teachers' salaries were reduced—one supposes as punishment for their meddling in the city's business. Again the teachers appealed to the NEA for help, but the prevailing power structure refused any action. At the time the leadership hierarchy dominating the NEA was largely in control of presidents of prestigious private colleges. Apparently they could not become excited about the plight of such modest people as the public school teachers.

These developments presaged a ferment in the NEA which ultimately was to result in a revolution and a change in its leadership. In 1910, the first woman president, superintendent of the Chicago schools Ella Flagg Young, was elected. And by 1919 the classroom teachers, who constituted the vast majority of the NEA membership, began to assume a more vigorous role. They succeeded in forming a Department of Classroom Teachers. True, no personnel for this department were employed until 1942, but the "rabble" (as some called it) was beginning to take over. The president of a great private university and a past president of the NEA, Nicolas Murray Butler, accused the NEA's membership of degenerating by falling into the hands of a very inferior class of teachers and school officials.[6]

It apparently never occurred to this university president, and his colleagues, that their obvious ignoring of the plight of teachers in the public schools was of any importance to education in the United States. Nor did it occur to him and his colleagues that they, too, might have sought positions of leadership in education to influence the trend of the times toward reverence for the great universities—and, incidentally, toward the denigration of those who taught in the lower schools.

Of course, this italicizes the indispensable, unstoppable power of freedom in a democracy. Even the humble have the legal right not only

---

[6] T. M. Stinnett, *Turmoil in Teaching* (New York: Macmillan, 1968), p. 21.

to protest their threatened degradation, but the power, by our Constitution and specific laws, to form their own organizations or associations to further their reach for better ways and improved circumstances.

Thus, in 1916, the American Federation of Teachers, as a national federation of state and local federations, became an integral part of the AFL-CIO, thus becoming actively involved in the union labor movement. It thereby affiliated with a power structure with legal rights to serve the interests of its members.

In June, 1915, existing teachers' federations were invited to send delegates to a national meeting, the purpose of which was to form a national federation. The newly formed American Federation of Teachers lists in its constitution the following goals, which were set forth in the constitution adopted at the formation meeting:

1. To bring associations of teachers into mutual assistance and co-operation.
2. To obtain for teachers all the rights to which they are entitled.
3. To raise the standards of the teaching profession by securing the conditions essential to the best professional service.
4. To promote such democratization of the schools as will enable them better to equip their pupils to take their places in the individual, social, and political life of the community.

Whether or not one favors teacher affiliation with organized labor (or with any other power or pressure group in American life), the AFT has had a great influence in assisting teachers to achieve improved working conditions, financial support of the schools, fairer treatment of teachers, and improved teachers' salaries.

First of all, the very organization of the AFT has had a tremendous impact upon stimulating the National Education Association toward more aggressive defense of teachers, toward preventing their outright mistreatment, in checking their wanton dismissal without real causes, and in many other ways. The very presence and the influence of the AFL-CIO has stimulated teachers' professional organizations at the local, state, and national levels to become much more effective representatives of teachers as they continue toward achieving professional status.

That the adoption of some procedural policies of organized labor by the NEA and its affiliated state education associations has some advan-

TABLE 8.1.

Membership Figures for the National Education Association
and the American Federation of Teachers

Year	NEA	AFT
1918	10,000	1,500
1920	53,000	10,000
1930	172,000	7,000
1940	203,000	30,000
1950	454,000	41,000
1960	714,000	59,000
1970	1,186,845	246,000
1980	1,900,000 (est.)	580,000*

SOURCE: Annual membership reports of NEA and AFT.

* In fairness to AFT, it should be pointed out that the exact membership of that organization is hard to come by. NEA reports that AFT estimates varied from 520,000 to 580,000. The variations appear to be the result of the lack of exact methods of determining the membership.

tages is attested to by vastly improved conditions for teachers during the years since the organization of the competitive labor affiliate, the American Federation of Teachers. The memberships of both organizations and their affiliates have also continued to increase. The comparative figures in Table 8.1 attest to these gains.

But the greater significance of the affiliation of teachers with labor organizations, and the reflection of the labor organization influence upon the aggressiveness of the National Education Association and its local and state affiliates, lies in the exercised right of teachers to affiliate with organizations of their choice, however militant and aggressive they may be. This is the right of free Americans as spelled out in our Constitution and interpreted by our courts.

9

Restricting Teachers' Private Lives

TEACHERS are full-fledged citizens, of course, and have all of the rights of other citizens. These rights are set forth in the Constitution. But the general public subconsciously tends to infringe upon those rights. Particularly is this true of the inclination to interfere with teachers' private lives and their freedom of speech.

Only a few decades ago a teacher's private life was subject to school board rules and policies. This was true especially in rural areas. Teachers dared not have dates, fall in love, ride bicycles, smoke cigarettes, drink beer, spend most of their income in another town, or "break" the Sabbath.

In all too many places, teachers can still put their jobs in jeopardy by engaging in political activities, expressing personal political convictions and choices among candidates for office, maintaining residence outside the school district, getting married, becoming pregnant during the school year, maintaining membership in certain organizations, engaging in certain religious activities, practicing certain hobbies, or engaging in certain social activities.

On many occasions when school boards have decreed that this or that aspect of a teacher's life constitutes "behavior unbecoming a teacher" or "unprofessional conduct," the boards have fired teachers or changed their job status. But the courts, especially federal courts, have been restraining boards from such actions in recent years. For example, the Supreme Court has decreed that teachers cannot be fired, non-renewed, or lose their teaching certificates for exercising rights guaranteed to all citizens by the Constitution—unless, of course, the exercising of these rights impedes the effectiveness of the teacher or seriously impairs operation of the school. Among the guaranteed constitutional rights most often violated are the due-process clause of the Fourteenth Amendment, freedom of association, the right to privacy, and freedom of speech under the First Amendment.

As mentioned in Chapter 7, through its DuShane Defense Fund the NEA has consistently backed court suits by teachers whose rights to teach have been violated by a school board, for conduct outside the classroom. Especially has this association come vigorously to the support of teachers who have been penalized for conduct that has no proven relationship to teaching. Some of the successful cases have included: (1) a Texas teacher and coach who was accused of driving with a waitress after games and parking on a country road; (2) a Georgia teacher refused employment because of her association with an interracial, religiously oriented communal farm; (3) a Wisconsin teacher who lived for a month in a room of the house of her fiancé, a divorced man. They were later married upon permission of a court; (4) a California teacher charged with a homosexual relationship with another teacher; (5) two Kansas teachers who violated the board rule that teachers must live in the county in which the district is located.

The American Federation of Teachers (AFT) and the American Civil Liberties Union (ACLU) have also vigorously participated in defending teachers against unfair or illegal treatment. Also, the NAACP (National Association for the Advancement of Colored People), while created for the protection and advancement of the civil and constitutional rights of all colored people, has on many occasions helped finance the court cases of Negro teachers.

FRANCES FISHER CASE

The subtle but cruel discrimination against women is clearly illustrated by the Frances Fisher case.[1] Mrs. Fisher was a high school teacher in Tryon, Nebraska. She was terminated from her position in the McPherson Rural High School District after a hearing before the school board. She had been employed as a regular teacher under continuing contract

---

[1] Kelly Frels and Ann R. Robinson, "Privacy," in *The Courts and Education*, Seventy-Seventh Yearbook, Part I, of the National Society for the Study of Education, ed. Clifford P. Hooker (Chicago: University of Chicago Press, 1978), pp. 294–95.

for the school years 1970–71 and 1971–72. She was fifty-five years of age and lived alone in a one-bedroom apartment. Her friends—both men and women—and occasionally friends from out of town, spent the night at her apartment, in the absence of motel or hotel space in the small community.

Her son, Gary Fisher, in his late twenties, was also a teacher, in another community. Often when his friends would come through Tryon, they would stay overnight at Mrs. Fisher's apartment; so did one young man who was serving an internship in the local high school as a part of his college requirements. In court, Mrs. Fisher testified that she had asked a member of the school board about housing for visiting guests. She was told that, since there was only one motel in town and it was usually filled each night, it would seem quite all right for her to furnish accommodations to visiting friends.

Almost immediately after the visit of the young man serving an internship, Mrs. Fisher was notified that her contract for the 1972–73 school year would not be renewed. Two grounds were given by the board: (1) failure to maintain discipline in her classes, and (2) conduct unbecoming a teacher.

Both NEA, through its DuShane Emergency Fund, and the Nebraska State Education Association furnished funds for Mrs. Fisher's appeal to the courts. The Eighth U.S. Circuit Court of Appeals found no proof of improper conduct, since the presence of guests in a home provides no evidence of immoral behavior.

THE ELAINE MURPHY CASE

Perhaps the most flagrant case involving both the private life of a teacher and the fabrications of a student failing her courses occurred in a little town in Arizona.[2] The case of Mrs. John (Elaine) Murphy of Mayer, Arizona, is classic in the sense that it demonstrates how an accused teacher is often at the mercy of those who want to believe any rumor, any allegation against a teacher—especially in a small community, where every whisper about the schools and teachers reaches the school board.

The American people have a deep reverence for justice. In a court of

---

[2] From Elizabeth Keiffer, "The Trial of Elaine Murphy," *Good Housekeeping*, May, 1969, p. 4.

law, one accused of wrongdoing must have a fair and open hearing, where the accused faces the accuser and presents evidence and witnesses to refute the allegations of illegal behavior. But too often this is not quite so with teachers. The most outlandish accusations can be made surreptitiously, and the teacher often has to disprove them—if he or she can. The parent often has but to beat a path to the office of the principal or superintendent with a child's charges or accusations, and demand that the teacher be fired in order to set the machinery in motion, most often putting the teacher under suspicious scrutiny. Any explanation of what happened and why is most often dubbed, in the community's mind, "trying to lie out of the incident." In other words, contrary to the fixed course of legal justice, teachers sometimes must prove that they are *not* guilty, whereas in legal cases the accuser (or the state) must make the charges and prove them before a jury of the accused's peers.

In September, 1968, Elaine Murphy, a thirty-six-year-old English teacher and mother of three teenage children, was called to her principal's office. When she reached the office, she was confronted by two officers, who informed her that they had a warrant to arrest her for furnishing marijuana to a minor.

The amazed teacher was dumbfounded. She said to the deputies, "I don't even know what marijuana looks like." The principal was equally shocked and unbelieving. He had high regard for Mrs. Murphy, as a person and as a teacher.

Yet, within a few minutes, Elaine Murphy found herself in the Mayer jail charged with a felony which could subject her to a penalty of ten years to life imprisonment.

As so often is the case, the teacher was being accused by a student. Barry Terrell had failed the English course she taught the year before, dropped out of school, and married. He drove to Prescott one night to attend a dance. During the course of the evening, he was arrested and jailed on a charge of illegal consumption of alcohol.

Infuriated by his situation, his wife suggested to the officers that his car be searched. This was done, and several hand-rolled cigarettes were found. When these proved to be marijuana filled, he was arrested again, this time on the charge of possessing the drug.

While he was released from jail to obtain $100, to pay the fine assessed on the liquor charge, Barry Terrell gave thought to what defense he might offer. When he was asked where he obtained the cigarettes, his answer was that his former teacher, Mrs. Murphy, whose English course he had flunked, had given them to him. He also stated that two of his cronies, Bruce Bennett and Donnie Halliburton, would verify this statement.

The fact that Barry Terrell and his brother Terry had both failed the English course taught by Mrs. Murphy gave some indication of the probable motive in the charge against her. The older brother had quit school, blaming his dropout on Mrs. Murphy. The other brother did graduate in 1967, but he retained his hatred for her. Since he spent a lot of time hanging around the school, he was able to spread his poison against Mrs. Murphy, thus helping to create a climate of dislike and suspicion of her among students.

He picked up support from Bruce Bennett, who was another problem student—and related to an influential member of the school board, a woman with numerous relatives in the town. Somehow this trio persuaded another future dropout, Donnie Halliburton, to join them in their conspiracy to defame Mrs. Murphy's character.

The prosecuting attorney at the preliminary hearing for the accused teacher formed the opinion that the boys were not smart enough to concoct a charge against her. But to Mrs. Murphy's defending law firm, it appeared strongly probable that the boy had concocted the story as a cruel trick on her—in an effort to get revenge for her failure to pass them all.

Fortunately, before her preliminary hearing, the Arizona Education Association joined the defense for the first time, immediately coming to Mrs. Murphy's aid with legal and financial help.

It should be added that Mrs. Murphy was something of a nonconformist; in a small town this is a decided handicap. Her father was an outstanding law professor. She smoked, was a moderate drinker, frequented the town bar occasionally, and played pool in a public pool room. While this was not enough to convict one of wrongdoing of any sort, it was enough to make many of her townsmen suspicious of her character. At her preliminary hearing her lawyer said: "I think it appropriate to consider Mrs. Murphy is a teacher here. She has a spotless record. . . . She owns her own home and is raising her family . . . of fine young children. Is she really going to risk all this to give some young punk marijuana?"[3] However, the justice of peace found probable cause to believe the story the boys told, stories that conflicted at some points. He ordered her bound over to superior court in Prescott. It may seem that many people in the community believed all the concocted charges against the teacher. That is a very human thing to do. Those who are deeply conscious of imperfections somehow gain great hope and confidence from believing that persons supposed to be near-perfect, such as teachers and ministers, have revealed human frailties. There is a sort of hidden pleasure to these people because, psychologically, it lifts them to a presumed level of performance which they probably will never actually achieve.

In the month before Mrs. Murphy could be tried in court, naturally the case was argued in every gathering in Mayer. So bitter did the debate become that, long after the trial was held and the teacher was declared innocent, strangers in the town who had heard of the case dared not ask questions about it. According to one story, the NEA sent a representative out to investigate the case while it was yet to be held. He went to a lawyer in Mayer and told him he was investigating the facts in the case. He was immediately advised that he had better get his information in a hurry and get out of town before dark, because the feeling was so bitter that somebody might kill him.

The trial of Mrs. Murphy began in Prescott on October 22. The courtroom was jammed; most of the population of Mayer were there. Barry Terrell testified that on the night of August 22 he saw Mrs. Murphy in the Mayer tavern, where she and her son were playing in a pool tournament. He testified that she asked him (Barry) if he would like some pot; that she had some at home which she would give to him, if he wanted to come to her house. "Then," he continued, "she drove me to her house, got the marijuana cigarettes and gave them to me." Bruce Bennett testified that he had been in the tavern that night and heard Mrs. Murphy's offer of the cigarettes to Barry, but he denied that they later shared the cigarette to measure the strength of the drug in it. Donnie Halliburton also claimed to have heard Mrs. Murphy's offer. Of all the witnesses who were in the tavern at the time, those three boys were the only ones who heard Mrs. Murphy's offer.

Rusty, Mrs. Murphy's thirteen-year-old son, seems to have made the best impression as a witness. He and his mother testified that they had

---

[3] Ibid.

been at the tavern on the night of August 29 (not August 22, as testified
by one of the accusers). Mrs. Murphy's husband John, her son Marvin,
and her eighteen-year-old daughter Mary Beth were at a horse show in
Flagstaff, or they would have been in the pool game, too. The event that
cracked the boys' accusation wide open was a witness Mrs. Murphy's
lawyer called to the stand on the fourth day of the trial. The witness was
a Prescott police lieutenant. He testified that after Barry Terrell's hearing
on the alcohol charge in September, he had warned the young man that
a marijuana charge might be brought against him. His arrest on this
charge occurred the next day.

Almost immediately the county attorney got to his feet and moved
that the charges against Mrs. Murphy be dismissed. Neither he nor his
office had known until that moment that there had been any chance for
Terrell to fabricate the story with the two other boys. Now it was clear
that they had had the time, and that they used it to concoct their cock-
and-bull story about the teacher and the marijuana cigarettes. The county
attorney stated to the court that to proceed with the trial would result in
a miscarriage of justice.

At this point, the Arizona Education Association entered the case.
Through its Commission on Professional Rights and Responsibilities, the
association granted $2,000 to pay Mrs. Murphy's legal costs. Soon after
this action the National Education Association granted Mrs. Murphy
$2,360 from its DuShane Emergency Fund, to cover the remaining por-
tions of her expenses in the case.

Of course, the case was dismissed, but this is not to say that "the
case is over." For the rest of Mrs. Murphy's life, the charge will follow
her and create suspicions in the minds of people about her.

This is the "hell-on-earth" for a teacher—any teacher, anywhere. Just
let somebody start a rumor, or suggest that maybe there's something not
just right with a teacher, and this will tend to dog the teacher's steps for
the rest of his or her life. Wherever this teacher may apply for a job, the
inevitable question will come up: "Have you ever been charged with or
convicted of a felony?" Either way the teacher takes is a devil's trap. If
she answers truthfully about being charged, she is already under suspicion; and no evidence on earth can clear her of the ever-expanding enlargement by others of her offense. Strange, is it not? Few other human
beings have so painful a cross to bear.

Several years ago the NEA went to the aid of two young women in a

Southeastern state who were accused of being Communists. They were cleared, and their teaching certificates were restored. But they declined to seek another position in that state because, they said, "Wherever we go in this state, this charge (although disproved) will go with us and bedevil us the rest of our lives." They appealed to the NEA to finance their transportation to a Western state, where they had job offers, and for subsistence until they could receive their first paychecks. This was granted.

Mrs. Murphy migrated to California, and is teaching in that state. One can only hope that this absurd charge does not crop up again there, thanks to some disgruntled student or vengeful parent.

EVOLUTION OF TEACHERS' RIGHTS

One aspect of the evolution of the teaching profession in the United States—in many respects, the most impressive of all—has been the growth in teachers' rights. The most striking part of that growth has occurred since the 1940s. From the earliest years of the free public school movement in the United States, it appears that teachers were rarely if ever thought of as having any of the rights of first-class citizens. Generally, they had only what rights a benevolent community was willing to give them.

It is a strange, puzzling bit of our history that teachers were generally deemed not to have those constitutional rights that other Americans possess, simply because they are leaders of our children. Largely, only in the last half of this century have even the federal courts generally upheld rights for teachers, rights such as the freedom of speech and expression under the First Amendment; the right to due process; the right to free political discussion and voting, and others. In fairness, it should be pointed out that relatively few such cases have ever reached the federal courts, because teachers previously tended to accept their low status. Either that, or they had no recourse to a powerful, well-financed professional association such as the National Education Association.

Why? Well, it's all rooted in our history, in customs and mores going back to and beyond the founding of this country. In the early years of the settlement of America, school teaching was neither a highly regarded nor a rewarding profession. With land to clear and crops to tend and cities to build, there was a premium upon physical strength. Emphasis upon education only began to grow as population and industries developed. Cities came into being, and the types of jobs that proliferated increasingly required the development of mental abilities.

The furor in the 1976 Olympic Games over the charges of racial discrimination by one nation, prompting the withdrawal of some twenty African nations and their athletes, shocked many people and was the cause of agonized hand-wringing by millions. This serves to remind Americans of lingering mores which we forget were once the accepted practice, instead of the exception. What we are inclined to forget is that, in the beginning of the Olympic games, only citizens of Greece were allowed to compete. No outsiders from any other nation could be admitted. This has its parallel in the treatment of teachers. While a new era is rapidly being born in society's attitudes toward teachers and teaching, history reveals the sordid story of widespread and harsh treatment. In the United States, teachers in several colonies were predominantly indentured servants, often bought (for the amount of the debt owed to their owners) at shipside like slaves. It is reported that in Baltimore, for example, there was a common expression when a subscription school was founded; someone would say, "Let's go down to the docks and buy a schoolteacher."

As for the status of women, in the earliest years of our country few were allowed in teaching. This seems a far cry from the current very vocal, animated and justified hassle over equal rights for women in virtually every aspect of our national life. But, of course, we must remember that women were not even allowed the right to vote until the adoption of the Nineteenth Amendment in 1920, almost a century and a half after the Declaration of Independence. For all those years we had lived as a democratic nation, with the right of citizens to be free, to select those who were to pass laws and those who were to see to their enforcement. Yet when we talked of the glories, the rights, and the privileges of free men, of self-government, the exalted status of free enterprise, and equality of opportunity, we still felt little or no sense of guilt, or even discomfort, that women were treated as an underprivileged and unfit minority. Even today, in many segments of our society, there is quiet grumbling and often loud complaint about the federal government seeking to enforce equal rights for women and for blacks. For too many of us, this smacks of the bungling and tyranny of "big government."

The scant employment of women as teachers in the colonial years is indicated by the fact that the commonly used term for a teacher was "schoolmaster," not "schoolmistress." Because education of women was not considered essential at that time, very few women were deemed to be qualified. Also, the almost sole dependence for proper discipline of the unruly was upon whipping, which required the physical strength of a man. This was a big element in the preference for male teachers.

There are still other considerations among the duties of these pioneer teachers in America which tended to favor men as teachers. In some school districts, especially in New England, the teacher was often expected to serve as sexton and gravedigger, and to perform the janitorial duties of the school. This is not to suggest that the employment of men was universal, for a relatively few women did find employment. Even in the lifetime of many, only three positions in the relatively small towns in which they grew up were occupied by or available to women: (1) that of operating the central telephone switchboard; (2) that of being the milliner and dressmaker; and (3) that of teacher in the local school.

In some small school districts, where split terms were used to adjust to the planting and harvesting of crops, women were employed in the summer because all male power was needed for work in the fields. But wherever women were employed, their pay was about half that of men. Of course, that practice continued until about the middle of the twentieth century, when teachers' organizations finally were able to secure the adoption of the single salary schedule. But this did not end pay discrimination against women.

Also, it should be noted that in the early colonial period relatively large numbers of women were employed in dame schools and assigned to classes of beginning pupils. Too, it is interesting to note that the Quakers in Pennsylvania employed many women as teachers. This probably explains why Pennsylvania had the largest proportion of women teachers of any of the original colonies. The Quakers seem to have had less bias toward women than prevailed among many of the other religious groups.

Treatment of Women in Professional Associations

A prime example of the treatment of women teachers as inferiors was that accorded them by the original professional associations, beginning about the middle of the nineteenth century. Rhode Island and Massachusetts formed state teachers' associations in 1845. By the time the National Teachers Association (now the National Education Association) was formed in 1857, some seventeen such state teachers' organizations had been formed, as follows: in Rhode Island, New York, Massachusetts, Ohio, Connecticut, Vermont, Michigan, Pennsylvania, Wisconsin, Illinois, New Jersey, Iowa, New Hampshire, Indiana, Missouri, North Carolina, and Alabama. (Some of these were reorganized later and formed new bodies, and their dates for organization may be found elsewhere as being later than those given here.)

In most of these associations women were admitted, but they were far from being considered as full-fledged members. Usually they could not vote or hold office, nor could they speak or present papers to the groups. This simply was conforming to existing public opinion of the times. Women rarely were permitted to appear on the programs of the associations. Actually, the NEA, which was formed in 1857, did not admit women to membership until 1866. Often, women were permitted to persuade men to present their viewpoints or to read papers prepared by them, but they could not appear in person or speak themselves before meetings of these associations.

Even after women became the majority in education associations, especially state associations, they were long treated as second- or third-class citizens. A woman officer in an educational association was a rarity, and remained so until recently. Actually it was about 1940 before women, who by then probably constituted 80 percent of the association membership, began to be elected regularly to leadership positions. Even in the 1950's and 1960's, it was common for one who was to address the convention of a state education association to observe that virtually all presidents of district or county units of the association were men.

MISTREATMENT OF TEACHERS

The people of the United States have at long last moved to eliminate the record of discrimination against blacks, and to abolish second-class or no citizenship. But these discriminations against women in many areas of American life have continued longer, still existing to some degree in many places.

Of course, the discrimination in terms of pay scales has constituted a chronic mistreatment of all teachers until recent years. The historic discrimination against women teachers still exists, although not as flagrantly in recent years. But widespread differences in the pay of men and women teachers still exist in many places and in many specific positions. To be sure, the origin and gradual acceptance of the single salary schedule, and the pressures on legislatures of well-organized professional associations and their lobbyists, have largely eliminated the once widespread and cruel discrimination against paying female teachers salaries comparable to those of other professional workers, even when preparation requirements were the same.

The petty restrictions and prohibitions placed upon teachers in our early schools, and especially in the one-room rural school, are well known. Many of these prohibitions were often included in teachers' contracts, but many more were simply verbal, representing the thinking of school patrons. Some of these were: no dating by women teachers of men in the community; compulsory church and Sunday school attendance; compulsory residence in the school district; mandatory trade in local stores. Marriage of women teachers during the school term often was a cause of dismissal, as was pregnancy during a school term (the popular idea apparently being that this reflected a bit of the seamy side of life to which children should not be exposed).

Then, during the great witch-hunt of the McCarthy era, when the American people were led to believe that Communism infested our society, many states passed laws requiring loyalty oaths of teachers. One by one, these state laws were declared unconstitutional by federal courts.

CHICAGO TEACHERS FEDERATION

Another effort at teacher repression was the prohibition against forming or joining unions. This all seems to have begun (or to have come to a head) in Chicago. As already noted, in the last years of the nineteenth century teachers' salaries there had been at a standstill for about two decades.

The Chicago Teachers Federation, formed in 1897, came into being as an independent organization not affiliated with labor. For nearly twenty years prior to this, teachers' salaries had changed little. The federation began at once to fight for change, but after they had secured some adjustments, the school board inaugurated a new economy program and reduced the salaries of teachers again. Low-tax advocates managed year after year to secure and maintain control of the school board. The Chicago Teachers Federation began a counter action by instituting (in 1902) studies of the tax system, resulting in a suit against tax evaders. It soon became evident that the teachers had to look for allies to fight the interests which were controlling the school board. Thus by 1903 the teachers became affiliated with the American Federation of Labor. By 1916, a total of twenty such groups had joined together to form the American Federation of Teachers, a national association. In 1915 the Chicago School Board adopted the Loeb Rule, which would have prohibited teachers from being members of labor unions, but the teachers secured a temporary injunction against its enforcement. This hassle resulted in the firing of sixty-eight teachers who were members of the union. The conflict became so intense that the Illinois legislature abolished the Chicago School Board in 1917 and established a new board with a new set of laws governing their powers and duties.

So the new movement progressed, always against the bitter opposition of many influential newspapers, employee groups, and industrial groups particularly. So bitter did the opposition become that during both World Wars teacher unionism became the target of charges of anti-Americanism and un-Americanism. In the meantime, the American Federation of Teachers has continued to grow, and its membership has increased so much that NEA has been forced to compete vigorously with it, especially in the large cities.

10

Restricting Teachers' Freedom of Speech

THE very first amendment in the Bill of Rights guarantees to the American people free speech in all its positive and productive forms. The colonists knew from history, and from their own experience with their mother country, that denial of the right of ordinary citizens to speak out concerning things they don't like, the things they fear, or the rights or liberties they want but don't have is undemocratic. Enforced silence is the easiest of all routes to the establishment of tyranny in places and ways that are most often subtle and ostensibly harmless.

Any nation that would be free must first guarantee freedom of speech to all citizens. Conversely, the quickest and easiest route to autocratic, unjust, and dictatorial government is to prohibit the right of freedom to speak to the mass of a nation's citizens. Especially would this apply to teachers.

It is obvious that the free speech and free assembly were cornerstones of the new nation. It is a regrettable commentary that public school teachers often appear to be about the last group in American life to achieve this right in full—in fact, and not just in theory. The first aspect of this freedom for which teachers fought hardest through the years was that of academic freedom. The second was the right possessed, theoretically, by all Americans—that of the personal right to take sides on issues of whatever nature, and to express them.

HOW THE BILL OF RIGHTS ORIGINATED

The founding fathers of the United States had an afterthought when they had already completed their final draft of the proposed Constitution.

It became apparent to the delegates that there were not sufficient provisions to protect the rights of the individual citizen, in whatever state he may reside, against an all-powerful national government. Thus, as indicated above, the first ten amendments to the Constitution were added. This cluster of amendments constitutes what is termed the Bill of Rights. It is of great importance that the First Amendment deals with freedoms guaranteed to the individual, especially the one guaranteeing freedom of speech and of the press.

This reference to the press has been interpreted to mean that a newspaper reporter shall not be required to divulge the source of information which formed the basis of a published story. Yet, to the surprise of many Americans, the U.S. Supreme Court in May, 1978, held that such information *must* be revealed, *if* the request for it is accompanied by a court order. (The court's vote was 5–4 on this issue.) This case involved more than 4,600 documents gathered in a three-year criminal investigation of a medical doctor who is alleged to have killed several patients with overdoses of an exotic drug. This was the second case in three months involving the forced surrender of confidential documents held by a newsman and/or newspaper, and the verdict was a totally new departure from past practices. One supposes this change arises because of the guarantee of the Constitution that an accused has a right to be confronted with evidence held against him (as in the Fourteenth Amendment), which has been generally interpreted as applying to an actual case in a court of law. There have been written intimations that the majority of the members of the Supreme Court are seeking revenge for the press's alleged mistreatment of former President Nixon. This suggestion is false, but the very application outside of the privilege of an accused in a court arouses suspicion.

FREEDOM OF THE PRESS

A long-standing (since 1799) part of the Bill of Rights, the First Amendment, seems at the moment to be in jeopardy. The amendment reads: "Congress shall make no law respecting an establishment of religion, or prohibiting the free exercise thereof; or abridging the freedom of speech, or of the press. . . ."

On Monday, July 25, 1978, Myron Farber, a reporter for the *New York Times,* was convicted of civil and criminal contempt and jailed, in an attempt to force him to surrender his investigative notes on Dr. Jascalevich, defendant in what has come to be called the Dr. X Murder Trial in New Jersey.[1] The court also assessed a fine of $5,000 per day against the *Times* until the court received the notes. The *Times* criticized the jailing and fine as a blow to freedom of the press.

An appeal to a three-judge panel in Newark was denied, and the court refused to suspend the civil sentence pending additional appeals. The judge also convicted both Farber and the *Times* of criminal contempt and ordered Farber jailed for six months and the *Times* fined $100,000.

This key test is a rather unusual one, since it has been generally accepted by the public and the courts that a reporter is privileged to protect his sources from imprisonment or revenge of any sort.

It should be kept in mind that the First Amendment, under its original interpretation, not only guarantees the right of free speech, and protection of sources, for newspaper people. It also means the right of the people to hear or to read—in short, the right to know all that is germane to public policy and/or the violations of the peoples' right to know. It does not give special protection to journalists.

Interference with the Press

As was expected, after the U.S. Supreme Court decision that an individual or firm could force a newspaper and/or reporter to reveal the sources of information contained in an article by obtaining a court order to reveal the sources of the information contained in the published account, several cases have transpired in which the reporter and paper have refused to reveal their sources.

Myron Farber refused to turn over his files in the Doctor X trial in New Jersey. The court assessed a fine of $1,000 against the reporter, and a $5,000 daily fine against the *New York Times*. On appeal, U.S. Supreme Court Justice Byron White and the New Jersey Supreme Court left Farber free for four days and suspended all fines.

Originally, the penalties were to continue until the material subpoenaed by defense lawyers was made available. The trial judge ordered the documents produced for his private inspection, so he could see if the defense should have them. The *New York Times* and Farber contended

---

[1] Leslie Oelsner, "Jersey Judge Jails *Times* Reporter; Refused to Yield Notes in Trial," *New York Times*, July 25, 1978, p. 1.

that a reporter should not be required to disclose his sources until a judge determines whether the material is protected by the First Amendment.

The Second Surprising Decision

A startling decision of the Supreme Court was rendered in July, 1978, in the *Stanford Daily* case. This decision held that police in search of evidence have the right to appear in a newspaper plant—or anywhere else, for that matter—and demand evidence which may be in the possession of the paper or any of its employees. There is an "if" here—if the police have in their possession an order from a judge who has issued a warrant "to search any property at which there is probable cause to believe that evidence of a crime will be found." This means that the Supreme Court rejected the traditional posture that police should first secure a subpoena which can be contested in court. Secondly, it means that freedom of the press under the First Amendment gives newsrooms more protection against unreasonable searches than, for example, private homes or doctors offices.

What does this mean? If the decision is allowed to stand, it means that information can be kept from publication and, therefore, kept from the people, thus weakening the chief safeguard of government. One writer lists the dangers of the Stanford decision as follows:

1. It dries up inside resources for potential news stories, once would-be informants find that their confidentiality would be exposed through police search of reporters' notes.
2. The dynamics of this loss of confidentiality, plus the police ability to harass and disrupt newspapers, could threaten the very viability of small independent newspapers in their community. As independent newspapers fail, safeguards against control of the press by government are weakened.
3. Stories can be shortstopped from reaching print in newspapers simply through seizure.[2]

In the third recent precedent-setting decision involving the First Amendment, the Supreme Court ruled that journalists can be forced to tell about the thoughts, opinions, and conclusions they felt while writing a published story. The court ruled 6–3 against the CBS "60 Minutes"

---

[2] Ann Melvin, "Stanford Decision Hurts You, Too," *Dallas Morning News*, July 17, 1978. Used by permission.

program in a libel case. This suit had to do with a libel suit by Lt. Col. Anthony Herbert, who had charged his superior officers with covering up war crimes in South Vietnam. Herbert claimed that the "60 Minutes" program falsely and maliciously accused him of being a liar.

This Supreme Court has, for the first time, given a public figure—a lawyer—the right to probe into the state of mind of the writer of the alleged libelous statement. But proving malice without probing the ideological process is virtually impossible. In light of two other decisions, this decision vastly increases the concern that this constitutional guarantee of freedom of speech may be emasculated.

This same court in the Farber case and the Stanford case aroused great apprehension that the treasure of freedom of speech and press, guaranteed by the First Amendment, may be jeopardized. Teachers, who have won many cases in recent years involving statements in the classroom, should be particularly apprehensive.

EXAMPLES OF FREE SPEECH FOR TEACHERS

In California, a federal court ordered reinstatement of three school-community workers who had not been kept on their jobs because the board had not considered the needs of the black community.

A federal court in Arkansas ordered reinstatement and back pay for a teacher with many years' service who was not renewed because of "insubordination." She had complained that fumes from an incinerator in the schoolyard spewed into her classroom. The court upheld the teacher on the grounds she was protecting the health of the children. The court said that a citizen, whether teacher or layman, has the legal right to seek redress for dangers or threats to health and safety.

New Hampshire Nonrenewal

A New Hampshire teacher of journalism and English, and a negotiator for his local teachers' association, was not renewed because (he testified in court) he had criticized the board before the local teachers' association, its negotiating team, and the superintendent of schools. The federal court overruled the board and ordered the teacher's reinstatement with back pay. The court held that his dismissal was due primarily to his exercising of his constitutional right of free speech. The decision stated that dismissal on the basis of uninvestigated complaints and unverified rumors is unjust, arbitrary, and capricious.

There are exceptions to the above ruling. For example, a woman teacher was dismissed for writing to a state legislator about inadequate funding of a program for handicapped children. Her letter was written on school stationery. The court ruled that, while she had the right to write the letter, she had no right to speak for the board or to misrepresent its position.

Also, the Alaska Supreme Court did not condone the right of two teachers to publish an open letter to the board criticizing the superintendent.

As a principle, courts often apply the cases in which free expressions by teachers interfere with functions of a government agency or other employing body. But a federal court in Connecticut did technically support a teacher who, at a school board meeting, accused his supervisor of being a liar, raised questions about his competence, and challenged the integrity of the whole administrative staff. The court ruled that these actions were permitted under free speech rights. Nevertheless, the court also held that to order reinstatement to his job would invite friction and destroy staff morale, which meant that the children would suffer.

A Texas university teaching assistant lost her job for making a severely critical (and reportedly obscene) speech to students attending a rock concert during a freshman orientation session. This diatribe was directed at the board of regents, the administration, faculty, students, and American society. She had also published an article containing many of the criticisms. The courts ruled against this teacher since the interest of the university outweighed her claim for protection.

The federal courts, especially, have tended to support teachers for expressing political beliefs on social issues unrelated to their employment. In Rhode Island a federal court found illegal the expulsion of a Peace Corps volunteer and university faculty member who had published in a newspaper in Chile a letter criticizing the war in Vietnam and Peace Corps policy on the right of volunteers to speak out on U.S. international relations. The court said to sustain a termination such as this would be to value bureaucratic paranoia over the central commitment of the First Amendment.

Also, a federal circuit court upheld the right of a New York teacher to wear an armband in class to protest the war in Vietnam. The court said that, without proof that the teacher's action caused disruption, prohibiting this conduct is not justified.

In 1969, a black elementary school teacher was not renewed because he participated in voter registration of blacks, in a successful effort to secure black representation on the school board. In ruling in favor of the teacher, despite a board policy prohibiting teachers from all political activities except voting, the court said: "The complete ban on the right of teachers to express political opinions and engage in political activity is inconsistent with the First Amendment guarantee of freedom of speech, press, assembly and petition."[3]

To further embellish the principle enunciated above, a North Carolina teacher participated in civil rights activity as an example of protected free expression which was upheld by a federal circuit court. This court ruled that a school board's refusal to rehire a nontenured black who had participated in demonstrations protesting racial discrimination, and in voter registration drives, was unconstitutional because its reasons were capricious and arbitrary, and particularly, because the non-renewal was a retaliation for the teacher's civil rights activity.[4]

Teachers' Freedom to Speak Their Views

The old, old notion that teachers are nonentities who know nothing about public affairs, and should remain silent on public issues, is rapidly disappearing from the American scene. The First Amendment declares the rights of *all* citizens, including teachers, to express their views. Yet one would surmise that teachers have suffered more for expressing views counter to prevailing opinion of the school board, or the superintendent, or the community in which they work than for any other cause.

Here is one court case in which a teacher fought the school board's cancellation of his contract for expressing his views. In 1968, Marvin Pickering precipitated the cancellation by writing to a local newspaper, charging that the public had been misinformed about the school budget in a proposed bond issue and stated that the superintendent had threatened to discipline faculty members who refused to support the board's position on the bond issue.

---

[3] Betty E. Sinowitz, "Court Ruling on Teacher's Right to Speak Out," *Today's Education*, Sept.–Oct., 1973, pp. 50–60.

[4] Ibid., p. 60.

The U.S. Supreme Court ruled that comments by a teacher on matters of public concern that are substantially accurate are not grounds for dismissal and that free and open debate is vital to informed decision making by the electorate. However, the court laid down two basics which might obviate a favorable decision: (1) If the school operation or the teacher's classroom functioning were disputed; and (2) if the comments were knowingly inaccurate.

State and federal court decisions now tend to follow the precedent established in the Pickering case.

Nepotism Criticized

A principal-teacher in Mississippi was not renewed after he criticized the school board and county government for violation of anti-nepotism laws. Along with a group of citizens, he signed a telegram to the state auditor, requesting that a special audit of the county supervisor be conducted. This same teacher ran for state senator and questioned waste and graft in the school system and county government. The court found that his charges of official negligence were basically true; he was reinstated.

Floating Teacher Upheld in Protest

Donna Johnson, a Roanoke, Virginia, junior high school math and science teacher, complained of her status as a "floater." She was a tenured teacher, but when she threatened to file a grievance to secure a permanent room, the school board did not renew her contract. The case was tried in a federal district court. School officials contended that her contract was not renewed because she was insubordinate and displayed a poor attitude. But the judge held that the right of a teacher to express concern about conditions which interfere with the education of her students falls within the protection afforded by the Constitution. He ordered her contract renewed and back pay for the 1976–77 school year.[5]

Teacher's Simulation Game Upheld

Janet Cooper, a Texas social studies teacher, used a Civil War simulation game in a class. Her contract was not renewed at the end of the school

---

[5] *NEA Reporter*, Oct., 1977, p. 20.

year. She won reinstatement on appeal to the U.S. District Court for southern Texas, claiming violation of academic freedom in an American history class. Her game involved assigning each student a role to act out in a historical incident—in this case, the problem of Reconstruction after the Civil War. The court on August 26, 1977, ruled that the teacher had lost her job for constitutionally impermissible reasons. The Kingsville Independent School District appealed the verdict. The case was eventually won by the teacher; the board was ordered to reinstate her and to pay her $15,000 in back pay and $4,500 in attorney's fees. The NEA DuShane Emergency Fund and the Texas State Teachers Association aided the teacher in the suit.[6]

Out-of-Class Speech

Dabney Lee, a great-grand-nephew of General Robert E. Lee, lost his job in Virginia in 1969–70 for protesting an action of the state education association. Lee, a teacher in Farmville, became active in the predominantly black education association. He taught two years in the all-black Luther P. Jackson School, where he was one of a small number of white faculty members. He took an active role in the affairs of the black Cumberland Teachers Association (CTA), especially in efforts to bring about merger of that association and the all-white Cumberland Education Association.

During this period Lee's association (CTA) nominated him for the office of treasurer of the Virginia Education Association. The VEA executive secretary, on advice of counsel, rejected the nomination on the grounds that it was received after nominations were closed; Lee's name, therefore, did not appear on the ballot. Lee threatened to sue the VEA and its officers. The executive secretary of the VEA, in an effort to avoid a possible suit, called Lee's superintendent and described to him the developments in the case. Also, the VEA secretary had a co-worker who knew Lee's principal telephone him and describe the events causing the threatened suit.

Lee lost his case in Richmond's Law and Equity Court. He also lost in the Virginia Court of Appeals.

The court order in the federal court case eventually filed by Lee, agreed to by attorneys for all parties, stated that the phone calls between

---

[6] Ibid.

the VEA secretary and others and the superintendent and principal resulted in a heated argument between Lee and the superintendent regarding VEA, and that because of Lee's activities Superintendent Smith did not recommend Lee for a new contract. Lee requested to know the reason for his non-renewal; he also requested a hearing by the school board. Two meetings of the board made no progress, so there were no reasons given for the dismissal.

The court awarded Lee a $4,500 stipulated settlement against the defendants (three members of the board, the superintendent, and the VEA secretary). The court also ordered the school officials to purge all school board records and personnel files of any derogatory references to the plaintiff. The school board also assured Lee of the offer of a new contract.[7]

FREEDOM OF SPEECH—ARTICLE I

The Farber–New York Times case, in which both were fined, has been previously described in this chapter. Further comment, however, is needed.

This case is different from virtually every previous case in which the courts, especially federal courts, had ruled that the First Amendment protected the rights of the investigative reporter and the publisher to secure and publish information involved in wrongdoing. In this case, the defendant had already been indicted for the murders. Thus, his lawyers eventually subpoenaed Farber's notes, claiming that they were absolutely essential to the defense of the accused. The trial judge ordered the notes turned over to him (the judge) so he could determine whether they were pertinent to the case.

This case, then, presented two conflicting rights. Both the defendants and the doctor have rights—the doctor has rights regarding fair criminal procedure, and the reporter and the newspaper have the right accorded a free press in the First Amendment. In case of conflict, the burden falls to the judiciary, which in this case ruled against the reporter and the publisher.

The fact that Farber had a valuable contract for a book on the case—

---

[7] Abstracted from *Case Summaries and Actions, June 1, 1969–May 31, 1970*, DuShane Fund Reports, June 25 (Washington, D.C.: National Education Association, 1970), p. 4.

which of course implied a profit motivation—tended to cloud the principle of freedom of speech in this case. In short, the court decision which seemed at first glance to conflict with the interpretation courts have consistently made—that the information collected for a story is to be protected from appropriation by others—was not in conflict with previous decisions.

SUMMARY OF CASES DEALING WITH ACADEMIC FREEDOM

Teachers today face a dilemma. They are urged to use innovative procedures, but some who have challenged the status quo suffer penalties, and a few actually lose their jobs. They are fighting back, with the support of their education associations, and are winning many cases in federal courts on the grounds that their First and Fourteenth Amendment rights have been violated.

In Arkansas, in connection with a second-grade unit on nutrition, the teacher's students had written a letter to the cafeteria supervisor expressing their preference for raw, rather than cooked, carrots. This teacher had twenty-six years of experience and top ratings but was not renewed because of "alleged insubordination, lack of cooperation with the administration and teaching the students to protest." She had also raised questions with school officials about possible pollution from an open incinerator in the schoolyard. She sued the school board. The court held that when a school board punishes a teacher who seeks to protect the health and safety of herself and her pupils, this can cause serious effects on free discussion of controversial subjects. Also, the Supreme Court, in a ruling on June 29, 1972, held that a teacher (even one without tenure) may not be fired during the school year or denied a new contract because he exercised a constitutional right. Gradually, the federal courts are spelling out the boundaries of academic freedom.

11

Mandatory Retirement Age
for Teachers

THE growing rebellion of teachers against school boards' blunt orders to retire promptly at sixty-five, or some other age that often is arbitrarily established, is rapidly being matched by other workers. The elderly are joining together to change retirement ages set a generation or so ago. They argue that the general and rapid improvement in health conditions has escalated the ages at which workers need to retire. The productive ages of older workers, including teachers, have steadily risen in recent years. So evident is this fact that mandatory retirement ages are rapidly diminishing and may soon become obsolete.

In this chapter will be found the accounts of some teachers who have taken their cases to the courts. Some of the cases involve teachers whose local school boards have compelled them to retire at sixty-five, although the state's mandatory retirement age was set at 70.

As the 1960s were marked by a revolt of the youth, so the 1970s are likely to be recorded as the age of revolt of the elderly against arbitrary treatment. Almost 10 percent of the population of the United States (about 23,000,000) consists of people who have reached the age of sixty-five or higher.

A forerunner of what may become a national trend occurred in Washington in early October, 1977. The U.S. House of Representatives passed, by the overwhelming vote of 359–4, a bill which extends the mandatory retirement age of workers in private industry from sixty-five to seventy and which completely removes the age for mandatory retirement for federal employees. Subsequently the bill was passed by the Senate and signed by President Carter, thus becoming law.

The age of sixty-five, which probably is the most commonly used one for mandatory retirement, appears to have been initiated in Germany by Bismarck, who originated a social security plan in 1884. In the United States, this age of sixty-five for mandatory retirement and the beginning of receiving benefits is the most common one. The rapidly increasing number of retirees at age sixty-five is creating a heavy drain upon the funds set aside decades ago for retirement benefits. Especially have these funds become inadequate in many cases because of inflation. Thus the trend toward extending the mandatory retirement age is likely to be generally endorsed; also, the increasing drain on Social Security funds will add to the trend toward acceptance of higher retirement ages.

In Bismarck's country and time, a much smaller percentage of the population lived to be sixty-five; life expectancy at birth was about thirty-seven years in Germany in the 1880s. Since then, thousands and millions of healthy, even robust, unemployed people sixty-five years of age or over have been forced to retire. The future seems certain to see a drastic increase in their numbers. Life expectancy in the United States in 1978 was sixty-nine years for men and seventy-seven for women.

Whether the new law will create a stampede of older people to stay on the job longer, thus filling posts that might otherwise provide openings for younger people, no one knows. This is going to be one of the great concerns about such a change. If raising the retirement age causes a great pile-up of unemployed or unpromoted younger people, this could be a great tragedy, if society cannot find another remedy for that problem.

Any way the problem is examined, this educational fear of pile-up of youngsters who have completed preparation for jobs but who can find no jobs, because only a few have been vacated by retirees, is real. Also, those who doubt the wisdom of postponing retirement fear that adding older workers to our work force will slow down the pace of change.

Society has got to find a way of eliminating deadwood from the work-force, a way to encourage new ideas and new methods of work. There are other disadvantages (real or imaginary) to the plan for later retirement, but this much appears at the moment to be certain: The mandatory age for retirement, in private business and in government, will now be raised to seventy years of age. And provisions will be made for determining who could be allowed to continue employment for a specified number of years, or until the circumstances change so as to make the need for retirement obvious.

Of course, there are different opinions about retirement. Some workers, whatever their occupations, are impatiently waiting for age sixty-five to roll around so that they can retire and enjoy the leisure they have earned. Others are so enamored with their jobs that they look with sadness upon the prospect of life dropping a curtain at 5:00 p.m. some day— a curtain that will separate them from what they have been doing all their adult lives, and from friends of many years.

SOME PROBLEMS OF TEACHER TENURE

In any informed discussion of teacher rights and teacher mistreatment, questions about tenure are bound to arise. For years, the public tended to be pretty solidly against tenure, but since midcentury, the pendulum has swung in favor of such legislation. Almost all states now have tenure provisions, or continuing contract laws, or tenure laws applying to the state or its largest school districts.

However, the concept of tenure for teachers today tends to be under rather widespread criticism, and among certain groups it is under vehement attack. Leading the opposition are, perhaps, school board members, followed closely by state education officers, and by some administrators who tend to abhor the notion that they should share authority to manage the school system with anybody. But in recent years the rise of discipline problems, vandalism, and actual crimes committed by students have been so widespread as to shock the nation. It is natural for the public to lay the blame at the feet of teachers. The throwing off of their shackles to a great extent, especially the proliferation of teachers' strikes, has helped to create the image of irresponsible school staffs. Of course, there must be some degree of soundness in this judgment of the general public, but that charge appears to be too easy an answer. The widespread multiplication of the crime rate in our society and the constant picturing of violence as a way of life in television shows are bound to have devastating effects upon children's concepts and behavior patterns. Making teachers the scapegoats for all that is untoward in our homes and in society as a whole is a very easy and very appealing answer. But it is too unfair for us to return to discrimination and abuse of teachers. Thus, the use of tenure is likely to increase.

TENURE SAFEGUARDS

More likely and solid answers probably are to be found in adopting some safeguards to tenure. The first is to understand the basic purpose of tenure. It was originally to spell out fair and equitable rules for the dismissal of teachers, *not* to protect the jobs of incompetents. Tenure probably came into being in an effort to protect public employees from bossism and the spoils system. Certainly, these were major causes of the innovation. Jobs were generally looked upon by political bosses as rewards to be conferred upon the faithful: "To the victor belong the spoils." The intent of tenure, first of all, was the employment and retention of capable professionals, with freedom to teach without fear of arbitrary actions by employing officials. It must always be remembered that having the great power of awarding jobs, or the right to fire people from jobs, gives many supervisors who are elevated to this seat of power a sense of infallibility. The smaller the caliber of a person, the more intoxicating is the power. Also, such power tends to give some people a sense of arrogance—rather than a sense of humility, as it should—and their sense of values becomes skewed. Doubtless, one of the elements in the appeal of slavery wherever it has existed has always been the heady sense of power which it gives to the one who holds others in bondage.

Second, tenure will stand or fall, will work or fail, on the basis of whether the school boards and the school administrators maintain a sound professional system of selection in the employment process. A poor system inevitably will select people who will not deserve to be retained in their jobs. Of course, no system is infallible in this regard, but hiring too many second- and third-rate people and later having to let them go sours administrators and boards on the idea of tenure.

Because a faulty system of recruitment and selection will guarantee the failure of tenure, there is the imperative that the administration develop an effective, thorough system of annual evaluations of the work of teachers during the probationary period, in order to screen out the misfits and incompetents. Such a system will help prevent the traumatic experience of teachers achieving tenure, then having to be dismissed on the charge of incompetency.

Third, a perceptive, constantly tested development of better personnel policies is a must for the competent school administrator to make tenure work to the satisfaction of the board and the public. These are the elements treated in a timely, courageous booklet, *Teacher Tenure Ain't the Problem*, issued by the American Association of School Administrators.[1]

Last, but by no means least, teachers themselves ought to assume major roles of responsibility in making tenure work. This can be done by being sensitive to the responsibilities and duties they are expected to perform. They must demonstrate in their attitudes and performance the value of legal permanence of their positions—not by an attitude of fawning subservience, but by one of diligence and good-faith performance.

A Forced Retiree Fights Back

The following statement is by Thelma Davis, a veteran teacher in the Griffin-Spalding School District in Georgia. The zeal with which Mrs. Davis fought her enforced retirement reveals the extent of the hurt when a highly competent teacher, who has many years of excellent service still ahead, is cast out.

When I was called into the principal's office, I had no idea what the meeting was to be about. The assistant superintendent informed me that on that particular evening a recommendation was to be made to the board of education of the county school system that forced retirement in this system was to be set at 65 years of age and that all teachers who came in this category were to retire at the end of the current year. I knew nothing about the fact, but was informed later that this same thing had been suggested or brought up before the board at the previous monthly meetings.

I had taught in the Griffin-Spalding Consolidated School system 21 years, plus three years in the vicinity making 24 years. I had never received anything except above average evaluations from any of the principals that I had worked with. I thought that after 24 years, if this is the way they felt, I just did not feel that I could stay.

Then into my mind flashed this thought: If I quit or if I resigned, I had no right to fight this forced retirement which I knew was below the state retirement age. I made three trips to the superintendent's office. On the first trip I asked for a hearing. I was told that I didn't need a hearing, and the essence of the conversation was that I should

[1] *Teacher Tenure Ain't the Problem* (Arlington, Va.: American Association of School Administrators, 1973), p. 31.

retire. After I was denied a hearing through my visits to the superintendent's office, I contacted the Georgia Association of Educators and
the National Education Association. The National Education Association was more than glad to defend me. They assigned one of our
NEA lawyers to my case. In addition, they hired an Atlanta law firm
to represent me.

The court judgment was rendered in my favor. The final judgment
entitled me to back pay with interest, increased retirement and social
security benefits, and costs of the action to a very limited amount.[2]

Another Mandatory Leave Policy Voided

Catherine Delores Tondeved, an elementary teacher in Blaine, Washington, failed to have her contract renewed in 1977 because the school board
had adopted sixty-five as a mandatory retirement age. She won reinstatement in the Superior Court of Washington in May, 1977—plus back pay
in excess of $13,000, plus legal expenses of over $9,000. This board decision was based on a unilateral policy of retirement at age sixty-five, but
the teachers' contract did not have the mandatory policy in it.

AGE DISCRIMINATION IN EMPLOYMENT ACT

The Age Discrimination in Employment Act of the U.S. Congress—and
court suits alleging denial of equal protection—are now available to teachers who have evidence that they have suffered discrimination on the basis
of age. In May, 1974, an amendment was adopted extending ADEA coverage to civil service employees of local, state, and federal governments.
This amendment protects teachers between the ages of forty and sixty-
five from age discrimination in employment, in such areas as hiring and
firing, promotion, compensation, leave provisions, and other conditions.
The Department of Labor (Wage and Hours Division) is charged with
implementing the provisions against discrimination.

Some examples: A professor in the University of Hawaii system secured a decision of a state court to continue his employment; the decision
also applied to his colleagues between the ages of sixty-five and seventy.

---

[2] Abstracted from court brief, *Thelma Davis v. Griffin-Spalding County, Georgia
Board of Education, et al.*, Civil Action no. C-75-6-N, U.S. District Court, Northern
District of Georgia, Newman Division.

He contended that he and all faculty members who had to retire at age sixty-five were being denied equal protection of the laws. Police officers in Massachusetts secured a decision from a federal court that mandatory retirement at age fifty was unconstitutional.

Comparative Data on Ages of Employment[3]

In 1948, almost half of all men sixty-five years of age and over were employed or seeking jobs. In 1978, only one man in five and one woman in twelve were in the workforce by that age.

People are now living longer. Presently, three-fourths of the population in the United States now reach sixty-five; those who do reach sixty-five tend to live on to the average of eighty-one years. In 1940, 7 percent of the population were sixty-five or over. In 1978, the figure was 11 percent; and in 2030, it will be almost 20 percent. Thus, it becomes apparent that the problem of age at retirement is whether the working force can support, through social security or other tax means, the cost. An ever-increasing proportion of the population consists of retirees. In 1978, six active workers supported one in retirement; it is estimated that by the year 2030 the proportion will be three workers to one retiree. To state the problem another way: Today, the cost to the federal government of supporting retirees is $112 billion per year; by 2030, it will be about $635 billion. This would mean an increase in cost from 24 percent to 40 percent of total federal spending. Thus there are two great problems, both of which really argue for raising the average age of retirement. (1) Where does the increased support money come from? (2) Where will jobs for young people come from, if retirement ages are raised?

PROVISIONS OF THE 1978 FEDERAL RETIREMENT LAW

The law states that beginning in 1979, employees in private businesses that have as many as twenty employees cannot be forced to retire until age seventy. Federal government workers, effective October 1, 1978, cannot be forced to retire at any age.

To turn the provisions around, the law also provides that the em-

---

[3] Data from United Press International newspaper release, July 20, 1978.

ployer cannot compel employees to work until age seventy before being eligible for retirement benefits, because revision laws require 100 percent vesting by the time the employee is sixty-five. Thus the worker has the choice of retiring at sixty-five or seventy. It must be noted that persons in private employment who reached sixty-five before January 1, 1979, could be forced to retire at age sixty-five. The law did not take full effect until 1979.

One important question is, Will a worker's social security benefits be available if he or she remains on the job after age sixty-five? The answer is yes, according to previous legislation. If a worker earned over $14,000 in 1978, this would reduce social security payments by fifty cents for each dollar beyond this amount until age seventy-two, after which the worker would be free to make as much as he can, without penalty. The 1978 law also does not affect Medicare payments to workers who remain on the job past age sixty-five.

The law does affect state and local government workers, providing the same treatment for them as for private employees. It should be emphasized that the federal law did not change the status of some federal employees, such as air traffic controllers, foreign service officers, and law enforcement officers and firemen. Also, requirements already set by collective bargaining agreements were to remain in effect until January 1, 1980, when the age-seventy provision became effective.

About two-thirds of all workers in the United States are not affected by the 1978 law because they do not have any mandatory retirement age.

As to the problem of serious effects on the job opportunities of younger people, it is estimated by federal agencies that only some 200,000 older people might remain in the private workforce as a result of changes in the law. And only 1,500 federal workers out of a total of in excess of 2,000,000 affected by the new law will remain on the job until age seventy.

Does the 1978 law affect state and local governments? Yes, the law applies to them. What workers, if any, are exempted from the provisions of the law? One group—college professors—were exempt until 1982.

How many workers are there presently who have no mandatory retirement ages? It is estimated that about two out of three workers in the United States do not have any specified mandatory retirement age.

12

Racial Discrimination
in Employment

RACIAL discrimination in the United States is not a new thing. Indeed, it dates back to the beginnings of the nation, to the beginning of the importation and sale of black slaves. This discrimination was usually backed up by actual (and from the present viewpoint, brazen) spelling out of terms and conditions.

The equality of educational opportunity in the United States did not come into full flower with the general establishment of a free public school system. In fact, not until the 1954 decision of the Supreme Court in *Brown v. Board of Education* did the provision including all races and creeds become the immutable principle of the public school system.

LAWS PROHIBITING EDUCATION OF
THE CHILDREN OF SLAVES

Although South Carolina was the first to enact such a law, a total of twelve states at one time had laws prohibiting the education (especially in reading or writing) of slaves or their children. The twelve states were Delaware, Maryland, Virginia, North Carolina, South Carolina, Georgia, Kentucky, Tennessee, Louisiana, Mississippi, Alabama, and Missouri. To this group should be added the District of Columbia, because in February, 1901, Congress passed a law declaring that the portion of the District of Columbia which had been ceded to the United States by Virginia should be governed by the laws of that state. Public education, though supported in all the states by taxation, was denied the slaves (and free blacks) and their children in the slave-holding states. Legislation regarding this prohibition was inaugurated by South Carolina in 1740 and revised in 1800. In essence the act provided:

> Whereas the having of slaves taught to write, or suffering them to be employed in writing, may be attended with great inconveniences. Be it enacted, that all and every person and persons whatsoever who hereafter teach or cause any slave or slaves to be taught to write, or shall use or employ any slave as a scribe in any manner of writing hereafter, or taught to write, every such person or persons shall for every such offense forfeit the sum of one hundred pounds current money.[1]

Added to this provision in 1800 (leaving the Act of 1740 in force by this enactment):

> Assemblies of slaves, free Negroes, mulattoes and mestizoes, whether composed of all or any such description of persons, or of all or any of the same and of a proportion of white persons, met together for the purpose of mental instruction in a confined or secret place . . . are declared to be an *unlawful meeting*; and magistrates are hereby required to enter into such confined places . . . to break doors, if resisted, and to disperse such slaves, free Negroes, etc.; and the officer dispersing such unlawful assemblies may inflict such corporal punishment, not exceeding twenty lashes upon such slaves, free Negroes, etc., as they may judge necessary for deterring them from like unlawful assemblages in the future.[2]

Virginia passed a similar law in 1849, which stated in essence:

> Every assemblage of Negroes for the purpose of instruction in reading or writing shall be an unlawful assembly. Any justice may issue his warrant to any officer or other person, requiring him to enter any place where such assemblage may be, and seize any Negro therein; and he or any other justice may order such Negroes to be punished with stripes. If a white person assembles with Negroes for the purpose of instruction either to Negro or white, he shall be confined to jail not exceeding six months, and fines not exceeding one hundred dollars.[3]

---

[1] George M. Stroud, *Sketch of the Laws Relating to Slavery* (New York: Negro University Press, 1968), sec. 3. pp. 58ff.

[2] Ibid., p. 58.

[3] Ibid., p. 61.

Georgia passed three separate statutes, the first in 1770, the second in 1829, and the third in 1833. North Carolina, Louisiana, and Alabama had enacted legislation similar to that of the states as described above. Kentucky, Tennessee, Mississippi, Missouri, Arkansas, Florida, and Texas seem to have had no specific state laws dealing with this subject; they tended to rely upon local communities to enact their own laws.

BUSING

Although the intent of the Supreme Court in ordering busing of children across school district zones and boundaries was to assure fair treatment of minority groups, especially of black children, the decision has in some instances failed to achieve its purpose.

The Rand Corporation released the findings of an in-depth study of the effects of this ruling on September 7, 1978. This report says that such busing, based on court orders to desegregate the schools, has resulted in "white flight" from increasingly black cities to predominantly white suburbs. The Rand study involves fifty-four school districts, each with at least 20,000 students. Whites fled from public schools shortly after desegregation orders were issued, either moving to the suburbs or sending their children to private schools. In Boston, the report said, white enrollments dropped 14.9 percent in the first year of desegregation and 20 percent in the second year. Denver's white enrollments dropped 13.2 percent; Pontiac, Michigan's dropped 18 percent. Voluntary busing plans, such as that adopted by San Diego, do not appear to have affected the white flight. These cases seem to indicate that mandatory, court-order plans have been the cause of accelerated white flight in school desegregation.

In this connection, officials of the U.S. Conference on Civil Rights report that white flight has been in progress since World War II, a decade or so before the Supreme Court's 1954 decision in *Brown v. Board of Education.* Therefore, the revolt was largely against forced busing, and not bigotry. Also, part of the cause of the white flight has been the rapidly rising cost of living in the big cities. In fact, the vast majority of whites throughout the nation will support busing if it is brought about voluntarily.

PROGRESS IN SCHOOL DESEGREGATION

In 1954 the famous *Brown v. Board of Education* decision of the Supreme Court declared that separate schools for the races are not equal and, therefore, are a violation of constitutional guarantees. That decision, of course, came as a shock to millions of Americans. The 1898 *Plessy v. Ferguson* decision of the Supreme Court, that segregated schools were constitutional if they were "separate but equal," had been repeated as a litany so long that the phrase had taken on the sanctity of scripture to most Americans. The *Brown* decision was received with stunned disbelief in many quarters of this country. Only in the late 1970's did the majority of the American people regain a measure of composure and accept the decision in good faith and spirit.

The intervening years were turbulent ones, beginning with rather open rebellion in some parts of the country, and there ensued a painfully slow and tortuous search for means of tolerable compliance and reluctant acceptance.

By 1975 the South, where the shock was most violent and the resistance doggedly persistent, had begun to comply with growing good spirits, while some pockets of violent rejection were most evident in the North and Northeast, taking the special form of violent resistance to busing.

In the interim, here are some of the steps toward reconcilement of the issues: (1) The slow but orderly dismantling of the dual school system in the South. Of course, almost every step of the way to progress has had to be cleared by decisions of the courts, especially the federal courts. Also, court-sanctioned orders of HEW (U.S. Department of Health, Education, and Welfare) resulting from federal legislation have been very effective toward this end. (2) Then in 1971, the Supreme Court held that busing may be used to help desegregate the public schools. In addition, this same decision (*Swann v. Charlotte District Mecklenburg Board of Education*) supported other techniques, such as redrawing school district boundaries and pairing black and white schools. The burden of satisfying the courts that its policies have not been discriminatory, when a district's racial distribution of students is basically disproportionate to the existing ratios of the two racial groups of its student makeup, has been difficult. In several states in the South, federal courts struck down busing policies in which students were assigned to schools on the basis of test scores. Also, in one state, expulsions and suspensions of black students have been stopped, because the numbers of students receiving such treatment had become extremely high. Federal courts have also ruled that a state has a responsibility to integrate school districts across school district boundary lines.

Federal courts have also had to issue orders for desegregation in a number of metropolitan districts in non-southern states, such as San Francisco, Los Angeles, Pasadena, Las Vegas, Pontiac, Boston, Detroit, and Indianapolis.

Also, federal courts have assumed jurisdiction in a few cases, where parents of Mexican children and other nationalities have charged discrimination, but only where there is evidence that segregation has been caused by discriminatory school board policies.

DISCRIMINATION AGAINST BLACK TEACHERS

Many cases of alleged demotion, dismissal, non-renewal, and salary cuts of black teachers have been considered by the federal courts. As early as the mid-1960s the courts upheld the job rights of seven Giles County, Virginia, blacks who were dismissed when their small school was abolished by integration. In Jackson, Mississippi, the Singleton decision mandated the use of objective nonracial criteria in cases of faculty desegregation. In two other Mississippi cities the school boards sought to eliminate black teachers by use of the prescribed scores on NTE (National Teachers Examination) and GRE (Graduate Record Examination). The courts have generally held these criteria invalid.

In some cases state courts have ordered some school districts to relate, insofar as possible, the ratio of black to white teachers to the ratio of black to white students. NEA has argued in some federal court cases that seniority should be the basic principle in retention when there must be a reduction in the number of faculty members. It cited the fact that more than 1,000 black teachers lost their jobs in five Southern states between 1968 and 1971, while more than 5,000 white teachers were hired.

Also, a federal court has ordered HEW to begin cutting off federal funds to seventeen states that have not complied with desegregation specifications in the Civil Rights Act. This has been appealed by the Justice Department.

The Giles County Case

In July, 1964, the seven Negro teachers who constituted the faculties of the Negro elementary and high schools in Giles County, Virginia, entered suit for reinstatement. Their schools were to be closed and the students moved into a nearby town school, as a result of desegregation. The Virginia Teachers Association, to which most black teachers belonged, joined the suit as a plaintiff. The suit charged that the teachers had been terminated solely because of their race; the dismissed teachers sought reinstatement in the Giles County school system for the 1964–65 session, and other types of relief.

On June 3, 1965, the federal district court judge found that the superintendent of schools had deprived these teachers of their rights under the Fourteenth Amendment. But instead of enforcing their request for prompt reinstatement, the judge's verdict held out only the privilege of making application for positions which might become vacant during the next two years. On July 23, 1965, these teachers appealed the order of the district court judge.

The situation in Giles County throws some light on the mild decision against the school board. At the end of the 1963–64 school term there were only twenty-five black children attending the Bluff City elementary and high schools. No black children had attended school with white children, nor had any blacks been employed in Giles County to teach white children in the public schools. However, by the end of the 1963–64 school term twenty-three black children had been assigned to the Giles County High School by the state's pupil placement board. Thus, on May 5, 1964, the school board ordered the discontinuance of the Bluff City Schools for blacks and ordered the division superintendent to notify the seven black teachers that their services would not be needed after the close of the 1963–64 session. Before the schools had opened for the 1963–64 session, four new elementary teachers and four high school teachers, all white, had been employed. The record showed that in several instances the dismissed black teachers had better collegiate preparation and more teaching experience than some of the newly employed white teachers.

The district court carefully avoided rendering a verdict on the real issue—that is, whether the seven dismissed teachers were denied reemployment because of their race. On May 15, 1964, the superintendent of schools notified each of the seven teachers that the closing of the Bluff

City schools and the placement of the black children in other schools made it necessary to abolish their jobs.

The appellate court's decision, while going much further than that of the previous court, ordered that in the filling of any teaching vacancy the superintendent must write to the dismissed teachers to see if they are available. If he chooses another he must explain in writing the reasons for his preferences.

The Case of Two Black Teachers Dismissed

The NEA's DuShane Emergency Fund filed a complaint in federal court in Albany, Georgia, on behalf of two black educators, Trulie Hammond and Albert Rauls. Miss Hammond had thirty-one years' experience, and twenty-three in the same school. Mr. Rauls had served as either high school or elementary school principal for fourteen years. The court action was against the Baker County superintendent and the school board, on grounds of racial discrimination and failure to provide procedural due process. Reinstatement and back pay were sought for each.

In 1969, a federal court ordered the state of Georgia to desegregate school faculties and student bodies. In the plan submitted by the Baker County School Board, the white faculty would be increased by ten; the black staff would be reduced by eleven.

The court suit contended that racial discrimination and not professional competence caused the dismissal of the two blacks, both of whom held college degrees. Also, the suit claimed that Miss Hammond and Mr. Rauls were denied due process under the Fourteenth Amendment, as neither was given the cause or causes for their dismissal, and neither had an opportunity to be heard.

Demotion of Blacks Overruled

Two black principals from Decatur, Alabama, William L. England and C. Leon Sheffield, won favorable decisions in federal court. The two, who had been demoted as schools were desegregated, were reinstated as principals. Alfred Sims of Clay County, who had been reassigned as a classroom teacher after his junior high school was closed, is now assistant principal in the Clay County High School. The court ordered that he be placed in the next vacant principal's job and paid a principal's salary in the meantime.

Blacks Restored to Positions

In April, 1973, the Fifth U.S. Circuit Court of Appeals ordered reinstatement of four black teachers and an assistant principal who were not given new contracts for the 1970–71 school year by the Columbia, Mississippi, separate school district. Previously a district court had rejected back pay and reinstatement petitions. The school district contended that the non-renewals were due to merger of schools at the beginning of the 1970–71 school year; however, the court found that the teachers were given no reason for the non-renewals, and that their requests for an explanation were not answered. A federal court had held in a previous case (1969) that equal-protection and due-process clauses of the Fourteenth Amendment required that, in case of a reduction in the professional staff caused by a court-ordered merger, those to be dismissed must be selected on the basis of a comparative evaluation of all employees of the district at the same level, on the basis of objective standards.

Lawyers Win Fees in Racial Discrimination Suits

A five-year series of court battles was rewarded by a federal court in Mississippi in 1975 in a decision that the school districts of Columbus and Starksville must pay $106,000 to attorneys who handled successful cases of alleged racial discrimination which began in 1970. The award was for attorneys' fees, expenses, and court costs, in cases involving twenty teachers. Most of the teachers were reinstated. One teacher who was fired twice was reinstated and also will receive back pay.

All of these cases involved teachers dismissed during the desegregation crisis. Some involved teachers dismissed for not meeting the cut-off scores on the National Teachers Examination, and some for not achieving the minimum score on the Graduate Record Examination. Two white teachers were fired for expressing their concern for the rights of blacks during desegregation—one for distributing documents protesting the discriminatory treatment of black teachers. In addition, a black teacher who had been reinstated by a court decision was suspended and later dismissed for bringing suit.

In ruling for the teachers on the failure to meet the prescribed minimum scores of the examinations, the court held that the tests are to the disadvantage of black teachers, that they are illegal criteria for hiring or retaining teachers, and that their use violated the equal-protection clause of the Fourteenth Amendment. Attorneys' fees were based on the Emergency Education Aid Act of 1972, which provides for granting such fees in teacher race discrimination suits against school districts. While this act calls for attorneys' fees to be levied against school districts, a recent Supreme Court decision applied this retroactively to cover attorneys' fees before the act became effective.

SUMMARY OF CASES NEA SUPPORTED ON BEHALF OF DISPLACED BLACKS

Houston Bassett, of Atlanta, Texas, won a court suit that awarded him one of the highest settlements ever won by an educator—$26,000 for two years' back pay and $16,000 for lawyers' fees, or a total of $42,000. In addition, the federal district court ordered him reinstated to his position as principal in the Atlanta Independent School District. The court ruled that the school board, in failing to renew Bassett's contract for the 1970–71 and 1971–72 school years, had failed to follow the court's decree that objective and nonracial criteria be used in determining who would not be retained after desegregation.

In the summer of 1970, the Department of Health, Education, and Welfare decreed Bassett's firing discriminatory and ordered him reinstated. In 1971, Bassett brought his suit to enforce that order.

Bassett had more than thirty years in education, which included twelve years as a principal. He had been offered a contract in February, 1969, containing a condition that when desegregation plans were developed, he would become an assistant principal at his previously all-black school. Bassett refused to sign this contract because he considered it a demotion. The federal judge in his decision described the offered position as a combination bookkeeper–file clerk and errand boy for the principal. Bassett was continued as a principal without a contract for another year. Then, when HEW ordered integration, he was denied renewal of his contract.

In late 1972, a federal court ordered sixteen black Alabama teachers who were dismissed in July, 1972, to be reinstated by the Wilcox County school board. The sixteen teachers were to receive back pay. In addition, the court ordered the board to begin adhering to nonracial hiring practices, and to provide evaluation reports to all staff members it intends to demote. Also, the court ordered the board to seek to meet accreditation requirements, to rescind a $7.50 per semester student fee, and to make sure that all students receive textbooks made available by the state department of education.

The NEA and Mississippi Teachers Association (Association of Negro Teachers) have reported in a court brief that racial discrimination in the promotion and dismissal of black teachers continues despite court orders banning the practice.

The associations informed the Fifth Circuit Court of Appeals in New Orleans that many school districts in Alabama, Florida, Georgia, Louisiana, and Mississippi show an aggregate decline in excess of 2,500 black teachers between 1968 and 1972. During the same period, the figures show an increase of 3,387 white teachers in these school districts. Also, the same report shows that Florida, Georgia, Louisiana, and Mississippi—in 70 percent of the school districts, between 1968 and 1972—eliminated about 29 percent of black principalships, while the number of white principalships increased by 6 percent.

Forty Blacks Reinstated

According to the NEA *Reporter* (April, 1976), forty black educators who lost their jobs in Washington County, Georgia, between August, 1969, and June, 1976, have won the right to reinstatement. The court suit, financed by NEA's DuShane Emergency Fund, charged the Washington County Board of Education with racial discrimination in the termination of teachers, counselors, and administrators when dual school systems were eliminated. The *Reporter* quoted one of the district officials as saying that the decree containing remedies was one of the most far-reaching yet financed by NEA. The official said that the substantial awards for back pay and attorneys' fees should demonstrate that it is very costly for a school system to discriminate on the basis of race.

INTEGRATION MEANS ALL RACES

In February, 1974, the *Lau v. Nichols* decision of the Supreme Court held that the San Francisco school district failed to provide educational opportunity for about 1,800 Chinese students who did not speak English, and that this failure constituted violation of Title VI of the Civil Rights Act of 1964. This act bans discrimination because of color, race, or national origin in any activity for which federal funds are being received. NEA joined the California Teachers Association in urging the court to compel provision of compensatory English-language training. The district immediately began seeking the best means by which the court order could be met.

In the meantime, similar cases of bilingual-bicultural problems were given favorable court rulings in Denver, in Portales, New Mexico, and in New York City. In 1975, Congress passed the Bi-Lingual Practices Act, encouraging school districts with a certain percentage of children of immigrants to employ teachers who speak not only English but also the mother tongue of the immigrant children. For example, Houston, Texas, had 22,000 Chicanos (Spanish-speaking Mexican children). Naturally, a relatively large number of bilingual English-Spanish teachers were compelled to be hired under this act. This act also provided federal funds to enable school districts to employ bilingual teachers.

As compassionate and as enlightened as this federal legislation may seem to many, it should be pointed out that many Americans vociferously denounce the federal government for such profligate waste of tax monies for this purpose.

TITLE VII OF CIVIL RIGHTS ACT
BARS DISCRIMINATION

The denial of equal education opportunities because of race, color, religion, or sex now has possible remedies in the Civil Rights Act of 1964. Amended in 1972, the act prohibits discrimination in hiring, firing, layoff, recruitment, wages, and conditions of employment, among other factors. The Equal Employment Opportunity Commission (EEOC) guidelines on sex discrimination include policies relating to marital status and to pregnancy, childbirth, and child-care leaves. Evidence can be established, if there are different practices caused by real qualities that are non-discriminatory. The burden is upon the employer to demonstrate that only persons of a given sex, national origin, or religion would be able to do the job safely or efficiently. Unaccepted or unlawful practices include use of tests and job classifications not closely related to job performance.

Complaints of discrimination can be filed with the EEOC, in Washington or at any of its district offices; they must be filed within 180 days after the alleged discrimination took place, unless the discrimination is continuous.

IMPLEMENTING SCHOOL INTEGRATION

The historic *Brown* decision that segregated public schools were unconstitutional is just now becoming universally observed, if not universally accepted.

The "dodges" adopted to avoid complete integration have been many. The latest involves fighting the use of school busing in the large cities to obtain reasonably equal numbers of, as well as opportunities for, each of the races. This latest gimmick has met with violent reactions in some northern cities.

It took several court orders to institute the busing of children over wide areas, in order to obtain racial balance in classrooms. It became necessary in many instances to bus children across boundary lines of school districts to obtain a reasonable racial balance.

A historic case was *Swann v. Charlotte-Mecklenburg Board of Education*, in which the Supreme Court upheld school busing as a means of desegregating public schools. This 1971 decision affirmed several devices to achieve this end; among these were crosstown busing across non-contiguous school zones, the rechartering of school boundaries, and pairing of white and black school systems to dispense with dual school systems. Federal courts in Georgia, Louisiana, and Alabama have ordered formerly all-black schools to remain open on an integrated basis in order to help equalize the burden of desegregation of black communities. Several gimmicks to block all-out integration have been negated by court actions. A Louisiana court decision struck down policies based on student assignments to schools by test scores. In Texas, a federal court has overruled suspensions and expulsions of students. Doubtless, since 1954, thousands of black students in the South have been victims of such tactics.

In Richmond, Virginia, where predominantly black core city schools existed within white suburban metropolitan areas, federal courts had to intervene. In 1972 U.S. District Judge Robert Merhige, Jr., ruled that the state board of education must combine the Richmond school system with school systems in two adjacent counties, in order to create a system that would be 66 percent white. This meant that 78,000 of the 104,000 students in the merged areas had to be bused. This order was later overruled by a panel of the U.S. Court of Appeals. But large school districts, like San Francisco, Los Angeles, Detroit, and Indianapolis have been ordered to desegregate their schools. The Detroit desegregation case was an important one. In 1972, the Sixth U.S. Circuit Court of Appeals approved a federal court order enforcing metropolitan busing to achieve desegregation.

THERE IS A "BLACK FLIGHT," TOO

In recent years, there has been much newspaper publicity about "white flight" to the suburbs in order to avoid integrated schools. This white flight became extremely serious in the 1960s and 1970s. Whites tended to have the money or the credit to purchase desirable homes in the suburbs. Also, many whites possessed transportation (i.e., automobiles) so that the working members of the family could reach their job locations within the inner cities, while their children attended nearby schools in the suburbs. According to recent studies, blacks will be the great "flight" of the 1980s. Instead of being beset with white flight alone, cities will now become the victims of both white and black flights to the suburbs.

Should this black flight occur in the predicted proportions, the inner-city schools are going to be in real trouble, with increasing numbers of poor black families, while the white families remaining in the cities will be largely childless. If these things occur, by the mid-1980s the urban schools will experience rapidly declining enrollments. Declining white birth rates will be followed by (less steeply) declining black birth rates. This inevitably means the larger cities' schools, sooner or later, are going to be in great financial trouble.

In Cleveland, the urban school districts between 1968 and 1976 lost 31 percent of their white students and (surprisingly) 20 percent of their black students. On the other hand, suburban Cleveland districts reflected a 14 percent drop in white students during the same period and an 80 percent increase in black enrollments, resulting in a suburban student population that was 10 percent black in 1976 compared with 5 percent in 1968.

This is an interesting and easily explainable development. When blacks become more affluent, they want the same things the prosperous whites want; and the gradual disappearance of discrimination is very definitely occurring. The whole rapidly changing, complex picture portends a wholesome, improving future. At the same time, it presents a series of most difficult and growing problems to solve.

SOME IMPACTS OF EQUALITY OF EDUCATION

In the years following the *Brown* decision, there followed much turmoil, especially in the southern states. But as of 1979 there were considerably more nonsouthern school districts which have all-black schools. This is caused, of course, not by legal desegregation but by the grouping of the two races in separate areas of certain cities. This de facto segregation is due to white (and later, black) flight to the suburbs.

On the twenty-fifth anniversay of the *Brown* decision, some interesting newspaper comments appeared. In one paper, there was a picture of Orval Faubus, the governor of Arkansas in 1957 who supported the defiance by Little Rock Central High School of a court order to admit seven black children. This caused a serious riot of white citizens, including many militants from other states. The 1957 riot was so serious that President Eisenhower felt compelled to send in federal troops to put it down. The 1979 picture showed Faubus shaking hands with Terrence Roberts, Ph.D., who was among the first blacks to be admitted to Central High School, in 1957.

Those in close touch with the situation in Little Rock—those who favored a mild start toward the full, ultimate integration of Little Rock schools (and this included the superintendent of schools and others)— felt a deep sense of bitterness toward President Eisenhower's refusal to intervene before the riot. When the riot did occur, the president intervened by (1) federalizing the Arkansas National Guard (when the Little Rock Police were overwhelmed by the crowd which formed to prevent the admission of the black children); and (2) sending in the 401st Airborne Division of the U.S. Army. Those in Little Rock who supported the gradual integration plan contend that this federal intervention need never have happened, if Eisenhower could have been persuaded to intercede sooner. Also, they claim that the hostile crowd consisted largely of "rednecks" imported from three or four nearby southern states.

Universal, free education and the abolition of segregation begin to pay remarkable dividends, at a time when such education is under fire and is being denounced in all directions. President Carter, in a twenty-fifth anniversary celebration of the *Brown* decision, said in a public address that our nation must still struggle to achieve integration and true equality in education, in housing, and in other areas.

On the same day, there appeared in daily papers a picture of Charles Lasley, a fifteen-year-old black sophomore in a Detroit public high school, who was the first student to win four individual championships in the National Academics Olympic Games, including the title in high school mathematics.

And, if further evidence is needed to demonstrate the priceless value to America of universal education, from the first grade through the university, one product of these schools—with a hit-or-miss, more or less accidental acquisition of the learning provided by both systems of education—is George Washington Carver, whose contributions to humanity are still one of the great wonders of the world. One's mind is irresistibly drawn, in horror and incredulity, to the fact that at the outset of the Civil War twelve states had hard-and-fast laws prohibiting the teaching of black children to read and write. Yet in the face of these illustrations (which could be matched, or at least approached, by an incredible number of other examples), there are some self-elected elitists who still hoot at the education of the so-called lower classes as a futile waste of public money.

Currently, there is a new outcry against higher education—and its costs, of course. One part of this outcry is against our higher education institutions providing scholarships and other types of subsidies for foreign students which enable these students to complete degrees in this country. Whether this is a waste of public monies (or private, for that matter) is answered by a simple recollection of our "brain-drain" students' contributions to our economy and to our national defense in medicine, science, and a multitude of other fields. These contributions are immeasurable.

Actually, the United States can and is counting education as one of its most valuable exports. President Carter asserted that the federal government should invest *more* in foreign students coming to study in the United States. At present, less than 5 percent of the total cost of foreign students studying in the United States is provided by the federal government. More than 60 percent of the foreign students pay their own way, and about 15 percent of support is provided by the students' home governments.

The rapidly growing overseas demand for American higher education has created a market that cannot be ignored. The number of foreign students studying in the United States increased from 34,000 in 1955, to 154,000 in 1975, to 235,000 in 1977; the enrollment presently exceeds 250,000. But as enrollments in higher education decrease in the next decade or so because of skidding U.S. birth rates since about 1957, there are constantly rising criticisms against colleges and universities.

13

Restricting Teachers' Political Activities

DURING the approximately seven years in which Billy Don Montgomery taught in the Tatum, Texas, Independent School District, his close friend and mentor was his former teacher, J. C. Beckworth, who had been principal of the Mayflower High School in the same district. Beckworth was fired by the school board in the summer of 1967. It was Beckworth who had encouraged and guided Billy Montgomery to become an active participant in the civic programs of the Mayflower community.[1]

The two major campuses in the Tatum Independent School District (Tatum campus and Mayflower campus) were located about seven miles apart. One of the campuses, which was operated for white students only until the late 1970s, was centrally located in Tatum; the other campus, which was operated only for black students, was located in the predominantly black farming area localized in the Mayflower community, about seven miles northwest of Tatum.

A major portion of Billy Don Montgomery's civic activities involved encouraging the black residents of the Tatum school district to take a more active interest in the affairs of their schools, their local government, the state and national governments, and the pressing issues of fundamental citizenship.

Increasingly, until about 1967, it had become the custom of the candidates for the board of trustees of the Tatum Independent School Districts to seek out the endorsement of J. C. Beckworth and his co-workers by going to the Mayflower campus and addressing the faculty there. Then, on the night of April 25, 1967, Superintendent Rex N. White and the

---

[1] Abstracted from trial brief, *Billy Don Montgomery v. Rex N. White*, Civil Action no. 4933, U.S. District Court, Eastern District of Texas, Tyler Division.

members of the board of trustees of the Tatum ISD planned to strike a blow to the black political leadership of that district by adopting a policy prohibiting teachers from engaging in any "outside political activity." On the night of July 20, 1967, they further effectuated their plans to disorganize and render helpless the political leadership of Tatum's black community by terminating the employment contract of J. C. Beckworth— after thirty-eight years of service to the Tatum district, and one year before his scheduled retirement.

The following school year, 1967–68, witnessed many statements by the Tatum ISD superintendent to that district's black teachers, to the effect that their violation of the Tatum school board's policy prohibiting the engagement of Tatum School District employees in outside political activities would result in a speedy termination of the offender's employment contract. Such threats by the superintendent and by the individual board members created an atmosphere of suspicion, anxiety, and job insecurity among the black teachers employed by the Tatum School District.

However, Billy Don Montgomery and other teachers who were active under the leadership of J. C. Beckworth in the political organization of Tatum's black community persisted, in their private hours, in urging their neighbors to involve themselves in the responsibilities of an active citizenry.

In the early spring of 1968, there emerged two black candidates for the board of trustees of the Tatum Independent School District. Both were successful in their bids for those offices, primarily because of the intensive efforts of Eugene Edwards, J. C. Beckworth, Billy Don Montgomery, and others. The efforts of Billy Don Montgomery in securing the success of Lester Sparks and Nathan McAfee in their races for the school board consisted of his registration of voters, providing transportation to the polls for prospective voters, soliciting campaign funds to cover the various expenses involved in political races, and distributing campaign materials for the two candidates. However, Billy Don Montgomery's efforts in the 1968 political race for trusteeships of the Tatum Independent School District never conflicted with his professional duty as a classroom teacher.

In May, 1968, Billy Don Montgomery, having been equipped with a miniature radio transmitter, had a conversation with Superintendent Rex N. White in the latter's office. Superintendent White stated that the principal reason Montgomery was not recommended to be rehired in the

Tatum Independent School District for the 1968–69 school year was because of his violation of the school board's policy prohibiting teachers' engagement in outside political activities. The conversation between Montgomery and the superintendent was tape recorded.

Billy Don Montgomery subsequently obtained employment in the Community Action Program for Rusk-Cherokee Counties. He was then hired to teach in the Dallas Independent School District in 1968–69, and was subsequently rehired to teach there for 1969–70.

Montgomery was forced to move to Dallas, where he and his family obtained an apartment to live in during the week. Every weekend he was compelled to drive the approximately 220 miles to Tatum, in order to supervise and attend to his property interests. In court, Billy Don Montgomery was finally awarded $3,700 in moving and travel expenses, and for the mental anguish caused by the Tatum ISD's policies.

CONTESTED ISSUES OF LAW

The chief issue involved in the Montgomery case was set forth clearly in the brief of the suit: Public school teachers have a special position, uniquely sensitive and subject to pressures against which the courts must protect them.

The U.S. Supreme Court has recognized both the special vulnerability of a teacher to certain types of pressures and his special importance in the exercise of his rights. In one case the court, while recognizing the application of constitutional rights to all persons, said that "inhibition of freedom of thought and of action upon thought in the case of teachers, brings the safeguards of those amendments (Amendments 1 through 8 and 14) of the United States Constitution vividly into operation."[2] In another case the court enjoined the operation of a statute requiring teachers to denominate organizations to which they belong. The reason for the decision was stated as follows:

> Such interference with personal freedom . . . is conspiciously accented when the teacher serves at the absolute will of those to whom disclosure must be made . . . those who can any year terminate the teacher's employment without bringing charges, without notice, with-

---

[2] *Wieman v. Updegraff*, 144 U.S. 183 (1952).

out a hearing, without affording an opportunity to explain. . . . Public exposure, bringing with it the possibility of public pressure upon school boards to discharge teachers who belong to unpopular or minority organizations, would simply operate to widen and aggravate the impairment of conditional liberty.[3]

This ruling, while supplying what is now the governing language in this area, was by no means an innovation. Chief Justice Warren, with Justices Black, Douglas, and Brennan concurring, had noted that "scholarship cannot flourish in an atmosphere of suspicion and distrust. Teachers and students must always remain free to inquire, to study and to evaluate."[4] In a separate, concurring opinion, Justice Frankfurter, joined by Justice Harlan, wrote: "These pages need not be burdened with proof . . . of the dependence of a free society on free universities. This means the exclusion of governmental intervention in the intellectual life of a university. It matters little whether such intervention occurs avowedly or through action that inevitably tends to check the ardor and fearlessness of scholars, qualities at once so fragile and indispensable for fruitful academic labor."[5]

This concept of the special role and responsibilities of teachers is very vividly set forth in *Wieman v. Updegraff*:

To regard teachers . . . in our entire educational system from the primary grade to the university . . . as the priests of our democracy is, therefore, not to indulge in hyperbole. It is the special task of teachers to foster those habits of open-mindedness and critical inquiry, which alone make for responsible citizens, who, in turn, make possible an enlightened and effective public opinion. Teachers must fulfill their function by precept and practice, by the very atmosphere they generate; they must be exemplars of open-mindedness and free inquiry. They cannot carry out their noble task if the conditions for the practice of a responsible and critical mind are denied them.[6]

The above declarations, as a part of the decision of the Supreme Court, spell out the legal rights of teachers against arbitrary dismissals by school boards, thus confirming that teachers are full-fledged citizens.

---

[3] *Shelton v. Tucker*, 364 U.S. 479, 490 (1960).
[4] *Twilly v. New Hampshire*, U.S. 234, 250 (1957).
[5] Ibid.
[6] *Wieman v. Updegraff*, 144 U.S. 183 (1952).

CONSCIENTIOUS OBJECTOR GETS TEACHER'S CERTIFICATE

A former Georgia teacher, now living in Oregon, won his fight for a teacher's certificate in Georgia. A federal district court in Atlanta ordered the Georgia State Board of Education to grant him a certificate within sixty days, and to pay legal costs.

Weldon A. Lodwick had been denied a certificate because he refused, on religious grounds, to be inducted into military service during the Vietnam war. After reviewing Lodwick's record as a teacher in a church-supported academy, the court found the board's action arbitrary, capricious, without rational basis, and therefore in violation of Lodwick's due-process rights.

The presiding judge stated that all of the evidence demonstrated that the plaintiff was an outstanding, well-respected teacher. In no way did his refusal to serve make him unfit to teach.

POLITICAL ISSUES

A non-tenured associate professor of philosophy at a southern state college alleged that his services were terminated at the close of the 1965–66 academic year because he exercised his rights of free speech. He claims he is a pacifist, and that he was dismissed because he founded an independent faculty-student publication which criticized the Vietnam war, supported a student who attempted to register with a draft board as a conscientious objector, criticized an English department textbook, and objected to the disqualification of an applicant for a position in his department because the candidate was an Oriental.

The Tenth Circuit Court of Appeals ruled that the expectation of continual reappointment to a teaching position is not an interest protected by the Constitution. The NEA presented an *amicus curiae* brief requesting that the Supreme Court review the case. The NEA claimed that established law *supports* the position that the continued employment of teachers at public educational institutions may not be lawfully conditioned upon their relinquishing constitutional rights. Further, the NEA asserted that the issue involved constitutional rights, rather than contractual rights.

Punishment for Political Participation in Texas Case

The Roma Independent School District dismissed four teachers in 1972, allegedly in retaliation for their support of a candidate who opposed the town's power structure in a school board election.

The four teachers alleged that the school board's failure to rehire two of them and its issuance of one-year probationary contracts to the other two were in retaliation for their association with an unsuccessful candidate for the school board who also opposed the party leader supported by the town's power structure.

The judge found that the only credible explanation for the nonrenewal and/or demotion of the four teachers was their association with this candidate; all circumstances pointed to political retaliation. Furthermore, the judge pointed out that the United States had a long judicial history of protecting the rights of teachers. He ordered the board to reinstate the two teachers who had not been rehired, and to expunge from the records of the two other teachers any evidence of having been returned to probationary status. Also, the school board had to pay about $15,000 for attorneys' fees and other court costs.

Beware of Political Power

Any organization finally awakening to the facts of political life discovers that power in government (especially in Congress) all too often is lodged squarely in the hands of those who are able to contribute significantly to the campaign expenses of candidates for important offices. For example, there have been published in many newspapers (some, incidently, well known as mouthpieces for "big business" of one form or another) vehement reactions to opinions of public employees, strong and quick enough to justify the designation of "knee jerk" reactions.

After President Carter's election in 1976, and accelerated by the 1978 general elections, there appeared a series of articles (amazingly alike in language and argument) denouncing the National Education Association for its use of membership dues to support the election of representatives pledged to support the creation of a federal Department of Education. Heretofore education had been lost in a jumble of the Department of Health, Education, and Welfare (HEW). There, traditionally, it had been assigned the leftovers (if any) from the demands of the other two huge constellations.

Here is a quotation from one article bearing the signature of Howard Jarvis, the backer of the California Proposition 13:

> In the last few years a new political power has quietly elbowed its way to the head of the line of special interest groups who are trying to get their hands into the taxpayer's pockets. That group is the militant National Education Association, which represents 1.8 million of the nation's 2.2 million teachers. Politicians all across the country are terrified of this new lobbying giant, and no wonder. In the 1976 Congressional elections less than 20 percent of the candidates who failed to win the NEA endorsement managed to get elected to office. . . . The NEA is now the second largest labor union . . . its annual budget is 10 times that of AFL-CIO.[7]

Nothing is said in this article about a major share of the concerns of the NEA being involved in improvement of education for some 50 million children of the United States. The assumption appears to be that NEA is fighting solely for the selfish aggrandizement of public school teachers.

MISCELLANEOUS CAUSES OF TEACHER DISMISSALS

Teacher Fired for Criticizing Board

A Colorado teacher, Kenneth Bretz, filed suit for reinstatement and $200,000 in damages and costs in October, 1974. Bretz was a mathematics teacher in the North Junior High School in Brighton, Colorado. His suit was supported financially by NEA and the Colorado Education Association.

Bretz claimed in his brief that his nonrenewal stemmed from his objection when the board delayed for several hours a presentation in his behalf by a group of faculty members and students. The day after this occurrence, his principal informed him that the superintendent and board wanted to dismiss him, and that he should apologize for his action the

---

[7] Howard Jarvis, "NEA Has Quietly Slid into Position of Power," *Atlanta Constitution*, Dec. 19, 1978.

previous day. He apologized to the superintendent for "any language that may have given offense," but the following April he still received a notice that he would not be rehired. This notice reached him a few days after he had received a superior evaluation from the principal.

Bretz's suit contends that he was deprived of the rights of free speech and expression under the First Amendment. Further, the suit alleges that, under board policies and the existing collective bargaining agreement, he is entitled to continued employment in the absence of sufficient cause, and his nonrenewal had deprived him of property without due process.

Firing for Conduct Outside the Classroom

Nicholas Mescia, a white teacher in Florence, South Carolina, was fired by his school board beginning with the school year 1972–73 because his "out-of-school" activities and personal associations were jeopardizing his influence as a teacher. At a board hearing, he was criticized for associating with a black teacher and for residing in a black housing project. No charge of incompetence was made at the hearing. The outcome of this case seems to sustain the viewpoint that a teacher cannot be fired for conduct outside the classroom which has no demonstrable relationship to teaching. The Constitution guarantees the citizen the right of free association and assembly, free expression, residency and privacy. (See the First Amendment.)

Professor Fired for Demonstrating against Advocates of Racial Segregation

A University of Missouri visiting professor of political science was fired in 1970 for lying down on the ground, in the path of the university marching band, as a gesture of protest against a racially segregated group. Patrick T. Dougherty, a white, first protested by letter to the university band when he learned it would be marching in a St. Louis parade sponsored by the Order of the Veiled Prophet, a group of approximately 1,000 white men. Later, when he attempted to interfere with the parade, he was arrested. Dougherty had been studying the secret order, and its effect upon the black community, for several years.

He claimed he was suspended from his job without notice or an adequate hearing. Later hearings were held by the political science department, the academic tenure committee, and the hearing committee of the University Board of Curators. Each of these groups recommended that he *not* be dropped from his position. Nevertheless, the Board of Curators voted to dismiss him.

The NEA DuShane Defense Fund financed Dougherty's defense in federal district court in Kansas City. The circuit court of appeals in St. Louis, to which an appeal from the lower court was made, ordered that he be reinstated, back pay for the suspended period be paid, and his record cleared.

Teacher Fired for Use of "Profane Materials"

Mrs. Deena Metzger, an instructor at Los Angeles Valley College, was dismissed after she assigned an English class to read a poem she had written. It was claimed that the poem contained profane language. Also, she was alleged to have distributed a picture book on sexual love. She had used these materials in a unit on censorship, pornography, and obscenity. She was reprimanded in May, 1969, by the college president; subsequently, the board dismissed her on grounds of immoral conduct and "unfitness for service." The NEA DuShane Emergency Fund financed an appeal to the courts. The Los Angeles Superior Court found that Ms. Metzger was a permanently certified teacher, and ruled in her favor. The California Supreme Court sustained the decision of the lower court by holding that the teacher's conduct did not justify the charge and did not warrant dismissal.

Teacher Fired for Association Activity

With the aid of the DuShane Emergency Fund, the Ohio Education Association, and his local Conneau Education Association (CEA), Roosevelt George won reinstatement to his position, back pay, and attorneys' fees. He had not been renewed for the 1970–71 school year. As a non-tenured teacher, he challenged his nonrenewal after he served as chairman of CEA's Professional Rights and Responsibilities Commission, and he also served as advisor to the negotiating committee of his school district. He had served his school district for seven years.

The court ruled that the Conneau Board of Education violated the teacher's First Amendment rights by firing him for a constitutionally impermissible reason. The specific reasons cited for his nonrenewal were: His teaching was not commensurate with his ability; he failed to make an effort to grow professionally; he demonstrated an uncooperative attitude toward administration and board policy. The court found that George had been evaluated during the previous year and no criticisms had been made of his ability or adequacy as a teacher. During the negotiating sessions, he was informed by the superintendent that his position was negotiable; there followed an intensive evaluation, resulting in his discharge. The court ruled that the teacher was dismissed because of his representation of the teachers in the contract negotiations.

Teacher Awarded Back Pay and Damages

A federal court jury in Atlanta awarded back pay and damages to Luke T. Calloway for his illegal firing by his school board. Calloway, the chairman of the English department of Clayton County's Forest Park Senior High School, was fired in March, 1970, for the alleged use of *Playboy* magazine and a 1928 Salvador Dali film as teaching aids.

His court suit, charging denial of constitutional rights to due process, named the former county school superintendent, the high school principal, and members of the Clayton County school board as responsible. The federal judge ruled that Calloway's firing was illegal. The jury awarded him damages of $5,000. He was also awarded back salary from March 19, the date he was fired, to August 31, 1970, the date of the end of his contract.

These verdicts seem to indicate that even in the absence of tenure laws, teachers cannot be fired without legal cause or due process.

Collective Bargaining Law Causes Dismissal

A Wheeler, Oregon, elementary school teacher claimed he was fired for his actions in negotiations under Oregon's new teacher collective bargaining law. Jeff Bourland had taught for nine years in the Mitchell School District when he was dismissed. He had been selected in September, 1973, to represent Mitchell teachers in bargaining with the board. In March, 1974, he received a letter announcing nonrenewal for the ensuing year. No reasons were given (as is often the case). According to the testimony of a board member, Bourland was fired because of conflicts with the superintendent; the superintendent was later fired by the board. The federal court granted Bourland's reinstatement with back pay for the 1975–76 school year. The court ruled that the board's firing of Bourland included a desire to retaliate against him for his negotiations and his speech on behalf of teachers. The fact that the board may also have been motivated by a desire to improve the school by removing both of the perceived troublemakers—Bourland and the superintendent—did not obviate the retaliatory motive.

Personal Appearance as a Cause of Teacher Dismissal

Three black teachers who had been dismissed by the Columbus, Mississippi, school board for wearing moustaches were restored to their jobs by a federal court in October, 1972. The court found that the board had applied regulations included in student-personnel regulations to the cases of the teachers. The men were dismissed by nonrenewal for the school year 1972–73, and missed work in September and October. The court ruled that a moustache, beard, or sideburns do not affect a teacher's performance of his job. Back pay for these months was ordered by the court, and $2,000 in attorneys' fees.

Teacher Dismissals Overruled

In Wyoming's Sweetwater County School District No. 1, Bruce Lee, a non-tenured art teacher, was not renewed after three years service because his principal resented his complaint that the principal did not comply with school board policies in two instances. The principal gave improper discipline to students buying marijuana, and he changed a student's grade from failing to passing without the teacher's consent. Lee was awarded $34,500 in compensatory damages and attorneys' fees against the school district by a federal court.

A second Wyoming teacher, Betty Jean Coyne, who held a continuing contract in the Meeteetse School District, won reinstatement and $49,000 in settlement. She was given notice of nonrenewal in March, 1977, on the charge of bearing negative attitudes toward the administration. But the board was unable to cite instances to sustain charges of unsatisfactory teaching performance, or that she had violated administrative directions in school policies. The state district court found insufficient grounds for her termination and ordered her reinstated, with back pay and fringe benefits.

THE REDUCTION IN FORCE (RIF) LAYOFF PROGRAM

The current financial squeeze on public funds due to inflation, unemployment, and the generally unfavorable economic situation has resulted in unemployment for many teachers. In a sizable number of cases, layoffs or dismissals involved teachers who were tenured or under continuing contracts. Most of these layoffs were doubtless due to conditions beyond the control of the school districts involved. However, in numbers large enough to be significant, teachers have had their legal rights violated by using the lack of finances as an excuse, or by cutting back on the educational programs resulting in the abolition of the jobs of people who were covered by tenure of one form or another.

Here are some cases where RIF has been used as a means of dismissing teachers who had claims to continued employment.

In one state, where the voters in some districts failed to vote for annual tax levies, the resulting reduction in teaching staffs in some districts was challenged by the state education associations and the NEA. The ensuing litigation has resulted in restoring the jobs to a large number of teachers.

Financial shortages were given by the University of Wisconsin as the reason for massive layoffs of tenured faculty members on a number of campuses. In Wisconsin, decisions relating to the use of budgeted funds for actual faculty positions rest with the chancellor of the university system, not the legislature or the Board of Regents or the central administration. Thus, the decision that financial exigencies existed at their campuses, necessitating termination of some tenured positions, was often used. On all but one campus, faculty committees recommended recision of layoffs because there was sufficient work. Some faculty members were restored to work; some were not. A court suit is pending to review this decision.

In several cases, a review of the facts has revealed data with which to challenge RIF layoffs. A private college dismissed thirteen tenured faculty and granted one-year contracts to over fifty tenured members of the faculty. A state court ruled that cash flow to the college could have been improved by the sale of real estate being held for real estate development. Also, the court found that the college had set as one of its goals the abolition of tenure. The court ordered reinstatement of the terminated, and restored tenure to those on one-year contracts.

A non-tenured teacher in Washington, D.C., was terminated without a proper notice or hearing, on RIF grounds because of financial difficulties. The federal court of appeals has renewed that case for trial.

Voters in Reston, Washington, failed to approve a local levy for their school district in 1972, so the district issued notices of nonrenewal to teachers and failed to fill sixty-six vacancies. An investigation, including depositions from school board members, established that sufficient funds were available and expected. The case is now in the state courts.

All of the foregoing and other similar cases lead to the conclusion that RIF reasons based on the claim of lack of financial resources are not necessarily conclusive in favor of school boards.

ACADEMIC REASONS FOR DISMISSAL

The Constitution does not require a public university to provide a hearing before dismissing a student for "academic reasons," the Supreme Court held in the March 1, 1973, landmark case of *University of Missouri v. Charlotte Horowitz*.

Shortly before graduation in 1973, Horowitz was dismissed from the university's medical school on grounds of poor clinical performance. She was near the top of her class academically, planned a career in neuropharmacological research, and seems to have had scant interest in developing a bedside manner. She contended that her expulsion without a hearing constituted a denial of due process, and the Eighth Circuit Court of Appeals upheld her.

The University of Missouri appealed to the Supreme Court, which voted unanimously to overturn the lower court ruling. The series of warnings Horowitz had been given about the faculty's dissatisfaction with her clinical progress, the high court said, constituted "at least as much due process as the Fourteenth Amendment requires." The justices went on, by a 5–4 majority, to state a broader rule of constitutional law: that "academic" dismissals, unlike disciplinary ones, do not require a hearing.

The ruling has generally been reported as a setback for student rights and a victory for educators who don't want judges becoming involved in academic judgments. The case is a murky one, however. The American Civil Liberties Union and other organizations which supported Horowitz contend that her dismissal was essentially for "misconduct," including poor personal hygiene and lack of rapport with patients and peers, and that to characterize such reasons as "academic" was "sleight of hand" on the Supreme Court's part.

GAY RIGHTS QUESTION DODGED

In another recent case appealed by a major university, the Supreme Court by a 6–3 vote bypassed an opportunity to rule on homosexual rights, declining to decide whether the university violated the First Amendment by denying formal recognition to a homosexual students' organization.

The non-action is seen as a limited victory for the homosexual cause, as the Circuit Court ruling (which the high court let stand without comment) held that the university violated constitutional guarantees of free speech and assembly when it refused to provide a meeting place on the campus for a "Gay Lib" organization. The university had contended that to recognize the group and provide it with an on-campus forum would increase the likelihood of violation of the state's sodomy laws.

The Supreme Court's refusal to accept the case leaves the appeals court ruling as the law of the circuit (covering seven states), but postpones setting any national precedent.

TEACHERS' CONSTITUTIONAL RIGHTS

The questions that arise in any discussion of the role of public school teachers in political activities are numerous and provocative. The public climate about these rights has been greatly clarified in recent years, but the basic question still remains: Should public employees retain the right to engage in political activities? (A more specific question is: Do public school teachers have the right to vote in the selection of school board members who employ them and determine their salaries?) David Rubin has stated the problem well:

May a teacher be dismissed or disciplined for taking an active part in politics during off-duty time?

Only if the restriction is justifiably a countervailing state interest. . . . The Courts have made it clear that the right to engage in political expressions and association is protected by the First Amendment. In a number of cases the courts have dealt with the question whether . . . a public employee may be compelled to relinquish these rights. . . . A school board in Texas, relying upon its own regulation banning all political activity by teachers except voting, refused to re-employ a teacher, at least in part because of his participation in political activities. Ruling for the teacher, the federal court held "that the complete ban on the rights of teachers to express political opinions and engage in political activity is inconsistent with the First Amendment guarantee of freedom of speech, press, assembly and petition.[8]

Rubin probably was referring to the Tatum (Texas) case (see page 157). At any rate it is a good example of how teachers may wittingly or unwittingly be drawn into activities that are often considered to go beyond the confines of their firm constitutional rights as citizens and voters.

---

[8] David Rubin, *The Rights of Teachers* (New York: Richard W. Baron, 1973), pp. 71–72.

14

Sex Discrimination
in Teacher Employment

THE persistence of discrimination because of sex continues to plague women in the United States. Especially is this noticeable in education. By Title IX of the Education Amendments of 1972, as strengthened by regulations issued by the Department of Health, Education, and Welfare in June, 1974, sex discrimination in education, including admissions and treatment of students, was made illegal in federally aided institutions. Sex segregation or restricting admission to members of one sex is illegal in vocational, high, and post-secondary schools, and in public undergraduate colleges. Under Title IX these schools may not set quotas based on sex or prescribed test scores. Prohibited, also, is sex discrimination in employment in educational institutions from preschool to university. These regulations reflect guidelines of the Equal Employment Opportunity Commission. Separate career ladders and tenure systems based on sex are prohibited; so are different retirement ages or pension plans. Fringe benefits must provide either equal benefits to male and female staff or equal contributions by the employer for members of each sex.

Pregnancy, for purposes of leave, must be treated as a temporary disability, with disability pay and fringe benefits. Advertising sex preferences or specifications is banned in the employment area, as are making inquiries as to marital or parental status and unequal compensation practices.

DISCRIMINATION AGAINST WOMEN IN TEACHING

Even as recently as the latter part of the nineteenth century, women in general—and teachers in particular—were supposed to look wan, never vigorously healthy. The woman's body was supposed to be shaped for childbearing and some doctors and health specialists believed that physical or mental exertion could destroy female health and beauty. Thus, formal education of the female was believed by many to trigger mental deterioration. The "hour-glass" model became associated with the female from prepuberty (and often almost from infancy). Girls were fitted with hour-glass shaping corsets, tightly drawn to affect body growth. The inevitable effects of all this "shaping" of the human figure were drastic. Ribs were turned inward, organs were displaced, and some females developed curvature of the spine.

Despite the fact that doctors in general knew or suspected that all of this forced shaping had disastrous effects on the body in general, the practice persisted. The dictates of custom and fashion were more powerful. In fact, the tightly laced corset became something of a symbol of wealth, or at least of economic security. Likewise, because small feet were a mark of distinction, women often deliberately wore tight-fitting shoes, in adherence to style or custom. A suntan was considered ugly, so women found it fashionable to use an umbrella on the beach. Women were told that laughter would stretch their facial muscles and cause them to be ugly with wrinkles.

For most women, the eventual liberation from these now unbelievable dictates did not arrive until about the advent of World War I. The absence of men, who had gone to be soldiers, created jobs in industry for women. In such employment the existing modes of dress were a hindrance and women gradually discarded them. By midcentury, the unbound, naturally shaped body came into style; it was accompanied by a sense of freedom, both intellectually and physically.

Women Teachers Need Not Apply

In the very early days of America's public school system, it was almost impossible for a woman to secure teaching jobs. The first schools were, of course, one-room schools, in which all grades were taught. Usually these schools were isolated in farm settlements numbering a few families. Due to the rugged nature of the environment, usually a man had to be employed as teacher in order to maintain any degree of order in these schools. In such an environment the prevailing philosophy was the old biblical injunction, "Spare the rod and spoil the child." Ganging together of the

TABLE 14.1

Changing Percentages of Male and Female Teachers
Employed in Elementary and Secondary Schools

	1929–1930		1939–1940		1949–1950	
	Elem.	*Sec.*	*Elem.*	*Sec.*	*Elem.*	*Sec.*
Males	9.8%	35.2%	11.0%	41.8%	8.8%	43.2%
Females	90.2%	64.8%	89.0%	58.2%	91.2%	56.8%
	100.0%	100.0%	100.0%	100.0%	100.0%	100.0%

	1959–1960		1969–1970		1973–1974	
	Elem.	*Sec.*	*Elem.*	*Sec.*	*Elem.*	*Sec.*
Males	11.6%	51.3%	15.0%	53.2%	16.0%	53.3%
Females	88.4%	48.7%	85.0%	46.8%	84.0%	46.7%
	100.0%	100.0%	100.0%	100.0%	100.0%	100.0%

NOTE: Reprinted from National Center for Education Statistics, *Digest of Education Statistics, 1976 Edition* (Washington, D.C.: United States Government Printing Office, 1977).

larger boys for the purpose of running off the schoolmaster was the event of the year in most of these little schools.

Women had little hope of securing jobs in such schools. A woman's great hope was to find a two-teacher (or larger) school where a man was head teacher and able to handle the discipline problems. Of course, in the multi-teacher town schools, women teachers early came into the majority. Table 14.1 shows the employment of men and women teachers over time.

FIGHT FOR EQUAL TREATMENT OF WOMEN IN EDUCATION

In 1972, Title VII of the Civil Rights Act of 1964 and the Equal Pay Act of 1963 were amended to include coverage for educators on all levels. Also, sex bias in admissions, treatment of students, and employment of staff were outlawed by Title IX, and coverage was extended to colleges and universities.

In the meantime, many women are resorting to federal court action to achieve fair and non-discriminatory treatment in colleges and universities. Under Title VII, for discrimination against women, courts may award up to two years' back wages and attorneys' fees and court costs. Proceedings were instituted against the University of California at Davis by Susan Reagan McKillop, an assistant professor in the art department. The university refused to award tenure and promotion to her in 1971, although it was alleged that she demonstrated outstanding ability and performance in surveys of teaching effectiveness. Her suit, with support from NEA, alleged a variety of unfair practices; because personnel procedures are conducted in secrecy, they provide tenure candidates no opportunity to be heard or to ascertain the reason for denial of tenure. It was alleged that these procedures violated due-process and equal-protection rights under the Fourteenth Amendment. Also, the brief alleged that, despite the fact that women received 43.5 percent of Art Ph.D.'s in the United States in 1969–70, the Davis campus had no ranking female staff members, while at least five members of professorial rank should be women, if the available pool of qualified women were drawn upon.

In another case, Annie Laura Keyes, a tenured professor of education, in March, 1972, was advised that her contract would not be extended beyond the following academic year, when she would reach the age of sixty-five—this despite the fact that the college continues to employ male faculty members sixty-five and older by means of yearly extensions based on teaching effectiveness and health.

Dr. Keyes filed a Title VII suit. In her class-action suit, she charged the college with discriminatory practices based on age and sex, contending that as a tenured employee she is entitled to be retained in the absence of just cause and to be given due process prior to dismissal.[1]

New Rights for Women

Recent laws and regulations pointing to equal rights for women are as follows: (1) Executive Orders 11246 and 11375, and Revised Order No. 4; (2) Equal Pay Act of 1963, extended in 1972; (3) Title VII of the Civil Rights Act of 1964, extended by EEOC Act of 1972; (4) Title IX of the Education Amendments of 1972.

Executive Order 11375 became effective on October 13, 1968. It pro-

---

[1] *Today's Education*, Sept.–Oct., 1974, pp. 58–62.

hibits employment discrimination on the basis of sex by federal contractors and subcontractors. A previous executive order (11246), issued in 1965, barred job discrimination by contractors on the basis of race, color, religion, and natural origin. Under these orders, institutions awarded federal contracts of $10,000 or more must agree not to discriminate against an employee or job applicant.

The Department of Labor has responsibility for enforcing these orders and has issued regulations and guidelines for contract compliance review investigations. These will require the following types of data: employee inventory, written affirmative action plans and evaluation list of new employees by classifications, date of employment, race, sex, ethnic origin, and pay rate; tests and other criteria for hiring; faculty manuals and administrative practice guides.

To terminate a contract, HEW must grant a hearing, and the contract may be terminated if non-compliance is found.

Under Revised Order No. 4 (1971), the Department of Labor issued criteria for affirmative action by contractors. Affirmative action goals must be on file for review by the federal compliance agency. Moreover, employees must periodically analyze staff to decide whether women are being underutilized, and to establish timetables for correcting deficiencies. Failure to develop an affirmative action plan can lead to contract cancellation.

Teacher retirement systems that appear to discriminate against women are also being subjected to legal examination. For example, some state systems require male and female members to contribute equally but do not provide equal benefits for each. Larger payments go to males than to females, supposedly based on the fact that on the average women live longer than men. The (EEOC) guidelines indicate that to treat men and women unequally with respect to benefits or retirement ages is illegal.

In Virginia, a class-action suit against that state's higher education system was instituted in 1973. This Fourteenth Amendment suit, backed by NEA, attacked the board's discriminatory provisions against women in areas such as recruiting, salary, promotion, tenure, retirement, and exclusion of faculty wives from being members of the faculties (nepotism).

One of the plaintiffs, a former professor of foreign languages, claimed that due to sex bias she was employed at a lower salary than men and was denied comparable raises or promotions, although her credentials, publications, and teaching performance exceeded those of her male colleagues.

Another woman plaintiff alleged that she was excluded from employee management programs and was given a larger teaching load than was usually given to faculty doing research. A third woman charged that she was forced to retire at age sixty-five, while male faculty members are usually permitted to teach through age seventy or longer.

Court Is Puzzled

The Supreme Court has been edging step by step and case by case toward an outright declaration against sex bias, but apparently it has not found a clear case to this end as yet. The justices have been probing to find a new rationale, a simplified means to look at laws that treat men and women differently, but have been repeatedly frustrated by subtleties and complexities. The Supreme Court seems to be faced with a great opportunity to make an unprecedented and unequivocal new declaration against sex bias, but it has been unsure of how or whether to do it.

A recent case illustrates the complexity of the problem. An Oklahoma law involves the age at which young people can buy low-alcohol-content beer. Under this beer law, women may legally buy 3.2 percent beer at age eighteen, while males cannot until they reach age twenty-one. In trying to find grounds for declaring a case of sex bias against men, the court pressed a well-proven civil rights lawyer (a woman) for an expression of what standards should be used. The lawyer argued that all laws that seem to discriminate against men are actually based upon discriminatory theories about the role of women in society and, therefore, there is no such thing in law as pure anti-male discrimination. At the time, the woman attorney was representing a man, a retired government worker, who was suing because he was denied a social security pension after his wife died.

Thus the matter of sex bias being unconstitutional is left in a lingering state, for the future to settle definitely, although recent decisions have tended heavily toward the females' side.

Sex Bias in Education Prohibited

Discrimination because of sex is illegal in federally aided educational institutions according to guidelines established in 1974 by the Department of Health, Education, and Welfare. The regulations will provide women students, especially those employed in education, with the means to file complaints of denials of equal opportunity. Remedial action is provided through administrative proceedings by which federal funds are withdrawn, or referred for court action to the Department of Justice.

While most federally assisted institutions are covered by Title IX (of the Education Amendments of 1972), military and religious schools are exempted if the regulations conflict with religious tenets.

Interpretations of Equal Pay Act

The 1963 Equal Pay Act was amended in 1972 to apply to professional, executive, and administrative personnel. This includes the staffs in both private and public schools from preschool through college and university levels. One result of this amendment will mean that women will, in time, be paid in accordance with requirements of the job, instead of according to their sex.

This act prohibits salary and other benefit differentials based on sex. Generally speaking, the law requires equal pay for men and women performing work in the same institution under similar working conditions, assuming the jobs require equal skills and responsibility. This does not mean their jobs have to be identical; nor do job assignments and titles. But job content does—"equal skill" means equal experience, training, education, and ability to perform the job held. Differentials in pay are legal where they are paid as a consequence of a merit or seniority system, or a system which either measures earnings by quantity or quality of production, or some factor other than sex.

The following may be considered violations of the Equal Pay Act: (1) paying unequal wages and promotional or other increments to similarly ranked employees; (2) paying unequal salaries to coaches of men's and women's sports, custodians and maids, male and female bus drivers, and male and female teacher aides; (3) providing unequal expenditures or benefits in retirement plans; (4) paying less to female supervisors, deans, researchers, and administrators than to male ones; (5) denying female teachers an opportunity to obtain family health insurance and other coverage on the same basis as male colleagues.

Responsibility for enforcing the act is vested in the Wages and Hour Division of the Department of Labor. Complaints may be filed by individuals or organizations. If it is determined that the law is being violated, efforts are made to secure voluntary compliance. When employers fail to comply with the law, the Secretary of Labor may initiate federal court action to secure back payment of wages and changes in future pay rates. Private suits may also be initiated, but only in state courts. Under the act, private suits must be brought within two to three years of the discrimination.

The act bars labor organizations and agents from inducing employers to institute or maintain wage differentials. This prevents organizations from justifying wage differentials based on sex, on the ground that it is part of a negotiated contract.

Some precedent-setting decisions have been rendered under this act. A federal court in Delaware found that pay differentials between a female teacher and softball coach and between a male teacher and baseball coach were not justified because the jobs are substantially equal, requiring equal effort, skill, and responsibility. Also, the two teams had the same limitations on hours of practice, numbers of players, rules, and length of season.

A&M Consolidated District Ordered to Equalize Pay

The A&M Independent School District, College Station, Texas, on June 28, 1977, was ordered by the U.S. District Court in Houston to pay back pay of $35,674 (which included $8,061.92 in interest) to 123 female teachers for the school year 1972–73. The court ruled that the $300 "head of household" increment paid to male teachers amounted to wage discrimination based on sex; that payment for extra duties (such as selling tickets to football games and other such duties) was to be equalized. The court found that *all* teachers performed extra duties, and that the duties were not substantially different. The claim that men were "on call" for additional duties as needed was not necessarily extra work, as no woman was given the opportunity. Thus, the Equal Pay Act of 1963 as amended in 1975 was violated. The federal suit was sponsored by the Department of Labor, after an investigation by the department's Wage and Hour Division.

ANTI-NEPOTISM REBUFFED

At the University of Massachusetts in 1973, an out-of-court settlement restored a faculty wife to a full salaried professorship, with full retirement and health benefits. Mrs. Aino Jarveson was denied tenure in 1961 due to the fact that her husband was already tenured. In 1965, she was fired when only twenty-three days from qualifying for retirement benefits. She was told that the university would not grant tenure to two members of the same family or permit two members of the same family a rank above instructor.

Sharon L. Johnson, on the School of Medicine faculty at the University of Pittsburgh, achieved tenure as the result of an injunction just one month before her dismissal was to become final. She had been denied tenure and promotion for alleged deficiencies in her teaching. In issuing the injunction, the judge cited evidence of reasonable probability of her success on the merits. The suit presents evidence as statistical proof of discrimination in the School of Medicine. Over a six-year period when many women were eligible for tenure, seventy men were given tenure while only three women were.

Courts seem to have upheld outspoken women who have suffered reprisals for questioning practices at the institutions where they were employed. For example, in February, 1973, Shirley Schell, with about 40 percent of the faculty of the Northern Branch of Delaware Technical and Community College, filed charges of race, sex, and religious discrimination against the administration of the colleges with appropriate state and federal authorities. Although she had received written notification that she was to be retained in her position for the following academic year, in May she was given notice of her immediate suspension, with pay and termination, and ordered to vacate her office and not come back on the campus. For this sudden action no reason was given except that of insubordination. Less than two months after her dismissal, a federal court declared that Ms. Schell had been deprived of right to due process. Her termination was arbitrary and capricious and a violation of her right to substantial due process. A negotiated settlement resulted in her being awarded $30,600 in damages.

The reduction in force (RIF) dismissals, enhanced by declining student enrollments and the pressures of reduced budgets, have had several impacts upon women faculty members. So often denied tenure and full-time positions, women are less likely to receive the benefits of collective bargaining provisions for job security rights. Unless master agreements exist—and this is typical in higher education institutions—women have often suffered job losses. This is not likely to happen in public schools for the simple reason that women outnumber men employees. But the reverse is generally true in colleges and universities.

NEA is receiving complaints from women in many universities on this kind of discrimination and is mobilizing its DuShane Emergency Fund for their aid in taking grievances to the federal courts. In the four-year period 1970–74 about $200,000 from this fund were committed in support of women's rights. Such issues as maternity leave, unemployment compensation during pregnancy, use of sick leave during pregnancy, anti-nepotism rules, salary equality, promotion, and equal pay supplements for female referees have been involved.

RIGHTS OF PREGNANT WOMEN

A signal victory was won for pregnant teachers in Connecticut in 1973. Mrs. Sabine Jordan, a member of the faculty at Connecticut College, had been denied unemployment pay because state laws provided that pregnant women were ineligible for unemployment compensation for two months before and two months after childbirth. The federal district court agreed that Mrs. Jordan had been discriminated against because of sex and denial of due process. The court also held that any woman who could establish eligibility could obtain benefits retroactive to January 1, 1971.

Maternity Leave and Pregnancy Laws Challenged

The discriminatory practice of barring teachers from their jobs because of pregnancy was sooner or later bound to come under attack in the courts. The act of barring childbearing women from earning a living seems rather cruel, in addition to being immoral—if it is remembered that female teachers are, by their being forced to give up their jobs, barred from tenure and other rights of male teachers, if and when they return to teaching.

Two teachers who are wives and mothers challenged a federal court ruling and the maternity leave policy of the Cleveland Board of Education on their rights to bear children. Mrs. Jo Carol La Fleur and Mrs. Ann Elizabeth Nelson are high school teachers. Their court brief labels the board rule unfair to female teachers and detrimental to the educational process, as well as being unconstitutional, forcing thousands of teachers out of their jobs each year. The board's contention, based upon a 1952 document which forced pregnant teachers to withdraw from teaching before the fifth month of pregnancy, is based on such justifications as preventing unseemly remarks by children, protecting the health of the teacher, eliminating teachers who are physically incapable of performing their duties, and administrative necessity.

The court's ruling, against the teachers, based on a twenty-year-old decision, is now outmoded. Medical evidence does not support the point of justification of protecting the health of the mother and unborn child. Furthermore, mandatory leave based solely on pregnancy is discriminatory.

On January 21, 1974, the Supreme Court overturned the cases against the Cleveland teachers, and a teacher in Chesterfield County, Virginia. The high court ruled that the rules enforced by the respective school boards regardless of the teacher's ability to continue work violated the Fourteenth Amendment's guarantee of due process. The ruling obviously means that the pregnant teachers who want to work and who can work will no longer be required to observe a leave rule based upon arbitrarily fixed dates.

Childbirth Sick Pay

Female teachers are entitled to receive sick pay for absence due to childbirth, the Connecticut Commission on Human Rights and Opportunities has ruled. The commission ordered the Bristol Board of Education to provide back pay to two teachers to the extent of their accumulated sick leave for the time they were disabled from working due to maternity. One case was that of Mrs. Bonnie R. Ferrante of West Hartford. The Connecticut Education Association and the NEA DuShane Emergency Fund financed the case. The ruling held that the board had violated the Connecticut Fair Employment Practices Act. This is a companion victory to one in January, 1973, which held that firing a teacher for pregnancy or forcing her to stop work after an arbitrarily prescribed number of months was illegal.

Kansas Teacher Denied Sick Leave

A precedent-setting case in Kansas was that of Joan McCarthy, of the Hutchinson School District. This teacher twice became pregnant and was denied sick leave benefits; she was forced to take maternity leave each time. She sued for back pay, alleging that denial of sick-leave benefits for those forced to take a maternity leave constitutes sex discrimination and that this is a violation of the Constitution and Title VII of the Civil Rights Act of 1965, as amended in 1972, and Title IX of the Education Amendments of 1972. The school district's policy provided for unpaid maternity leave for pregnancy and sick leave for virtually all illnesses and disabilities which required absence from work, with the exclusion of maternity and its physical accompaniments.

The court ruled that Joan McCarthy had a right to relief under Title IX, which outlaws exclusion of pregnancy as a disability.

UNEQUAL SPANKING—A NEW FORM OF DISCRIMINATION

In early August, 1978, a startling new example of discrimination in the operation of schools was uncovered by the Department of Health, Education, and Welfare. Some newspaper editors across the country had a field day, as the finding was widely circulated by the press. HEW, in a 1975 survey of the Washington, D.C., school district, found that teachers in the district had spanked thirty boys and only two girls. According to HEW, this is clearly sex discrimination, and federal funding could be affected.

III

A NEW PROFESSION
OF TEACHING

15

Indicated Reforms
in the Public Schools

IT would be much quicker, perhaps easier, to list some sure-fire, instant cures for the weaknesses of the public schools which are presently drawing criticisms, than to list a series of obvious things and processes which must be changed in their concepts, approaches, and operational features. But the problems the United States faces in reforming its educational system are much more complex than that. Simply tinkering with a few obvious facets of the system would, of course, have a few noticeable and somewhat dramatic effects. Some of these would be constructive and effective. But such instant remedies would bring about only temporary and minor changes in the whole system. The need is far greater than that; it must therefore be dealt with in two phases or aspects. Chapters 16 and 17 are devoted simply to designating some of the needed changes.

First it is necessary to list some obvious approaches or adjustments that need to be made now. Some of these may be lasting, but the changes of much longer duration must be dealt with more in depth and more in detail. This chapter will deal with things of a minor nature, but obviously of great need and urgency.

Deeper, longer-lasting, more basic changes must be more comprehensive and harder, but more fundamental and more lasting. There are two firm and substantial approaches to the essential problems of reform of our schools.

THE SCHOOL AS A MIRROR

The first firm foundation can be established by ascertaining or describing the fundamental bases for the existence of the public schools in America.

There are many ways to describe their fundamental purposes. Basically, the public schools are and must always be a mirror that faithfully and accurately reflects the society they were founded to serve, for the purpose of (1) identifying educational needs and (2) seeking to serve (or correct) these needs.

All Americans are somewhat given to blaming their public (tax-supported) institutions for weaknesses and failures in the body politic. Not often does it occur to an American to scrutinize himself and his neighbors to discover the fault. This is certainly one of the hardest comparisons for the average citizen to face up to. It is but human nature to blame someone or something else for whatever goes wrong in society.

STEPS IN REFORM AND RENEWAL

Such vital institutions as the public schools must have constant and critical examination looking toward relevant renewal in their operations. Here are some suggestions for progress in this endeavor.

1. INCREASE THE MINIMUM REQUIRED PREPARATION OF TEACHERS. Viewed from any perspective, a giant overhaul of our school programs is indicated. This should begin with raising the minimum level of preparation of teachers. The present minimum of the bachelor's degree or higher is now universal among the states. A proposal made in 1978 by Lawrence A. Cremin, president of Teachers College, Columbia University, that this minimum be set at the doctor's degree level may not be attainable immediately. It may be that even a decade or more will be required to support and establish a series of basic reforms which will give a roughly defined pathway to the future of public education in the United States. It is quite evident that an intense reformation is necessary, as the data contained herein demonstrate. Here is part of Cremin's proposal:

> The time has come to require the doctorate for all who would seek entry into the educating professions. Many states already require five years of preparation for a permanent school certificate—the requirement is most often satisfied by four years of undergraduate education joined to a fifth year of professional preparation. I would argue for redesigned programs, not unlike the six-year B.S.–M.D. programs at

Northwestern University and Boston University, in which the B.A. and Ed.D. could be obtained at the end of six years.[1]

There are many good reasons for proposing this seemingly far-out, difficult step. And it will come in time. *But for now it would appear to be feasible to move almost immediately to requiring at least the master's degree for all beginning public school teachers.*

First of all, we have been accumulating every year (since the declining birth rate began about 1957) an annual surplus of teachers, until there is now a huge surplus of qualified teachers under the existing preparation requirements. We have been producing each year, in the last decade or so, from 50,000 to 100,000 new teachers who could not find jobs. Second, we must find some way to reduce this surplus. Some other professions, notably medicine, have followed the practice of raising standards of preparation and, thus, of admission to practice. Such a step could be taken by the respective state legal authorities within the next two or three years. It is true that enrollments in the elementary schools will probably begin to increase again by the middle 1980s, but as great as is the problem of the numbers of teachers to be prepared at a higher level, the nature of the preparation will be more difficult. This has to be changed drastically; stated below are some of the elements that deserve to be given great consideration.

2. REDUCE THE PRESENT OVERLOADING OF TEACHERS. Especially in the elementary schools, with thirty, forty, or sometimes even fifty pupils per teacher, the class size must be reduced to a manageable level. For the best possible teaching results this load should be reduced to twenty pupils or fewer per teacher. This step would serve to reduce the teacher surplus, but above all, it would serve to improve the quality of teaching and learning.

3. FIND APPROPRIATE AND EFFECTIVE MEANS OF PUBLICIZING THE GRAVER FORMS OF VIOLENCE IN THE LOCAL SCHOOLS. Evidence continues to be produced challenging the assertion of the superintendents or other administrative officers in many school districts that discipline is not a serious

---

[1] Lawrence A. Cremin, *The Education of the Educating Professions* (Washington, D.C.: American Association of Colleges for Teacher Education, 1978), p. 22. Used by permission.

problem. For example, the Orange County (Florida) Classroom Teachers Association conducted its own survey over a period of eighteen months. More than 100 teachers reported that they had been physically assaulted by students—three times the number reported by officials of the schools. In addition, 200 teachers reported that students had damaged teachers' personal property because of disciplinary action against them by the teachers involved. The National Education Association is convinced that only about 10 percent of the violent incidents are ever publicly reported. Also, it is reported that principals, as well as teachers, tend to keep quiet on student violence. And there are charges that the chief administrator does not present the full truth to the school board. Therefore, quite innocently the board often fails to present the truth of the situation to the community. The really alarming aspect of this entire situation is the growing attitude that nothing can be done about the problem. Many teachers are quitting and going into other fields: The number of teachers with twenty years or more experience has been halved since 1961, with the greatest decline occurring in the last five years.

Parents and other responsive citizens must get the facts about this situation and move to stop it, or we Americans can surrender, too, the Great American Dream. At the heart of that dream has always been (and probably always will be) a universal, free—and hopefully a rigorous—system of education.

Of course, this proposal will find immediate and vigorous rejection by many, both in the schools and among the public. But the public schools cannot survive with the present alleged wide prevalence of extreme misbehavior.

Change Induces Change

Cremin has commented that in 1910, when Abraham Flexner's report[2] on the need to improve medical education was published by the Carnegie Foundation for the Advancement of Teaching, this report exerted profound influence on medical education.[3] Flexner did not propose an entirely new model for the preparation of medical doctors, nor did he advo-

---

[2] Abraham Flexner, *Medical Education in the United States and Canada*, Bulletin no. 4 (New York: Carnegie Foundation for the Advancement of Teaching, 1910), p. xiii.

[3] Lawrence A. Cremin, *The Education of the Educating Professions* (Washington, D.C.: American Association of Colleges for Teacher Education, 1978), p. 9.

cate disbanding all existing programs. Instead, he worked toward the ideal of keeping the best practices—the proven, effective practices in existing programs—and substituting new ways to replace the old ones which were clearly not working, or clearly outmoded. With something quite far afield from precise accuracy, he proceeded to search for procedures that were considered to be workable and to add new ideas and practices as the need arose.

4. DEVELOP MORE REALISTIC TEACHER EDUCATION REQUIREMENTS. As a part— and maybe a very important part—of the need for some new approaches and new techniques, there can be but little skepticism concerning the need to supplement present practices in the preparation of teachers. This is not to be considered as a proposal to stampede educators into a hurry-up, frantic effort to overhaul the preparation of teachers just for the sake of change—as if any kind of change, in any aspect of the practices of society, is bound to be an improvement. This simply is not true. But what an interesting and informative book it would make should some author bring forth a volume identifying the discarding of existing techniques and devices which seemed to offer promise to improve the performance and, at the same time, depicting the instrumentalities that were brought into being by presumed efficiency of new devices which proved to be utter failures. Every new thing is not necessarily a good thing or an improvement over what exists. Neither is every new thing a bad thing; nor is a second-rate thing good simply because it is new.

At least, we know this: The world has moved so fast since the close of World War II, so many new instruments of power have come into use, so many new concepts have been proposed that promise to enrich human life immeasurably, that the process of formal education in the basics has become essential to the realization of peace.

There are many ways of approaching this task of revising the preparation of teachers. Perhaps the easiest is to begin with the length of the formal period of preparation, then to use a step-by-step approach to a description of the total constituents of preparation.

We would begin with the blunt proposal to seek to persuade the respective states to adopt the minimum of the master's degree—five years of college preparation—for the initial certification of teachers.

Quite naturally there would arise the question, Why? After struggling for a century and a half to require all beginning teachers to have completed the bachelor's degree, why turn almost immediately to requiring a still new and higher standard?

The answer is simple. First, the body of knowledge which children are now expected to acquire (or seek to acquire) has increased by such proportions, in the last half of this century alone, as to require one who would seek to teach to have finished the studies symbolized by the bachelor's degree, at the least. Second, the increase in the number of teachers who can qualify for the present relatively low levels of attainment has created a surplus, leaving thousands of teachers each year who cannot find jobs. They are forced to throw away (to some degree) the value of years of preparation which, to say the least, cannot be used for the purpose for which they were acquired.

Beginning in 1957, the nation experienced one of its many fluctuations in school enrollments. This decrease in school enrollment, at the elementary school level quite naturally, began with decreasing birth rates. A number of factors can cause such declines, such as war, the prospect of war, or economic "hard times." The present decline in the elementary school enrollments which began in 1957 is expected to continue for a few more years. The figures in Table 15.1 indicate quite clearly the nature of the enrollment changes:

TABLE 15.1
Summary of Trends in School Population in the United States

Age of School Population	Fall, 1961	Fall, 1971	Fall, 1981 (Projected)	Percent Change
5–13	33,461,000	35,790,000	24,025,000	2%
14–17	1,219,000	16,343,000	14,734,000	10%

Source: *Projections of Educational Statistics to 1981–82* (Washington, D.C.: U.S. Department of Health, Education, and Welfare, 1972), Table 1, p. 9.

Shape of Things to Come in Teacher Education

Previously, we have proposed that because of (1) the existing overload of our teachers almost everywhere, (2) the abnormal numbers of teachers who have met the bachelor's degree requirement but who cannot find jobs, (3) and the overwhelming expansion of knowledge that all teachers must master, all beginning teachers should have completed the master's degree, the contents of which will be suggested below.

5. SCHOOL ADMINISTRATORS ALSO WILL HAVE TO MEET HIGHER STANDARDS. This will probably mean that states will move soon to requiring six years of preparation, in some states qualifying for the specialist in education degree for principals. In addition, states will begin to require completion of the doctor's degree for superintendents of schools. Many school boards are already requiring this for employment.

6. WHAT WILL BE THE INCREASED REQUIREMENTS IN TEACHER PREPARATION? No one can predict in full what the new requirements will be, when the goal is completion of the master's degree. There are several choices here. One would be full accreditation, including state, regional, and National Council for the Accreditation of Teacher Education for the preparing institution. And, of course, each institution must first be approved by its state department of education, as well as receiving approval for its proposed program of studies for the preparation of teachers.

For beginning teachers, major concentration should be upon general education, with special emphasis upon subject field to be taught, if preparing for high school teaching. This will consist of major and minor subjects, with a prescribed minimum number of hours in education, and including observation (under supervision—at least one semester during the senior year of the bachelor's degree course) in the college observation school.

During the graduate year, the candidate should spend about half-time in completing graduate work in the subjects to be taught or at the level of the elementary grades for which the student is preparing. The other half-year should consist of a well-planned, thorough internship, under experienced and qualified supervisors. This internship should be partially financed by the state in which this preparation is pursued with appropriateness specifically designated for this purpose. In all instances, the college or university and the state should help underwrite board and lodging for the student for that required period of internship, if pursued off campus (which will happen in probably the majority of cases, because only a small fraction of observation schools are maintained on campuses). The vast majority of observation work will be in the public schools, carefully selected for being near the campus or for possessing unusual features necessary for full preparation of teachers in certain fields.

As the preparation for beginning teachers, principals, and superintendents is lengthened, the handling of violence and discipline in the classrooms and among school activities should have top priority, if we are to restore the behavior considered essential for effective teaching. Moreover, colleges and universities preparing teachers should not only offer regular courses in their teacher-education curricula, but should make available such courses for full-time teachers to pursue when they can be absent from their classrooms—in-service courses offered at night, on Saturdays, and at other convenient times.

The practice teaching, or student teaching, or internship, or apprenticeship—whatever the designation of the sponsoring institution—should be under the guidance of a highly skilled classroom teacher who holds a regular teaching position in one of the schools selected by the preparing college or university. In fact, the first consideration in selecting a school to be a student teaching center should probably be the availability of superbly competent teachers. And such teachers should be paid for this additional and highly important responsibility. Supervising interns should not be an extracurricular activity for teachers but part of their regular load for which they receive adequate remuneration.

Skilled Teachers to Guide Student Teaching

It is high time that colleges and universities that prepare teachers make the student teaching or internship the center of teacher education. Much of what has traditionally been taught as a textbook course of information in methods, in discipline, and in stimulating interest must be shifted to the internship. In short, interns must learn how to handle and revise a classroom whatever the grade level or subject—to the point that each succeeding period becomes an adventure—in the achievement of expertise in the teaching process.

A first step toward that end is placing at the center of this responsibility, the very best, the most qualified, the most appropriate and challenging classroom teacher at the appropriate grade or subject level. Of course, this does not necessarily involve abandoning the careful supervision and assistance of appropriate professors from the staff of the preparing higher education institution. Under such an arrangement, the classroom teacher should serve as an adjunct member of the staff of the preparing college or university. This arrangement should not carry any nuance of denigration of either the teacher or the supervising college teacher. It is simply a recognition of the differences in both skills and subject mastery in each position. What university professor would claim competence in teaching skills at the kindergarten or first-grade level? Conversely what first-grade teacher would lay claim to the full range of skills and subject matter competency of the subject field professor?[4]

Under present preparation requirements for beginning teachers, surpluses of teachers as high as 100,000 a year are produced. This surplus was in some years during the 1970s at least 50,000 teachers. This is a waste of talent which ought to be stopped. The chief weapon or remedy that any of the professions have to rectify such a situation is to set higher preparation standards for initial certification. To raise standards of preparation and admission to practice is virtually the only recourse a profession has if it is to avoid the slide into low-quality performance. Of course, those who were promised certification by existing state regulation or law should be certified. Otherwise, the courts must rule that the *ex post facto* law has been used, which is unconstitutional. And this would probably apply to college students who have already declared their intent to prepare for teaching careers.

Medicine has consistently followed this practice. Of course, enforcement of higher standards is never an easy thing to accomplish. In about 1910, when Abraham Flexner made the historic survey already referred to, he found to his horror (and much more so to the public's) that about one-half of the then existing 160 or so medical schools in the United States were really little more than diploma mills. These schools admitted a class in October—even high school graduation was not required for admission—and graduated the class the following April as full-fledged doctors. Flexner recommended that these diploma mills be abolished, and in a few years, they were, when the AMA (American Medical Association) started enforcing higher requirements. Many people believe that teaching may be repeating this ploy by tolerating institutions offering the external doctor's degree in education.

A presentation by Sister Mary Emil summarized effectively the kind of teachers this country seeks:

---

[4] For elaboration of this point, see Novy Bowman, "College Supervision of Student Teaching: A Time to Reconsider," *Journal of Teacher Education*, May–June, 1979, pp. 29–30.

The most fundamental thing, I believe, that is to be done about teacher education, must first take place not in some college but in society generally. We must restore the image of the teacher as someone who has wisdom as well as knowledge who can impart not only science but some ability to judge of all lesser things in the light of great unifying truths.

Throughout history we have wanted to think of our teachers like this. Is the idea of the *magister, doctor*—a kind of ministry to be exercised toward others, and the highest relationship which one man can stand to another. If society wants such teachers for all its schools— public, parochial, and private—we in teacher education will find a way to produce them, but society must be convinced that it needs them. And so, *if I had my way,* our best resources of intellect and eloquence in universities, journals, and TEPS conferences, would be devoted to the problem of how we can make it evident that if our values are muddled, if we have no very clear understanding of even our American traditions, if we do not know how to convince ourselves that we should be responsible for anything; if service, sacrifice, dedication, are no longer driving forces for our youth, then we should look to what our teachers believe and what our teachers know.[5]

Securing the Best Possible Process of Preparing Teachers

Contrary to widespread belief, Horace Mann was not originally an educator but for much of his life a lawyer. Because of his interest in the newly founded public schools, he became a member of the state board of education in Massachusetts. Also, he became during the 1820s and 1830s an ardent advocate of the creation of schools especially designed to prepare skilled teachers for the newly founded free schools. He perceived the gulf then existing between the well-financed and well-established private schools and the public schools. Becoming concerned for the very survival of the fledgling public schools, he became a militant advocate of the creation of normal schools (which he studied in Germany) to prepare teachers for the public schools.

In his crusade to establish and support the common schools, he said:

> I believe Normal Schools to be a new instrumentality in the advancement of the race. I believe that, without them, Free Schools themselves . . . would at length become mere charity schools and thus die

---

[5] Sister Mary Emil, "If I Had My Way," *The Education of Teachers: Curriculum Programs* (Washington, D.C.: National Education Association, 1959), pp. 78–82.

out in fact and form. Neither the art of printing, nor the trial by jury, nor a free press, nor free suffrage, can long exist, to any beneficial and salutary purpose, without schools for the training of teachers; for, if the character and qualifications of teachers be allowed to degenerate, the Free Schools will become pauper schools, and the pauper schools will produce pauper souls, and the free press will become a false and licentious press, and ignorant voters will become venal voters, and through the medium and guise of republican forms, an oligarchy of profligate and flagitious men will govern the land; nay, the universal diffusion and ultimate triumph of all-glorious Christianity itself must await the time when knowledge shall be diffused among men through the instrumentality of good schools. *Coiled up in this institution, as in a spring, there is a vigor whose uncoiling may wheel the spheres.*[6]

ABOLISH CORPORAL PUNISHMENT

Many people are not aware that the courts have ruled several times that thrashing a public school student is not illegal. But the time will come—and probably not far in the future—when the courts will ban corporal punishment as essential to good discipline in the schools.

In 1970, a fourteen-year-old boy lingered in the school auditorium after a program. Two school officials held the boy while the school principal, using a wooden paddle, spanked him. Blood clots formed on the boy's body as a result of the beating, and he was in bed for several days after the spanking. His mother filed a suit against the three men involved. Finally (in April 1977) the case reached the Supreme Court, which held by a 5–4 vote that the beating by school officials did not violate the Eighth Amendment ban against cruel and unusual punishment. The majority voted that this amendment applies only to criminal proceedings. *One court member said that schoolchildren don't need the same protection as criminals in prison, because schools are open institutions that receive community supervision.*

Such decisions usually stir up further controversy. Only three states (New Jersey, Massachusetts, and Maine) ban corporal punishment. Hawaii has a moratorium on such punishment. Maryland has an anti–corporal punishment law, but the law allows counties to supersede its

---

[6] Horace Mann, as quoted in Charles A. Harper, *A Century of Public Teacher Education: The Story of the State Teachers Colleges as They Evolved from the Normal Schools* (Washington, D.C.: National Education Association, 1939), pp. 21–22.

effect, and all but two counties do this. Also, many city school districts have abolished corporal punishment.

NEA Opposed to Corporal Punishment

At the annual meeting of the NEA Representative Assembly in 1971, there was a special committee created to study corporal punishment in the schools, including the extent of its use and alternative forms of punishment. In 1972, this task force reported that it was seriously opposed to corporal punishment. It urged the development of alternative disciplinary techniques, "and proposed a model statute that would prohibit all forms of corporal punishment." The proposed statute would permit only the use of " 'such amounts of physical restraint as may be reasonable and necessary' for a teacher to do the following: (1) to protect himself or herself, the pupil, or others from physical injury, (2) to obtain possession of a weapon or other dangerous object upon the person or within the control of a pupil, (3) to protect property from serious harm."[7]

On June 23, 1972, the NEA Board of Directors adopted the report of the task force on corporal punishment and referred it to the Executive Committee "for implementation as feasible." The proposal was supported by the 1972 Representative Assembly. The board also authorized the NEA president to send to all state officials a copy, and to urge them to work for passage of such legislation.

Thus the NEA is on record as opposing the use of corporal punishment in the schools. This is an important statement and position by an organization representing about 66 percent of the nation's public school teachers. This, we believe, will be enacted into law in the near future. The passage of such a law will set teachers, parents, and society in search of better means of discipline.

DEDICATION AND DISCIPLINE

"Teachers are not as dedicated as they once were"—this glib phrase is the perfect example of the critics articulating the charge repeatedly, but not once glancing into the societal mirror. An apt rejoinder might well be:

---

[7] "NEA Position on Corporal Punishment," *Today's Education*, Nov.–Dec., 1978, p. 55.

"Neither is the public." In the lifetimes of most of those who may read this, there will be the firm recollection of earnest parental support of the schools for the enforcement of discipline. But presently the general behavior of the public, and its toleration or acceptance of an entirely new pattern of behavior, both in society and at home or at school, tends to be shocking. Perhaps acquiescence is a more accurate designation than acceptance. The behavior pattern of the American people, who own the schools, is almost as much at variance with earlier days and practices as is that of the teachers. To state the premise with greater emphasis, it is utterly unrealistic to expect a pattern of permissive behavior (or tolerance of one) in the home and a more rigid one in school. As a plain fact, there is probably not much a family can do to alter practices and customs in society, either locally or in broader areas.

The efficiency of teaching and "discipline" tends to be in direct relation to the pupil-teacher ratio. One can imagine the highest type of discipline if a teacher has only ten students; this continues through the ratio of approximately 20–1. After that point, each student added to the class roll diminishes teacher control, thus diminishing the effectiveness of the learning process. To prove this point in an out-of-school setting, it is an accepted concept that a discussion group of adults may be quite successful if the number in the group is twenty or fewer. If there are thirty to forty, there is very little feedback and interchange of ideas.

It sounds too reasonable for people to criticize teachers for not being the strict disciplinarians they once were—generally, this means in the prevailing relationships when the critics were in school. And so often, particularly if it is a man speaking, this is followed by the comment, "When I was in school, I knew that if I got a licking there, another was sure to come at home—except a harder one."

SOME PRO–SOCIAL-PROMOTIONS ARGUMENTS

Many teachers are inclined to defend the automatic promotion of students from one grade level to the next at the end of the school year.

There is a story (probably apocryphal) as follows. In the 1930s an expert was hired to evaluate and recommend changes for the Detroit school system. In the course of examining the marks of pupils in grades 1–5, he was impressed with the omnipresence of one student by the name of Joe Louis. After some reexamination of the record of this boy, the expert discovered that he had the grade F for each of the five grades. So he wrote on his record, "This boy should be taught to do something with his hands." At the time the name of Joe Louis had not emerged into prominence, but he was to become the heavyweight boxing champion of the world.

Social promotion seems, on superficial examination, to be an outrageous miscarriage of justice, and another and devastating indication of the utter failure of the public school system. The criticism, and general public reaction, is all wrapped up in the seemingly simple (but actually indefensible) notion that all children must measure up to a set of immutable standards of achievement. A child is to be marked a failure or near-failure if his score falls at or below an arbitrarily designated point.

But what is to be the standard or the criterion for designating failure? Suppose for the moment that the public does force strict adherence to the concept of grading on the curve. What are the results? Well, one result is to tend to mark a child a failure, a miserable outcast, a sort of cast-off, a thing to be ridiculed. For what? So that others can be elevated to respectability and admired? Granted, there are gradations of native ability. For what? Here is where the confusion begins. For one student, it will be superiority in grasping the mysteries of foreign languages; for another, the unquestionable urge to know the hidden riddles of science; for still others the everlasting hunger to think and speak and write superior prose, or to march to the alluring rhythm of poetry.

What of the non-linguistic, the non-scientific, the non-lover of the beauty of the cadence of poetry? Do they have no abilities or aptitudes, no imperceptible urges for beauty, or fineness, or worthwhileness? Lacking such presumed areas of proven worth to society of the first category, is there nothing in them worth cultivating? Should society accept its own categorization (or that of a sizable section, if not a majority of it) of them as failures, people of no value, or dummies? If so, then the American Dream and all the worthwhile dreams grounded in the conviction that all free peoples, with a chance to grow and to reach for yet higher ground through the healing and uplifting power of education, most certainly would go out the window. Nations would again turn to reliance upon the elite, the aristocracies, made so by forcing their own concepts of the superior, as defined by *them*, as confirmed by *them*, as proof indisputable of superiority. Thus man—free man—would once again trade that freedom for the age-old lie that human superiority is based upon two things: birth, and one-track education.

TRUANCY

School officials in Houston, Texas, are giving serious consideration to requiring student absences to be made up by attending Saturday classes. The proposal also carries with it the possibility of denying passing grades to students who have more than six unexcused absences in a twelve-week quarter. The Saturday classes may be used to return to the good graces of teachers who post passing marks; they may also be used to excuse students from final examinations. Currently, the district already excuses from quarterly finals seniors who have high grade averages and good attendance records. It is possible that the district may extend this practice to all high school students.

A study showed that fifth- and sixth-grade students in the lowest quarter of their classes missed about thirty days of class during the last school year. On the other hand, students in the upper three-quarters only missed about ten days. This district reported that state law required that a student attend only 51 percent of the time in order to pass. A top school official was quoted as saying this would allow some student to miss a couple of years of instruction by absences in grades one through twelve. The district plans to identify school buildings well distributed throughout the city, for the Saturday make-up classes.

"MALPRACTICE SUIT" AGAINST STUDENTS

Suits against teachers for failure to teach students effectively were mentioned in Chapter 4, with the prediction that this movement will eventuate in what has been described in medicine as malpractice suits. Cases are now being reported of teachers suing students (and, of course, their parents) for physical attacks.

Here is one case in point. Reported in a news item from Corpus Christi, Texas, was a successful suit of a teacher against a teenage boy who had slugged the teacher in 1978. The teacher was awarded $2,396 in damages. This has been called a landmark case; educators say it is the first Texas case in which a teacher won damages against a student attacker. The comment of the boy was, "I'll never do that again." The attack grew out of the boy's smoldering anger for being suspended several months before this incident for misbehavior in the hallway. The high school boy said he did nothing wrong, and he took out his anger on the teacher. The boy stated his intention to get even at the time of the suspension. The teacher he hit was a man who was not involved in the hall episode.

This incident may well trigger the enactment of laws in other states providing recourse for teachers against violence by students. The thousands of teachers, the majority of whom are women, who have left teaching or who have suffered psychological loss of health and vigor will in time demand such laws. This development, alongside already enacted legislation (in some states) enabling parents to sue teachers for malpractice (as has become already a nightmare in the medical profession), will become general. Putting these two together, one may predict the ultimate abandonment of both corporal punishment by teachers and violence in schools by students.

REDUCE THE TEACHER LOAD

A major key to reform of the public schools, and a paramount key to improving their efficiency and their performance with the individual child, is to reduce drastically the teacher-pupil ratio. For the 1977–78 year, the situation was as follows: In the elementary schools, the pupil-teacher ratio was 21–1, down from 25–1 in 1970–71. At the high school level, the ratio was 19–1, down from 19.1–1 in 1976–77.

In 1977, the total production of newly qualified teachers was 213,054, all of whom had completed at least the bachelor's degree, but based on the then current pupil-teacher ratio only 84,900 were employed.

If the quality-criterion estimate (based on the requirement of maximum levels of quality) is used, 219,450 elementary teachers and 280,500 secondary teachers, or a total of 499,950 were needed. The total of newly prepared teachers in that year would have been 67,446 short of the number needed on the highest quality-of-instructional situation. Some studies propose a maximum ratio of 15:1 for elementary teachers, and for high school teachers an average of 20 students per class or a total of 100 per day for the five-period day.

The cost of adding 85,200 additional teachers (44,900 elementary and 40,300 secondary) would add some $834 million to the total public school budgets of the United States, based on the average starting salary of new teachers.

It might well be, however, that the decreasing annual enrollment figures will extend on into the middle of the 1980s. If so, these lower enrollments could cut the annual increase in the estimated number of teachers required to reach the new teacher-pupil load by about one-half the above-projected increase, thus reducing the annual increase in cost by that proportion.

16

Updating the Examination Syndrome

IT is little short of amazing how deftly the public can be sold on "nostrums" or "miracle drugs" which offer sure-fire solutions to whatever weaknesses or fancied weaknesses beset their public schools.

At the moment, the allegedly infallible remedy which the public seems to have embraced is that of testing. For once, the suggested device has much to support its advocacy. If there are measures for proving the possession of knowledge at several levels of schooling, why should anyone raise objections to being examined to substantiate the extent to which they have mastered the required knowledge?

There are many reasons why the answer to this question is not a simple one. In the first place, the acquisition of knowledge, in the form of facts to be digested and regurgitated on demand in the future, ought not and cannot be an automatic and unfailing formula.

THE OTHER SIDE OF THE EXAMINATION SYNDROME (OR HYSTERIA)

It would be almost a perfect educational situation in the United States if the obvious, profound, and newfound public faith in the miracle drug of standardized examinations—both for students and teachers—could actually live up to the highly advertised remedial effects on both. But experience teaches us that there is no such thing as a perfect examination that will prove to be satisfactory to *all* the people, regardless of the innate talents or the sky-high aspirations of the "public." There are inherent weaknesses in tests themselves, when laid alongside the wide variations in the talents and aspirations and studies pursued by innumerable students.

Ashley Montagu, the great British anthropologist who has spent sixty years studying education and the learning potential of human beings, states, "The human brain is the most educable of all the brains in the world. . . . He [the child] is capable of learning anything under appropriate environmental conditions. . . . Then we treat children of the same chronological age as if they were developmentally of the same age too. To treat children of the same chronological age as if they were all equal is to commit a biological and social absurdity."[1] This fact should serve to alter concepts about the fallibility of tests, and of the meaning of test scores at specific age and developmental levels.

The overreliance on exams as measures of academic talent and/or achievement goes far back in history. In the United States admission (or certification) to the various categories of teaching was achieved by the use of examinations—admittedly simple in construction, content, and usefulness. These tests date back to the earliest publicly supported (either by taxation or by subscription) schools. These schools were overwhelmingly of the one-room variety which at first almost universally employed male teachers.

Here is an example (maybe fictional, but realistic in all too many instances) of the early teacher examinations. It had been handed down through several generations of the family of one of the authors of the book cited:

> Grandfather was on the school board in the little rural community in which he lived. He and another board member had in mind a young man named Matthew as a teacher of their school. Matthew had little "book larnin." He attended church regularly and his character seemed to be quite satisfactory. So far as was known he did not use intoxicating beverages. . . . But he had only attended and finished the local one-room school. The certification law at the time stated that all candidates must be examined in respect to character, ability to teach, and soundness of knowledge of subject to be taught. . . . Matthew was examined by Grandfather—who commanded him to open his mouth. . . . Grandfather peered inside the tobacco stained cavity and then ran his fingers over the blackened teeth. Grandfather said to the other member of the Board present (the two of them made a legal majority of the three-member board), "Write Matthew out a certificate to teach . . . I find him sound in every way."[2]

---

[1] Ashley Montagu, "The Education I Believe In," *Today's Education*, Feb.–Mar., 1980, p. 48. Used by permission.

[2] Albert J. Huggest and T. M. Stinnett, *Professional Problems of Teachers* (New York: Macmillan, 1958), p. 416.

Ridiculous? Yes, of course, in terms of today's required levels of college preparation. But this type of certification (not so simplistic as this, of course) existed in a few places well past the midpoint of this century, at least in terms of the elementary subject matter included in the legally prescribed examinations for certification of teachers in the one-room rural schools. Ridiculous in today's America? Yes, in terms of the simplicity cited above; but not in terms of several hocus-pocus gimmicks that can be used by those with axes to grind.

But it seems appropriate to glance back briefly to the history of examinations for teachers in the United States. It will be recalled that the certification of teachers, i.e., legal certification, reaches back as far as ancient Athens. In Europe, the practice of certification or licensing originated with the church and was later adopted in England. When schools began to develop in the American colonies, this same process was transmitted to this country. The first teacher license in the colonies which became a part of the United States was issued in 1637 (one year after the founding of Harvard) to Adam Roelansten of New Netherlands (now New York). This license was issued by the Reformed Dutch Church in Holland, that being the predominant faith of the early settlers of New Netherlands.

As the colonies grew, the legal authority for the licensure of teachers was a haphazard, varied affair—in the hands of towns, churches, and governors. With nationhood, following colonial practice, authority was vested in local school officials. The examination of applicants for teaching was haphazard; nepotism was prevalent.

By 1850, it was evident that an improved system was imperative, so states began to assume authority for certifying teachers. Gradually this responsibility was placed exclusively in state departments of education. But for about a century a measure of authority remained at the local level, where licensure occurred via the examination route, or at the county level. The examinations were elementary in content, being based upon elementary school subjects. New York in 1841 and Vermont in 1842 were the first states to pass such legislation. By 1900, local certification still existed, but the examinations were beginning to be made out and to be graded and certificates for a given county issued by the state authority. As late as the 1950s, these certificates, valid only in specified counties and usually for the one-room rural schools, continued to be issued in a few states by the examination. But the certification of teachers has now been universally shifted to the state departments of education, and certification is based only on evidence of prescribed courses or degrees from accredited colleges and universities. Also, it is now virtually a universal practice for teacher certificates to be issued upon the recommendation of the college or university in which the preparation (degree) was secured. Presently there are over 1,200 higher education institutions approved by states for teacher preparation. Virtually all of these must be accredited by the appropriate regional accrediting association. By 1974, in addition to requiring that the teacher-preparing institutions must be accredited by their regional associations, almost half of such institutions were accredited by the National Council for the Accreditation of Teacher Education (NCATE). In that year at least 80 percent of the newly graduated teachers were from NCATE accredited institutions; by 1979, that proportion had increased to about 90 percent.

HOW SOUND ARE THE MEASUREMENTS OF TESTING?

Of course, certain standardized tests, carefully devised and carefully interpreted, can reflect a high degree of reliability. The great danger is that the meanings of many test scores may be grossly misinterpreted—even the old, prevalent and very popular system graded on a 100 percent basis, where every score below 60 was considered failing, and grades were rather arbitrarily assigned by percentage scores: 90 to 100 = grade A; 80 to 89 = grade B; 70 to 79 = grade C; 60 to 69 = grade D. Below 60 got an F. This is easy for every layman to understand, and one supposes that a sizable portion of the American public grew up on such an arrangement.

Unfortunately, the scoring of all examinations is not that simple. In virtually all modernized examination systems there are booby traps, possibilities of bias, and faulty interpretations of the results.

The notion that these processes are precise, accurate, and infallible is cleverly demolished in an editorial in a professional journal:

> My friend was a geologist. We were in his backyard, awed by the majesty of the Rocky Mountains. The monstrous, flat, sloping rocks that are the hallmark of Boulder, Colorado, were the subject of our conversation.

"Do you know how old those rocks are?" my friend inquired.

"I have no idea at all," I replied.

"They are about four hundred million years old," he said—"give or take a hundred million years."[3]

The editor then proceeds to point out that the statement "give or take a hundred million years" was a prosaic and normal way of indicating roughly how far off one way or the other the speaker could be in the accuracy of the judged age of the rocks.

It is obvious that this variation in accuracy, or lack of accuracy, also may apply in the judged meaning of examination scores. These scores are rarely precise; they could also vary widely and be even less accurately interpreted to the public. One of the most reasonable suggestions about the value of standardized tests was phrased by an expert in the field, who observed that these tests enable advisors to do a better job of guidance in evaluating the chances of students' success in college, and so forth.

There are guidelines spelled out by the editor quoted above. He writes: "Precision in the physical sciences, as in the social and behavioral sciences, is hemmed in and made more manageable by the concept of standard error."[4] This is a statistic which specifies limits within which the true score of measurement on a test of an individual actually lies. And he gave a simple explanation of interpretation of a derived score as follows:

If Becky Jones got a score of 107 on that test, Becky's true score can actually be assumed to be somewhere between 101 and 113 (i.e., plus or minus 6). And such an assumption will be correct two-thirds of the time. One-third of the time it will be wrong! One time out of six the score will be higher than 113, and one time out of six the score will be lower than 101.

The concept of standard error would not be particularly significant, if teachers or administrators did not use test data to make decisions about individual students in their schools. However, it is one thing to say that the average sixth grader in a particular school achieved at a 5.4 grade level in reading. It is a very different thing to note that Billy Johnson achieved at a 5.4 grade level in reading.[5]

---

[3] Jack Frymier, "On the Way to the Forum—It's a Very Standard Error," *Educational Forum*, May, 1979, pp. 388–91.

[4] Ibid., pp. 388–89.

[5] Ibid., p. 390.

THE TESTING OF INTELLIGENCE

The development of scientific approaches to the measuring of intelligence began in the last two decades of the nineteenth century. Galton and Cattell began the development of experimental procedures for measuring mentality during this period. This stimulated further development of differential psychology, which became the basis of aptitude testing.

Shortly after 1900, Binet began to devise the first scales for measuring the intelligence of schoolchildren. His consisted of thirty brief tests. An individual child's score was derived by determining the age of children who scored as did the child being measured. This technique became the basis for Terman's development of the Stanford-Binet Test, in which the concept of the I.Q. was developed. That is how a child's ratio of mental age to chronological age was determined. If the two were equal, the child's I.Q. was 100. From this eventually was developed the deviation I.Q., which gradually displaced the ratio score.

Throughout their lives in and outside the school, Americans have placed complete confidence in the "exactness" of intelligence tests. The following event, which occurred while one of the authors was teaching in the public schools, exemplifies this total confidence.

Ann was a student in my eighth-grade science class. Her parents were both college graduates. I hardly noticed Ann for the first few weeks of the term because she was very quiet. One day I received a note from the counselor's office asking me to return a call to Ann's mother. We scheduled a conference to discuss Ann's mediocre performance in my class.

When the time came, I was ready. I had studied Ann's cumulative records and her schoolwork over the past years. I found that the three I.Q. scores on file were 101, 103, and 102—remarkably consistent and also remarkably average. Ann's grades during the two previous years had consistently been B's, indicating that she was performing high in relation to her ability. Currently, Ann was taking five academic subjects and band. She had no study period. Her test scores in science had steadily declined from B to D—.

Both parents came to the session. As a matter of routine, I began the discussion by letting the parents talk while I listened. Right away, I saw that they had two things to say. They said them politely but with total assurance and confidence. Ann was capable of making top grades and she was doing her best. After she failed a test at school, her mother would often quiz her and find that she knew every answer.

When I showed these parents that her scores on the three most recent intelligence testings averaged 102, I thought that they would view this as average. But, to my amazement, because the score exceeded 100, they became further convinced that their daughter was above average. The daily work that she had done was obviously average; yet, it hadn't the power to convince that the I.Q. scores possessed.

This is but one case of millions throughout the country where educated Americans accept I.Q. test scores as gospel. Yet, if the facts were known, the predictive validity of these tests is very low. Upon retesting, a student may score dramatically higher or lower. Even the most popular of these tests have low correlations with each other. Two of the best-known and most widely used intelligence tests in this country (the WISC and the Stanford-Binet) have correlations between .60 and .80.

THE TESTING INDUSTRY

The examination (or testing) business has grown in recent years into an annual multi-million-dollar business. The testing industry has skyrocketed from small beginnings to a giant industry. This evolutionary process has not come to pass overnight; it probably had its beginnings with the development of the College Entrance Examination Board in 1900, which for a generation kept a close rein on the liberalization of the curricula of public high schools, holding the offerings of these (the people's schools) to the type of preparation which would tend to increase the likelihood of students' admission to the classical offerings of the then existing prestigious colleges.

But about the second decade of the twentieth century there began a mild public clamor for more practical subjects meant especially for the non-college-going group. At first these new offerings were in vocational education (the skilled trades in industry) and in agriculture. Both areas at the time were rarely if ever prerequisites for admission to college, or indeed rarely if ever acceptable for entrance to higher education. Of course, with the enactment of the Morrill Act (the Land Grant College Act) in 1862, the walls of objection to agricultural education began slowly to crumble. Congress passed legislation in 1914 (the Smith-Lever Act) providing some assistance to high schools for the teaching of agriculture; and in 1917 it passed the Smith-Hughes Act, providing assistance in offering vocational subjects.

The public demand for vocational education courses in the public high schools came much later than that for agricultural courses, when the United States began to shift from a predominantly agricultural economy to the establishment of industries, which in time began to demand preparation in certain skilled trades. Actually, this demand for such courses in the high schools did not become noticeable until about 1920. This demand was largely confined to the industrial areas in large cities at first; then it spread to embrace eventually the entire nation.

The conviction behind the development of the first standardized tests, to be administered to high school graduates who sought to be admitted to the colleges and universities, arose because of two circumstances. The concept of the nature and content of the then existing (roughly from 1870 to 1900—and later in many areas) curricula of colleges and universities was based on a conviction imported into the United States from the European universities founded during the Middle Ages. That conviction was that the function of the universities was to extend the education of the upper classes—or the small percentage with presumably the highest intelligence. And the accepted concept of the curriculum worthy of the designation of "higher education" was the classical concept—the study of Latin and Greek and philosophy and the arts and related disciplines. Of course, with time the colleges and universities in general began to revise curricula to meet new requirements, but many continue to emulate the offerings of the early Ivy League institutions.

Although the full flow of the demand for liberalization of the curricula of higher education did not begin until well into the twentieth century, there were, beginning about 1870, growing demands for the doors of higher education to be opened wider to admit a greater proportion of high school graduates. This caused some split in the ranks of the private and public high schools. About 1880 the principals of the private high schools began to complain that they were becoming confused as to what subjects would be required for graduation, and thus for admission to the prestigious universities, notably those of the "Ivy League." As a solution to their dilemma, they were advised to seek the establishment of a body which would seek betterment of the communication between the private high schools and the Ivy League institutions. Quite naturally, this system tended to favor those who had completed the parallel curricula offered by the private schools. Any tests based on these curricula tended to be biased against those who had not pursued them. This liaison, in time, resulted in the development of the Scholastic Aptitude Test (SAT) as an examination for admission to these select colleges and universities. Quite naturally, these examinations were based largely upon the curricula of the private high schools which, at a lower level, were largely based upon the courses offered by the Ivy League institutions. The SAT was the first of the standardized examinations used as an admission requirement by higher education institutions. Of course, with the rapid growth in the number of public high schools—especially after 1920, when these public high schools broke away from the straitjacket of the classical disciplines and began to broaden their offerings to include more practical subjects—this test tended to dominate the testing business, especially the college admission tests. This dominance was ameliorated somewhat by the development of testing programs at Stanford and Iowa, which became widely used as college admission tests, especially among the graduates of public high schools.

Gradually, the Educational Testing Service (ETS) became the developer and publisher of tests in the fields of education, both for schools and colleges and for admission to professions in general. ETS was established in 1927 in Princeton, New Jersey, but with no connection with Princeton University. It is an independent, nonprofit organization under the sponsorship of the American Council on Education, the Carnegie Foundation for the Advancement of Teaching, and the College Entrance Examination Board (CEEB). Its stated purposes were to improve and extend the testing programs of the sponsoring agencies, to conduct research in the field of educational measurement, and to provide leadership in the educational measurement field. While its beginnings were relatively modest, it has grown into a giant measurement firm with a research staff of more than 1,200. It has provided measurement instruments and consultant services for a number of national organizations and has led in the measurement of educational progress. It also provides consultants in the field in other countries. Widely used tests that ETS has developed are the SAT admissions program, advanced placement examinations, college placement tests, college level examinations, and so forth. In the field of teaching it has developed the National Teachers Examination, widely used to measure minimum competency in teaching.

As mentioned previously, the College Entrance Examination Board came into existence in 1900, with support from both higher education and secondary schools, to facilitate the movement of high school graduates into the colleges of their preference. Its basic function (among several related ones) was to provide a series of entrance examinations, national in scope, for admission to colleges and universities. CEEB was initially sponsored by twelve eastern colleges in conjunction with the National Education Association and the Association of Colleges and Secondary Schools of the Middle States. Presently, its membership includes many colleges, universities, high schools, and large city school systems. About 2,000,000 students from some 25,000 high schools participate in the admissions programs annually. In fact, approximately two-thirds of entering college students each year take one or more of CEEB's tests. These tests are offered in about 3,000 centers throughout the United States and in 70 foreign countries. The scores then are transmitted to the colleges designated by the candidates, and to the students' high schools, in approximately four to five weeks after the taking of the examinations. As a general rule, scores on the tests are not the exclusive factors in admission to higher education. But, of course, these tests carry great weight in the decisions.

A Sample of State Testing Legislation

The Florida legislature passed the Accountability Act of 1976. In part, the act provides for the state commissioner of education to implement a statewide program of assessment testing which shall provide for the improvement of the operation and management of the public schools. The act provides that districts should award certificates of attendance as well as differential diplomas, depending upon the achievement levels of high school seniors.

As a result of this legislation, the Florida State Department of Education instituted the Florida Statewide Tests of Basic Skills at grades three, five, eight, and eleven; plus the Eleventh Grade Tests of Functional Literacy. (Nowhere did the legislation define the methods for evaluating functional literacy.)

A panel to evaluate the Florida competency program was appointed jointly by NEA and its affiliated state teachers association in Florida. This panel consisted of Ralph W. Tyler, director emeritus of the Center for

Advanced Study in the Behavioral Sciences at Stanford University and senior consultant of Science Research Associates; plus an associate professor, an elementary and a high school teacher (both in Florida schools), and a professor of community medicine. In general, the panel endorsed the purposes of the Florida Accountability Act. It also endorsed the need for educational improvement in all the states, if the great expectations for education are to be met. However, it found the mandatory standards seriously faulty.

THE IMPACT OF SOCIAL AND ECONOMIC CHANGE ON TESTS

When everything is peaceful on the American scene—when there is peace, prosperity, and a smooth flow of ideologies among the population; especially when governmental budgets are balanced or nearly so—then everything tends to be agreeable concerning the public schools. But let any of those be upset—by depressions, recessions, uncontrollable inflation, war or threatened war, or annual escalations of the tax rates—and there arise painful howls from the general public. There must be a scapegoat upon which all or major blame can be focused. All of this is sometimes welcomed with great glee by some who think that the ideal system of education is not state-supported education for all. And, of course, the vested interests of some of the corporate rich or the land-rich or the resources-rich loudly protest the alleged failures of the schools.

When this occurs there are vociferous demands for either (1) return of the function of education to the churches or the privately supported education institutions; (2) widespread, drastic reforms in the public schools; or (3) tax reforms. Rehabilitation demands include standardized testing of both teachers and students—and for the latter, this fetish has generally advocated testing at the conclusion of every grade or class level.

Of course, it should in all fairness be added that the American public is no different in this respect from people in other free nations where universal education at public expense exists. And, as stated at several points in this book, this is as it should be. Instead of aimlessly griping about it, those who operate the public schools and those who are charged with directing the school programs—legislatures, school boards, administrators, and teachers—must seek (1) to understand the nature and portent of the public's criticism, and (2) to respond to those criticisms which are valid or partially so.

At this point, the efficacy of standardized (or competency) examinations appears to have been embraced by enough of the public to justify a fair, balanced experimentation by the schools. But at the outset some pitfalls and weaknesses should be critically examined, and the dangers of overemphasis should be clearly defined.

Just to mention some of the gimmicks used to correct the situations which are far from perfect: (1) The validity of tests applied to a diverse population is questionable. (2) Most, if not all, standardized tests are biased with reference to some groups. (3) The variability of the points at which the tests are administered to students: Shall they be at the end of each grade level, or at the end of the fourth, eighth, and eleventh grades?

One other caution should be recorded here, regarding the probable reaction of parents to the results of the tests. If parents now clamor for tightening up the standards of teaching and learning, what will be their reactions when their children fail at any of these points? What if their children must face the fact of doing additional remedial work at that point, or fail to be passed to the next level?

If the schools now engage in social promotions to avoid the ire of complaining parents, as is so often charged, will not the periodic competency testing arouse even more violent anger? If it is now relatively easy for the schools and teachers to compromise by passing students in order to avoid the anger of parents, will not they be compelled to find ways of resuming such practices to avoid the attacks of parents?

Of course, in time in America, there began to be pressures to incorporate more practical subjects—first in the high schools, and later in higher education. There is a historic example of the duality of concepts about education. In 1862, the Morrill Act (the Land Grant College Act) provided federal funds to assist in establishing colleges to develop scientific bases for the improvement of agriculture in the United States. While this act was on President Lincoln's desk in 1862 awaiting his signature, the president of one of the prestigious eastern universities supposedly wrote the president urging him to veto the act because "agriculture was not a fit subject for higher education." Of course, the liberal arts colleges which originally were founded largely by church organizations generally adhered to the classical concept. But toward the end of the nineteenth century and in the early years of the twentieth, the emerging demand grew in fervor for "practical" education, especially in agriculture, architecture, engineering, industrial arts, vocational and technical education, business subjects, and others. This schism became so great that the principals of public high schools found it necessary to establish their own organization, the National Association of Secondary School Principals (NASSP), in 1917. This was in major part a protest against accrediting and other standards which made it difficult for high schools to meet the demands of the public and industry for more practical courses.

The Committee of Ten, appointed by the National Education Association in 1892 to study the offerings of the high schools, also recommended a liberalizing of the secondary school curriculum. Considering the composition of the committee—largely college presidents and professors and teachers in private high schools—its recommendations, from the present vantage point, seem surprisingly liberal. The committee recommended that the chief function of secondary schools be not to prepare students for college, but to prepare them for life, whether they go to college or not. They believed in the academic disciplines and in the transfer of training; the same subjects prepare one for college or for life. It is not surprising that the report did not prove to be too effective, since the trend toward preparation for life via greater emphasis in high schools on technical and vocational subjects was gathering momentum. In other words, the new trend toward practical offerings in the high schools was already underway, and this trend would continue into the twentieth century.

But the critics of America's public schools love to compare progress in the United States with that in the Soviet Union, and to imply that Soviet gains are due to the shortcomings of our educational system. Especially do the alarmists like to praise the USSR's educational system for effectiveness; and they like to damn American schools as inadequate. On the matter of food production alone, the Soviets employ in excess of 60 percent of their working population in farming, against our 5 percent; and we experience food surpluses while the Soviets are plagued with persistent food shortages. Today one will find many land-grant colleges in the highest ranks among higher education institutions in enrollments. Indeed, many of the land-grant colleges now rank among the top 20–25 percent of the nation's universities in most measures of excellence. Only in the last few decades or so have many of these institutions emerged into acknowledged respectability. Thus the derision (they had been marked by such names as "cow colleges") aimed at land-grant institutions for over a century simply is stifled by the evidence—both of the caliber of their curricula and the quality of their institutional research and teaching personnel—and the fruitfulness of their contribution to the nation's needs.

New Testing Programs

In fairness, it should be said that the higher education institutions began to recede from exclusive emphasis upon the classical concept of higher education, and to make provisions for more liberal offerings, toward the end of the nineteenth century. Then, in the early years of the twentieth century, new testing programs developed at Stanford University (the Stanford-Binet tests), and similar developments at the University of Iowa by E. F. Lindquist, went a long way toward elimination of earlier elitist approaches by developing the Iowa Test of Basic Skills, which contributed greatly to the gradual shift to testing programs which measured the actual talents and achievements of the total student population. Where once the exams of the College Entrance Examination Board were virtually without competition, these tests came in time to be healthy competitive instruments.

It appears that the University of Michigan was the first to break away from the rigid standards of classification and accreditation of high schools by appointing a committee of its faculty which, on invitation, would visit high schools within the state. If this committee was satisfied with the quality of work in a given high school, graduates of this high school would be accepted for admission to the university, on the recommendation of the high school principal. These steps encouraged the high schools to broaden their curricula, leading to more practical courses and thus enabling them to meet the demands of the public. This step ultimately had some measure of influence in the founding of the presently existing six regional accrediting associations.

The most widely used tests for predicting success in college and thus as admission examinations are the SAT (Scholastic Aptitude Test) of the College Entrance Examination Board and the ACT (American College Testing Program). These tests, it is true, are used to determine college admission as a primary purpose. But there is a broader function of enabling college personnel to make better decisions on guidance counseling for each student.

WEAKNESSES IN COLLEGE ADMISSION PRACTICES

There is continuing skepticism concerning the infallibility, even the validity, of standardized tests. This is particularly true of college admission tests. It is quite evident that student performance in high school, as measured by aptitude tests, is often not an accurate predictor of performance in college. One of the astonishing facts is that students with excellent high school grades often do not perform very well in college. On the other hand, some with below-average records and low aptitude test scores perform beyond the measured expectations. Thus the single use of high school grades or admission test scores tends quite often to prove not only inadequate, but also unfair. Judging the promise of performance in the world of work by college grades also is often inaccurate, to say the least.

THE FLORIDA LITERACY TEST AND THE COURTS

In Tampa, Florida, in a state that puts its fervent trust in the efficacy of literacy testing, an important case reached a federal court in 1979. The case involved Gary Berrien, a seventeen-year-old black student, one of ten children of Ezell and Mildred Berrien. Gary had completed the twelfth grade but did not receive a diploma. He could not get into the army without that diploma. Gary's parents said they had no idea that the boy wasn't meeting the requirements for graduation and that he was a functional illiterate. The boy, according to some of his teachers, had great ability in music, woodworking, and carpentry. In fact, he played the organ in three different churches on Sundays and was paid for his work. The boy's parents were, of course, deeply upset about his failure to graduate from high school. His father was bitter about the boy being passed along from grade to grade, then being informed at the end of the twelfth grade that he couldn't graduate because he was a functional illiterate under the new statewide testing program.

In July, 1979, a Florida federal district court ordered that a diploma be awarded to the boy, and to the other 4,787 students (3,445 blacks and 1,342 whites) who failed the literacy test after three attempts. These 4,787 had met all other requirements for graduation.

This was the first federal court ruling on the new wave of minimum competency graduation requirements.[6] Also, the court ruled that the Florida testing program had begun in 1977, when Gary was a sophomore, and that the earliest this requirement could be enforced was in the 1982–83 school year. Otherwise, one assumes, this would be tantamount to imposing an *ex post facto* law. In addition, the federal court pointed out that the test discriminated against most blacks, who until 1971 attended segregated schools. The court's decision did not bar such testing per se, but only established the time element. North Carolina, for example, gave its students at least three years' notification of the new requirement for graduation.

ATTACKS ON TESTING CLAIMS

Under the Freedom of Information Act, the National Education Association in May, 1979, challenged the right of the Federal Trade Commission to withhold certain factual materials of a study on testing. That part of the FTC report released to the public indicated that students who attended costly private coaching schools achieved higher test scores on standardized tests than those students who had not had such coaching. These scores were reportedly on tests that the test-makers had claimed to be "coachproof." The NEA had twice requested all of the underlying data involved in the FTC study of coaching schools, but these data were not forthcoming, and NEA said that it will not drop its court suit until such data were provided.

The NEA claims that the data requested have great implications for the rights of millions of this nation's students and adults, at the turning points of their lives. It has consistently criticized the threatened excessive use of standardized tests to make judgments about human life and aspirations, and has repeatedly probed into the standardized testing areas. The NEA executive director also called for a thorough governmental and media investigation of the entire powerful but unchecked testing industry.

The NEA's request for data from the FTC, from which the conclusion allegedly was drawn that coaching boosts the scores of those taking standardized tests, has been denied. In the meantime several media concerns have filed requests for this information, especially in view of the

---

[6] "Tests on Trial in Florida," *Time*, July 30, 1979, p. 66.

fact that test-makers (including ETS) have consistently claimed that their tests are "coachproof." As a result of this refusal by FTC, not only is NEA pursuing its court suit under the Freedom of Information Act, but it has called for a major investigation of the testing industry, in view of the lack of regulation, and the possible impacts upon the students taking the tests.

The attack by NEA is aimed particularly at the Scholastic Aptitude Test (SAT), prepared and published by the Educational Testing Service—which, incidentally, became embroiled in several federal court cases regarding the charge of discrimination against black teachers, via the use of its National Teachers Examination (NTE). (These court cases are described in Chapter 7.)

Media Publicize Testing Hassle

Time magazine picked up the substance of the hassle between the National Education Association and the Federal Trade Commission's Bureau of Consumer Protection over the effectiveness of private coaching schools and their alleged effectiveness in enabling their students to outstrip those who did not have the benefits of coaching on SAT tests:

> Six times a year, high school students converge on test centers nationwide for a fearsome academic ritual: the Scholastic Aptitude Test (SAT) which helps to determine where tens of thousands of students will go to college. In theory there is little that students can do to prepare for the test since SAT supposedly measures innate ability, not learned skills; in practice, however, more students each year desperately cram for the SAT. A third of the public and private schools in the Northeast now offer some sort of preparation course. Elsewhere around the country, thousands of nervous scholars flock to commercial coaching schools, which drill and review them—and woo them with promises of striking results. The College Entrance Examination Board which sponsors the SAT has steadfastly tried to discredit cram schools, thus defending SAT's objective infallibility. But the coaching schools, which also prepare students for the Law School Admission Test and Graduate Record Examinations, have become more than a $10 million annual business. So the FTC's Bureau of Consumer Protection decided to investigate them.[7]

---

[7] "Coaching Daze," *Time,* June 11, 1979, p. 57. Copyright 1979 Time Inc. All rights reserved. Reprinted by permission from TIME.

The *Time* article mentioned one test-coaching concern which operates a chain of eighty-eight schools. This concern had once advertised that it can raise the SAT scores by at least 100 points. The fee charged for this coaching course was $275 per student.

The FTC report of its study on coaching schools indicated that after ten weeks of coaching the test-taker could improve both verbal and math scores by an average of 25 points, while the College Entrance Examination Board had never found an increased score due to coaching of more than eight to ten weeks. Also, *Time* reported that the Educational Testing Service, which derives and administers the test, admitted that "some students on some occasions may have increased their scores after attending some coaching courses." These admissions constitute a decided deviation from previous claims that "intensive drill is at best likely to yield insignificant increases in test scores." The most successful of these coaching schools holds that "so many people think that aptitude is innate . . . but a test just measures the level which you are at. But if you get an improved student you should have an improved score." And *Time* adds: "All of which seems to show that the distinction between innate ability and acquired skills is blurry, that college admissions officers should not rely too heavily on test scores, and anybody who wants to learn can learn."[8]

A question emerges: Since standardized scores are not completely trustworthy and since public schools are supported by public taxes, should poor scores on these tests ever be used as the sole criteria for admissions screening? The American people have a deep concern about its gamble on free public schools that are open to all and prepare students for the future. We are gambling that *this system of universal education is the basic foundation upon which a free, self-governing, independent nation, "with liberty and justice for all," can be built.* Is that gamble really a delusion?

The Federal Trade Commission, in releasing the report by its staff on May 29, 1979, shied away from any endorsements. Each year, more than a million high school students take SAT tests, some twice, at $10.50 a test. The FTC study said that 50,000 students are enrolled in commercial coaching courses that cost at least $10 million dollars annually.

General Omar Bradley once wrote, "Our parents are the authors of all our days. Our teachers are authors of all our deeds." This is a rather

---

[8] Ibid.

sweeping tribute, but certainly there is a great measure of truth in the statement. One thing is fairly certain—that kind of teacher competence can scarcely be measured by a test or a series of tests. A standardized test has not yet been devised that can measure or identify in a teacher that precious gift or trait of being able to touch the life of or urge a child to be infinitely greater than he is, or has been.

Excerpts of Use of Competency Testing

A realist looks at the worship of rankings on standardized tests as follows:

> Presumably, the almighty letter grade and SAT tell it all . . . we smile wryly when a speaker repeats the cliché: half the students will always be below average, and we never have most of the students above the fiftieth percentile. But the next day we're back in that old groove again, hard at work trying to get everyone above the mean. Clearly, by this criterion our schools will never be any better. . . .
>
> It seems to my associate and me that how a student spends precious time in school and how he feels about what goes on there is of much greater significance than how he scores on a standardized achievement test. But I am not at all sure that the American people are ready to put a rather straight-forward criterion such as this ahead of the marks and scores we worship needlessly in much the same way our supposedly more primitive ancestors worshipped the gods of thunder and fire.
>
> And so it will be difficult for schools to get better and even more difficult for them to appear to.[9]

Many of us, particularly parents and the general public, have been led to believe that the schools are failing if they can't enable all students to be above the mean (which is the fiftieth percentile on a normal-curve grading system). This, of course, is impossible. The median on the system would be that point at which one-half the children score above the half-way point and one-half below. To illustrate the error in interpretation in the simplest of illustrations: If a test has only a few questions as simple as "Add two and three," all pupils score perfectly, or nearly so. But in a much more complex problem, "Extract the square root of 2,500 and the cube root of 1,020, etc.," the grades among, say, 100 students would tend

---

[9] John Goodlad, "Can Our Schools Get Better?" *Phi Delta Kappan*, Jan., 1979, p. 43. © 1979 Phi Delta Kappan, Inc. Used by permission.

to be distributed on a normal curve, half scoring above the midpoint (or 50th percentile) and half below that mark. Thus, the ease of misinterpreting the realistic meaning of a given pupil's score, or rank in a heterogeneous group, is great.

Questions about Exams for Other Professions

The current furor over alleged excesses in the use of standardized exams in the public schools for admission to college and for teachers appears to be spreading to other professional groups. For example, suspicions about testing for admission to the practice of law seem to be growing.

This whole turmoil about standardized testing and the use of cram courses and shortcuts to achieve membership in a given profession seems certain to grow. It takes no prophet to suggest that the examination syndrome is likely to grow more muddled—eventually ending in scandal. Such a fiasco will force professional organizations to set up safeguards, such as placing full reliance upon colleges and universities through rigid accreditation, and the possibility of withdrawal of such accreditation in case of any hanky panky.

New York Law and the Testing Movement

With the passage by New York State of a new graduation requirement, effective in 1981, the continuing hassle regarding the secrecy surrounding standardized testing appears to have taken a step toward full public understanding of the purpose of such testing.

The basic question is whether the standardized exams for admission to colleges (both the questions and the answers) should be kept secret. The new state law in New York requires that, within thirty days of the administering of such exams, both the questions and the correct answers will be made public. Test-makers are protesting vehemently this new provision. The College Entrance Examination Board, which administers its SAT test to 1,000,000 high school seniors each year, vigorously opposed it. The reason: There is no bottomless pit from which to secure new questions. The Educational Testing Service says it spends two years developing each version of its SAT test; once both questions and answers are made public, the test must be discarded.

Segments of the press see this legislation as a victory for parents and student groups backed by Ralph Nader. The testmakers are warning that development of wholly new tests will increase the cost to each student by $2.50, up to $13.00 instead of the present $10.50.

The new law was also opposed by the American College Testing Program and the Law School Admissions Council. The most vehement protest came from the American Medical Association (a total of 125 medical colleges) and the American Dental Association (60 dental schools). These two apparently plan not to offer tests in New York, so it appears that the 5,000 applicants for admission to medical schools and the 1,000 applicants for admission to dental schools each year will have to go elsewhere to take the tests.

Since the passage of the New York law requiring testing companies to return to students their scores on all questions, there have been two cases of students protesting to ETS that their answers to given questions, which were marked in error, were in fact correct. ETS changed their grades as a result. Prior to the passage of this law, ETS furnished such data only to the college to which the student was seeking admission.

The NEA severely criticized Educational Testing Service, which threatened to raise its rates to students because of the legislation and possibly to reduce special services to handicapped students and those who, for religious reasons, cannot take the tests on Saturdays. More than 8,000 delegates to the NEA convention called for similar federal truth-in-testing legislation and a congressional investigation of the powerful but unchecked testing industry.

The New York law, which became effective on January 1, 1980, affects only standardized admission tests for colleges and graduate schools given in that state. It will have nationwide effects by making available closely guarded scores.[10]

TEACHERS SPEAK OUT

At the annual NEA meeting in 1979, teachers vigorously protested the misuse of standardized tests in the schools. They complained that these tests are unfair, especially to minority students, are often invalid, are probably coachable, and quite often are out of date. They adopted a reso-

---

[10] NEA News Communications, July 16, 1979.

lution representing the policy of 1,800,000 teachers, about three-fourths of the total public school teaching staff. The NEA convention statement also called for a moratorium on the use of SAT scores until adequate coaching is available *for all students eligible to take the examination.* Also, an NEA policy statement urges Congress to investigate the tax-exempt status of the testing business, and to consider the need for further truth-in-testing legislation to guarantee access to all tests and statistical data held by such agencies. The testing industry was criticized as unregulated, unquestioned and unaccountable to consumers—a business which controls the careers of millions of Americans at critical points in their lives via impersonal standardized tests.

An allegation—perhaps far-fetched—that indicates the fallibility of standardized tests in predicting the academic promise or ability of an immature high school senior (or graduate) is the old facetious comment, "A statistician drowned in a stream which he has measured extensively and found to have an average depth of four feet." Of course, these tests will tend to be accepted at face value, or more—by those who are convinced that the wrong people are teaching, going to school, and even being born.

It seems to be quite obvious, in view of the current controversy about the use of standardized tests largely to determine which high school graduates will be admitted to higher education institutions—as well as to measure, in a fashion, those who are to be permitted to graduate from high school—that some other and more satisfactory means must be found. Francis Keppel, former U.S. Commissioner of Education and dean of the Harvard Graduate School of Education, suggests a program comparable to the National Assessment of Education Progress. This program has been developed by the Education Commission of the States (consisting of the chief state school officers of the respective state Departments of Education). He suggests evaluation designed to assess student achievement by scholars and teachers and by representatives of the public interest.

> The key question of this process is how well are we doing nationally, by region, by age, by sex and race and other categories. . . . You will notice that I am suggesting such an assessment for the general or liberal and civic aspects of higher education programs. It seems to me that the professional and technical programs are being more rigorously analyzed by a variety of means, and perhaps do not require a comparable method of assessment. . . .

. . . please note that I do not suggest that all students be assessed on all subjects; quite the opposite, a small sample of students should be assessed every few years, usually on one subject only, chosen from the familiar list of language and writing, mathematics and science, social science and foreign affairs. We are not interested, in order to make policy and programs, on data on individual students; we are in need rather of knowing whether a reasonable degree of accuracy of what is being learned in the state and nation—and whether we are doing better or worse than in the past. Such data can guide policy decisions by higher education in general, and by state governments in decisions on governance and financing.[11]

Thus, in the United States, we seem to be approaching a solution to the problem of a fair and just system for assessing the real accomplishments of our public schools. This search has been a difficult one, often filled with rancor and with bitter, but honest, differences of opinions. But that happens to be the route followed by a real, practicing democracy. Thus, when people finally reach a consensus on a difficult issue, it becomes a matter of victory "at long last."

A BALANCED VIEW OF TESTS

The question of the specific types and costs of appropriate testing methods is debatable. Care should be exercised to avoid extreme positions with reference to these two great problems. To leave the matter as stated in the preceding part of this chapter could easily be interpreted as one-sided. In fairness, there are some valid points on each side. Here are the comments of one who has pursued thorough study of this subject as a vehicle for preparing teachers.

The Scholastic Aptitude Test (SAT) has been attacked by NEA as being coachable, even though the majority of evidence shows that coaching effects have generally been small to negligible. A part of ETS's keeping coaching effects small has been the keeping of test material secret and confidential—not releasing test item material so that test items become public—and apparently NEA wants ETS to release the material. One certain outcome of releasing test material

[11] Francis Keppel, "Basic Policy on Student Achievement: A New Agenda Item," Address before the American Association of Higher Education, Mar. 5, 1980, p. 19. Used by permission.

will be that the tests become more coachable, as test-coaching schools will be able to secure easily large amounts of test material.

Also, a test is a sample of behavior from which other behavior is inferred. If a person does well on a test, the inference is that he or she would also have done well in the large domain that was sampled by the test but not included in the test itself. Coaching, in one sense, is the providing of information that will cause a person to do better on the test but not necessarily have higher standing in the behavior or learning domain that the test is supposed to be sampling. In one sense, short-term coaching for better test performance shows coaching to be in a way analogous to vitamin pills; brief coaching can be of considerable aid to those with a severe deficiency in test wiseness—to those who have had little or no experience in taking tests. The majority of those who have had years of experience in test-taking in a variety of settings are not helped by short-term test coaching any more than well-nourished people who eat plenty of vegetables and citrus are helped by taking vitamin pills. Thus, whatever small gains in scores to be had on such tests as SAT are more likely to accrue to underprivileged, educationally deprived students who manage to take coaching courses, than those at the well-to-do level with better educational opportunities.[12]

This teacher added the following comment: "The demand for making public the questions and the correct answers to each, while having some advantages, most certainly will add significantly to the cost of such tests."

---

[12] Statement by Donald G. Barker, Texas A & M University, in a recent conversation.

17

The Human Equation
and School Reform

ONE of the major—if indeed not the greatest—needs of America's venture into free, universal, compulsory education is a clear and treasured public vision of what such a concept can mean to the individual. The basic key to the inculcation of that vision is the infusion of added emphasis upon the human equation in the teaching of all of the nation's children.

There is an old but touching anecdote of a little first-grade boy being unexpectedly called upon by his teacher to repeat the Lord's Prayer. (Presumably this antedated court decisions regarding prayer in public schools.) The little boy nervously stood and hesitated a moment to summon the scattered fragments from his memory. Then he began: "Our Father who art in heaven, How'd you know my name? . . ." This is, at first glance, food for a good chuckle at the youngster's mixing of alliterative phrases. But there is also there, the timid reaching into space for the unquenchable and everlasting search for identity, for recognition, for affection—which is an inherited attribute of every sensitive human being.

We are members of a society that tends to idolize—on the surface, at least—the tough-acting, tough-sounding competitors whose worshipful cult is "Nice guys finish last," or "The tough guys will come in first." This is, in essence, the religion of the cynic and of the would-be elite; and of those who make their living in occupations of violence. The heart of the implication is that our society is a rough and tough replica of the jungle. Education, or whatever formative influences there are, must shape children into hardened automatons who spout the wild-animal sounds of conflict, who blabber slogans of violence such as "the brutal will survive." Loren Eiseley refuted this predatory religion bluntly as follows: "The truth is that if man at heart were not a tender creature toward his kind, a loving creature in a peculiarly special way, he would long since have left his bones to the wild dogs, in the African grasslands where he first essayed the great adventure of becoming human."[1] This idea was translated to the schoolroom by Bel Kaufman in the following statement: "I've run the gamut of every kind of school from the toughest to the so-called best. But whatever the class, whatever the student—whether he was a window smasher or an apple polisher—each one it seems to me, in his own private wilderness, was crying: 'Listen to me, look at me, pay attention to me, care about me!' "[2]

At the heart of all worthwhile, individual-centered education, directed at freeing the individual child from the bonds of superstition and fear and from bondage to cults and from the world of crudeness and self-centeredness, has been—and always will be—an inspired search for the roads that lead to satisfying answers to the question: "How'd you know my name?" For answers that lead to recognition, to personal identification of each individual whose presence graces (or disgraces) the school.

What a world of needless fears, agonizing soul-searching, keen hurt, and bitter suspicions could fade into nothingness, and be replaced by deeper sentiments of gratitude of parents toward teachers who perceive their role as leaders in the search for the magic key to such fruitful development of children. The great teacher knows instinctively that to each child—however modest, however self-effacing, however aggressive—the most precious name in all the world is his own. The eventual sense of gratitude of each child for this sensitive approach of a teacher will come to the child—fully and completely—only after the passage of many years, but the warmth and depth of that gratitude will tend to outreach the ability of expression. This is not a sickly, sentimental thing. It is a practical, down-to-earth, heart-warming fact of life for any gifted teacher to seek with great zeal.

It is a very human trait to reflect on an outstanding teacher as a "born teacher." This is an overworked phrase. It is extremely doubtful that there is such a thing as a born teacher. Of course, we are all born— all human beings. And, of course, each of us inherits certain potentials.

---

[1] Loren C. Eiseley, "An Evolutionist Looks at Modern Man," in *Readings for College Writers*, ed. H. J. Sacks, John Milstead, and Harvey M. Brown (New York: Ronald Press, 1962), pp. 361–71.

[2] Bel Kaufman, "Education and Social Change: Symposium," *Teachers College Record*, Dec. 1966, pp. 230–31.

But none of us is a "born engineer," or a "born medical doctor," or a "born minister," or a "born artist." If this were the case, then it would appear that each human being would inevitably be, or overwhelmingly tend to become, whatever his parents were—ministers, doctors, lawyers, or whatever. No. What each of us becomes is influenced by natural inheritances, and greatly so of course. But as important—or in all probability much more important—is what we acquire by education, by subtle influences that stick with us, and we become the sum of any number of incidents and experiences we collect along the road to maturity. The old saying, "Each of us is the sum total of all those we have met or things and events we have experienced," contains elements of truth.

All this is to say, first, that there is little reality to the born-teacher motto; second, that how to become a master teacher is a complex and varied thing—certainly as much as the sum total of the experiences and activities which have come to us.

What a multitude of discipline problems could be eased by the sensitive teacher who instinctively senses that what frequently occurs in behavior, which on the surface appears to be rebellious and outrageous, is actually the overwhelming urge of an immature child for recognition, for a kind word, for praise, however meager! The wise teacher will seek to find something, however small, however inconsequential to praise. And, let's not kid ourselves, not only is this true of immature children, it is also strongly true of adults.

As Abraham Maslow has noted:

> To understand the breadth of the role of the teacher, a differentiation has to be made between extrinsic learning and intrinsic learning. Extrinsic learning is based on the goals of the teacher, not on the values of the learner. Intrinsic learning, on the other hand, is learning to be and to become a human being, and a particular human being. It is the learning that accompanies the profound personal experiences in our lives . . . as I go back in my own life, I find my greatest education experiences, the ones I value most in retrospect, were highly personal, highly subjective, very poignant combinations of the emotional and the cognitive. Some insight was accompanied by all sorts of autonomic nervous system fireworks that felt very good at the time and which left as a residue the insight that has remained with me forever.[3]

---

[3] Abraham Maslow, "What Is a Taoistic Teacher?" in *Facts and Feelings in the Classroom*, ed. Louis J. Rubin (New York: Walker and Company, 1973), p. 159. Copyright © 1973 by Louis J. Rubin. Used with permission from the publisher, Walker and Company.

In a society which is changing so rapidly, naturally the ideals and concepts of values change accordingly. This means that every succeeding generation of adults, especially parents, tends to judge children's progress in education, and especially their sense of values, by what the parents knew as schoolchildren. Thus there will tend to be a sense of conflict between the two in almost every published comment or judgment of the adult generation with regard to the upcoming generation. Especially will there tend to be great divergence in values. The ideological conflicts are inevitable, by the very nature of human beings as products of vastly differing societies as well as of differing systems of education. An article in a professional journal quotes a high school honor student as writing:

> I am a sick American teenager.
>
> I am sick of being treated as a person
>   apart from the human race,
>   instead of as a part of it.
>
> I am sick of advice from columnists
>   who tell me that my parents
>   don't understand me; that
>   my world doesn't understand me;
>   that I don't understand myself;
>   that only they—and their
>   advertisers—do.
>
> I am sick of pressures from my school,
>   my church, and my community—
>   to be always on the go, running,
>   running, running—of the pressure
>   to win at any cost.
>
> I am sick of public apathy
>   in the affluent society created
>   by my parents' generation.
>
> I am born of my mother. I laugh.
>   I cry. I bleed red when I'm cut.
>
> I am a person.
>
> Treat me as one.[4]

---

[4] Blanche J. Martin, "What Do We Do about Our Values?" *Delta Kappa Gamma Bulletin*, Summer, 1968, p. 10. Used by permission.

THE PROBLEM OF DISCIPLINE—AND
THE HUMAN EQUATION

The matter of discipline constitutes the second half (depending on the individual viewpoint and stance of the beholder) of the basic and most vehement criticism of the public schools—that of lack of discipline. (The first criticism, of course, is of violence in the schools.) This was dealt with only in terms of physical aspects in Chapter 2. Extended comment was intentionally reserved for this chapter. First will be stressed the basics of the "human equation" approach, followed by some suggestions as to particular techniques.

Basic to the humanistic, personalized approach is for school personnel to modify the overemphasis upon physical aspects of discipline that was reputedly so well-nigh universal in the earlier history of the public schools. Generally referred to as "spare the rod and spoil the child," this pattern has been cited repeatedly herein. This is a prime example of mores tending to be passed on to succeeding generations and to be accepted by them often as a mark of respect and affection for their forebears. This approach served well while the nation was slowly evolving, in a virtually universal agricultural economy—with physical, emotional, and religious unity of basic beliefs, including child-rearing practices and methods of enforcing good behavior.

But the entire world has changed drastically in this century, and this change of pace has gained momentum, especially since World War II. Thus has the behavior of youth been altered, and that changed behavior has invaded the schools.

It is quite probable that, with all its alleged weaknesses, teacher education is weakest at the point of dealing with the misbehavior of schoolchildren. When parents and the public speak of discipline, they tend to think in terms of inflicting corporal punishment, the use of the lick in quelling misbehavior. Thus when they talk of the "lack of discipline in the schools," they are bemoaning the disuse of the old rod. This simple answer to all the untamed behavior of children in home or school is shopworn and obsolete—as we have said previously in dealing with the now-bankrupt practice of flailing of children, which we politely call corporal punishment.

In all probability, the next significant phase of teacher education is going to be devoted to new approaches to discipline in the schools. Parents and adults in general, especially those who have no children in school (and this group is in the majority of our adult population), have set up a constant, repetitive refrain to bring vigorous discipline back to the schools. If this means a return to the beating of children, one might as well call for the return of the horse-and-buggy days of travel. The plain fact is that this way of life is gone. It isn't coming back, no matter how loud the clamor.

Teacher education in the future will be compelled to provide a larger proportion of the education courses devoted to psychology and human behavior, and those subjects dealing with understanding of minds and motivations. The constant public demands for a return to the outmoded physical punishment of unseemly behavior patterns are but the nostalgic pleadings for a return of an era that is over. In the first place, children will not accept a return to such an era of discipline—and neither will their parents (with special emphasis upon those who are shouting the loudest about bringing back such discipline).

A Positive Approach to Discipline

So often the endorsement of a positive approach to discipline is equated with permissiveness or lax discipline. This is a faulty interpretation. Discipline is not only a good thing in schools, but it is an absolute must, for without it the greatest lesson is for naught. While the number and range of student legal rights have mushroomed in the past two or three decades, no student has a moral or legal right to disrupt the learning process. This is a fact which must be recognized by everyone.

There are many who believe that the only way to achieve a classroom climate that is civil enough for productive learning to ensue is through the use of corporal punishment. The proponents of positive discipline do not believe this. They offer the following reasons why corporal punishment should not be used in our schools.

Corporal punishment at its best is an inefficient way to maintain order in the classroom. Its power to deter misbehavior rapidly diminishes with increased repetition. There are those who contend that some students understand only this type of treatment, and that it is the only thing that will work for these students. They recognize that some students are dealt with in this manner in their homes, but they believe there is a great difference between a teacher's administering a whipping and the child's parents doing the whipping. If the parent-child relationship is good, that parent mixes love and concern for the child with the punishment. But the teacher's motive may be simply to get the child off his (the teacher's) back. Furthermore, opponents of corporal punishment acknowledge that those students who know only punishment may even *prefer* a whipping to a more logical approach to the problem. Most of us can remember that those serious talks with our parents were even less preferred than the spankings we got.

Proponents of a positive approach to discipline oppose the use of corporal punishment because it does not address the cause of the misbehavior. In fact, it may feed the cause. The student who misbehaves to gain attention succeeds when the teacher resorts to corporal punishment. We believe that school is too important, too serious, to be filled with disruptions. We hire teachers for their expertise; we do not hire them to babysit. Teachers who spend their days yelling at students and giving whippings are short-changing taxpayers.

Those teachers who use corporal punishment frequently find it the easiest and fastest solution. But in reality it solves nothing. We believe that teachers who depend on the rod to educate do a severe injustice to those teachers who depend on an interesting lesson to do the job. Corporal punishment, then, discourages teachers from seeking more effective means of discipline.

Teachers who contemplate using corporal punishment should think about its effects on the students and on their perspectives. First, it teaches them that might is right. Current research continues to show that student behavior is affected more by what their teachers *do* than by what they *say*. When teachers use corporal punishment, it affects their relationships with all the class members. Students know that the really good teachers are smart enough to cope with their problems in more professional ways. Think of the other professions which use beatings. Perhaps this is necessary with hardened criminals, but do we want our schools to emulate prisons?

Corporal punishment is often used because of the frustration of the teacher. It may result from a bad evening the night before or from other personal problems of the teacher. Whatever the cause, the results are that it portrays students as less than human. There is no way to measure the emotional damage it may cause today, next week, or several years from now.

Finally, the teacher who contemplates using corporal punishment must realize that by doing so he places himself in legal jeopardy. Most teachers do not realize the legal ramifications. For example, let's take the issue of due process. Before a teacher can legally use corporal punishment, that teacher must first try other approaches to solve the problem. Second, the student must be forewarned that to continue to repeat the behavior will result in corporal punishment. When the punishment is administered, it must be witnessed by another teacher or administrator. If the parents request, the teacher must provide a written account of the events leading up to the paddling and the efforts made to avoid it. Parents are becoming more aware of their legal rights. Teachers should take more precautions.

The Teacher's Role

"But," asks the teacher, "if not corporal punishment, then what can I do to maintain discipline?" First we suggest that most effort should be placed on trying to avoid problems, rather than on trying to become an expert in solving crises. A good lesson must *involve* students. Even some adults can concentrate for only a maximum of twenty minutes; teachers should not dominate the lessons for more than ten to fifteen minutes at a time. The teacher's role is then to closely supervise the students, walking among them, answering questions, giving assistance and forever watching them. By staying alert at all times the teacher can nip problems in the bud, before they cause disruptions, by simply walking over near the potential problem area or by using nonverbal expressions to let students know that he is aware of their attempt to disrupt but that the lesson is too important to allow for disturbances.

When serious problems do develop, a private talk with the offender is a must. The teacher sets the tone for the discussion, and that tone is very important. He might begin by telling the student that, as you know, we have a problem. It isn't exactly the teacher's problem or the student's problem; it belongs to both. Then the teacher may wish to ask the student what he thinks they should do about it. If the student refuses to cooperate, the teacher must impress upon him that the issue is one that must be resolved. Perhaps the two of us will have to ask others for help? If so, the logical people will be those who understand the school best (the administrators) and those who understand the child best (the parents or guardians, and perhaps the school counselor).

But this does not suggest that the teacher should threaten to call such a conference. On the contrary, teachers should never threaten students. This is mentioned because it is a viable option and probably the most logical next step if the behavior is not corrected. If the problem isn't corrected, the teacher must take action.

On even more serious circumstances, expulsions or suspensions may be necessary. Historically, suspensions from school have not been effective. In-house detention centers where students are isolated from their peers seem to offer much more promise.

Discipline is a serious problem in our schools today, and it must be attended to. But whatever approaches are used, those should address the cause of the problem and attempt to correct it, rather than suppressing the symptom. The type of discipline that all teachers should strive to attain in their classrooms is self-discipline. This requires that students be involved in the solving of problems which concern them.

Discipline Then and Now

A comment by Abraham Flexner, who firmly established his position as an eminent scholar with his now famous study of medical education and the resulting overhaul in its content and substance, indicates his impatience with the idea of specialized preparation for teachers, and with the whole idea that teaching per se could ever be taught. He held that such preparation consists solely of the mastering of a classical field of study. He concentrated upon Latin and Greek at Johns Hopkins University; deciding that college teaching was not for him, he took a preferred position as "assistant professor" (the terminology used in that day) in the Louisville High School to teach Latin and Greek.

> As I reflect upon the technical requirements now made on teachers in high schools and upon the insistence on some sort of technical training even of college teachers, I am amused to remember that at nineteen, having had only two years of college education . . . I not only obtained a post, but at the end of my first term I was promoted to a "full professorship." . . . I confess that I am no friend of teachers colleges . . . they are absurd institutions . . . admitting huge hordes

of persons, mostly without backgrounds and usually without scholarly ambition; and undertaking by minute training methods and statistics to produce a good teacher. . . . In my judgment, teaching would improve at once if our present teachers colleges were abolished. My first problem as a teacher was that of maintaining discipline among boys . . . I recollect, the fact that on the first or second day a boy by the name of Davis began an uproar in a beginning Latin class numbering about fifty. I made a quick decision. I left the room and went to Professor [principal or superintendent] Kirby's office to ask his assistance in restoring order, promising if he helped me then I should never ask his aid again. . . . Entering the room he raised his cane and with flashing eyes asked me to point out the culprit. When I pointed out Davis, he made for him . . . but taking discretion as the better part of valor, Davis made for an open window and jumped out.

"Is there anyone else?" he asked.

"No," I said. "The others will now behave themselves."[5]

Here is a case in which a teacher who knew only enough about discipline to run for the principal when a problem arose sneered at the notion that a preparing teacher might be taught the basics of handling such a case.

The indispensable key to good education and to good discipline is now, always has been, and always will be the superior teacher. Consider the following quotation from John Steinbeck:

My eleven-year-old son came to me recently and, in a tone of patient suffering, asked, "How much longer do I have to go to school?"

"About fifteen years," I said.

"Oh! Lord," he said despondently. "Do I have to?"

"I'm afraid so. It's terrible and I'm not going to try to tell you it isn't. But I can tell you this—if you are very lucky, you may find a teacher and that is a wonderful thing."

"Did you find one?"

"I found three," I said. . . .

My three had these things in common—they all loved what they were doing. They did not tell—they catalyzed a burning desire to know. . . .

I shall speak only of my first teacher because, in addition to other things, she was very precious.

---

[5] Abraham Flexner, "Teaching Schools," ch. 5 in *I Remember* (New York: Simon & Schuster, 1940), pp. 66–73. Copyright © 1940 by Abraham Flexner; © 1960 by Jean Flexner Lewison and Eleanor Flexner. Reprinted by permission of Simon & Schuster, a Division of Gulf & Western Corporation.

She aroused us to shouting, bookwaving discussion. She had the noisiest class in school and didn't even seem to know it. We could never stick to the subject, geometry or the chanted recitation of the memorized phyla. Our speculation ranged the world. She breathed curiosity into us so that we brought in facts or truths shielded in our hands like captured fireflies.

She was fired and perhaps rightly so . . . for failing to teach the fundamentals. . . . She left her signature on us, the literature of the teacher who writes on minds. I suppose that, to a large extent, I am the unsigned manuscript of that high school teacher. What deathless power lies in the hands of such a person.

I can tell my son who looks forward with horror to fifteen years of drudgery that somewhere in the dusty dark a magic may happen that will light up the years . . . if he is very lucky. . . .

I have come to believe that a great teacher is a great artist and there are as few as there are any other great artists. It might even be the greatest of the arts since the medium is the human mind and spirit.[6]

If for one generation the United States could achieve the ideal rapport between parents and the teachers of their children, there would be a revolution in human relationships approaching the ideal. The parents could gradually and in good conscience drop the catchy slogans such as "the extravagant public schools," "the sloppy teaching in our schools," "the social promotion gimmicks schools have adopted to cover up their failures to teach well," and so forth.

Herein are comments some teachers have made about parents who have such easy answers for all the problems of discipline and of teaching. Of course, it is but natural for a mother to propose the tactics she has found effective in her own home with her own children. An entirely different set of circumstances arises in a schoolroom with twenty-five or thirty or more children and one teacher. The solitary parent—quite naturally—finds it difficult to visualize the diversity of conditions, behaviors, outlooks on life, and patterns of ideals in a group that represents as many homes as there are children in most public school classrooms.

The following are comments about given situations teachers face and the expected reactions of some parents. One teacher ends her case exam-

---

[6] Quoted in *The Education of Teachers—Curriculum Programs*, Report of the Kansas TEPS Conference (Washington, D.C.: National Education Association, 1959), p. 71. On this point see also Louise Sharp, ed., *Why Teach?* (New York: Holt, 1957), p. 260.

ple, directed presumably at a critical parent, with the rhetorical question: "Have you ever wondered what you [a parent] would do if you were confronted with a problem like that and it was your responsibility to handle it?"

Another teacher is concerned about the differing values from one home to another. She wonders about the boy who breaks his glasses at home; his mother requests the school insurance form for use in requesting payment for the glasses, saying they were "broken on the boy's trip from home to the school." Yet the same mother throws a tantrum if her son is dismissed from the school's athletic team for cheating on an exam.

Or consider the parents' organization which clamors for the schools to emphasize home-and-family-life education, because of the worsening divorce rate, child abuse, juvenile delinquency, and so forth. Members direct vitriolic criticism at the school board and the teaching staff for invasion of the privacy of the home.

Unity of Administrators and Teachers—Rapport in the Teaching Profession

Moreover, in the educational world which must come to the United States, there is an imperative. The gulf between administrators and classroom teachers, which at the moment in most schools and states appears to be widening, must be closed, and a genuine rapport must be established. This sounds like a rather elementary and easily soluble problem. It is not. One has only to review the worsening relationship which has split the two groups into warring camps. Since about the mid-1950s there has been an increasingly tense battle between the National Education Association and the American Federation of Teachers, with some significant gains by each organization. The NEA eventually (in the late 1960s and the early 1970s) was forced to adopt a steadily increasing posture of what appeared to the general public as radicalism.[7] In short, it was compelled by the flow of events and the dictates of its membership to condone—if not to advocate aggressively—the use of collective bargaining and the strike, under the softer-sounding names "professional negotiations" and "sanctions."

The process the NEA adopted in 1962 worked, *but all too slowly;* and

---

[7] T. M. Stinnett, *Turmoil in Teaching* (New York: Macmillan, 1968), p. 406. For a description of the battle for membership loyalty of teachers, see pp. 66–82.

the flow of the times, and its membership, dictated this action. Thus, whether administrators liked it or not, school boards and public opinion forced them to disassociate themselves from teachers' organizations, and from what was generally viewed as tactics of organized labor. This split only added to the age-old controversy regarding the development of status hierarchies in teaching.

Healing the Breach between Administrators and Teachers

Since the beginnings of the public schools in the United States, there has existed in varying degrees a hierarchical kind of relationship between administrators and classroom teachers. Historically, there has also been a hierarchical relationship between personnel in higher education, based upon ranks among the teaching staff. In the first case, the best way to describe the structure is to characterize it as prestige relationships—gradations in authority relationships. At the college level, the gradations are based on levels of preparation, years of experience, and judged quality of performance.

Of course, in the lower schools this relationship was handed down from the earliest one-room rural schools, where a man was employed to keep under control the larger boys. These days are often referred to as having the "Ichabod Crane" type of school setup. Here probably began the "spare the rod and spoil the child" philosophy of the function of the school, and the concept of the nature of disciplinary needs. Then, as years passed and the number of these one-room rural schools proliferated, and as the lowly subscription schools were replaced by tax-supported ones, women began to be employed. As towns and cities emerged, larger school systems had to be created. Again the hierarchical status of men, pretty well fixed in the public mind by now, became predominant—especially in the roles of superintendents and principals. As the nation's population grew and industrial development emerged, the cluster of larger schools grew, and the number of positions for women increased rapidly.

After 1900, two great changes occurred. First, the number of school districts and schools began to decline (through consolidations) (Figure 17.1 shows this decline between 1939 and 1976). Second, the education requirements for teachers escalated rapidly, both in general education and specialization, and in time in professional studies. Thus the number of both men and women employed in the schools increased. To cite the

FIGURE 17.1.
Number of Local Public School Systems: United States,
1939–40 to 1975–76

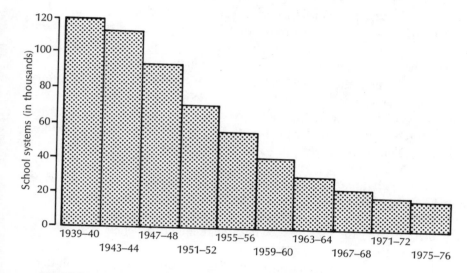

NOTE: Reprinted from National Center for Education Statistics, *Digest of Educa-tion Statistics, 1976 Edition* (Washington, D.C.: United States Government Printing Office, 1977).

extent of these growths: the number of school districts in the United States as late as 1930 was about 122,000. Consolidation had reduced this number to about 15,000 in 1979. Virtually all of these now are able to provide high school education for every child in the district.

For years many school districts existed legally without offering any schools at all. They existed simply as tax havens for large landowners, voting only such taxes as were needed to send the few school-age children on tuition to adjoining districts.

Modern centralization, of course, requires a sizable increase in the number of administrators as well as in the number and specializations of classroom teachers. But with the rising costs of living, the rapidly increasing industrialization of the United States brought on an increasing trend toward specialized preparation and job specialization, with a consequent decline in the commonality of job and responsibility concepts. In addition, in the 1950s, the impact of the organization of teacher affiliates with the AFL-CIO, with its labor union aggressiveness and tactics, began to appear among public school teachers across the country. Especially was this impact a powerful force in the larger cities.

The hopes of organized labor to make inroads upon the membership of the professional associations of teachers, both state and national, were brought bluntly into the open by James Carey, vice-president of the AFL-CIO, before the annual convention of the National Education Association at Denver in the summer of 1962. He criticized the teachers for thinking that their craft is a profession, and therefore somehow above the work of union members, and cautioned that both economics and integrity necessitate unionism in the teaching field. He referred to teachers' strikes in New York City in 1960 and 1962 and to recognition of the teachers' union (AFL-CIO).

Although James Carey's speech shocked most of the audience, it nevertheless had a telling effect upon teachers across the United States. It did not create a stampede to join the union organizations, but it certainly escalated the already growing impatience of teachers with the inactivity of their own organizations.

Thus, at the same Denver convention of the NEA, two resolutions were passed, "Adoption of the Use of Professional Negotiations" and "Professional Sanctions." These were weapons similar in purpose to those of *collective bargaining* (for agreeing upon terms of working conditions and salaries) and the *strike* (for enforcing the demands of teachers in cases of impasse or failure to reach mutual agreements). These two processes were not, at the time of adoption, backed by the force of law (as the two processes used by labor have been since 1935).

Until such legislation can be secured for teachers, there will continue to be wide schisms between classroom teachers and administrators. A basic reason for the development of a widening breach between administrators and teachers was, in the absence of federal or state laws sanctioning and requiring or permitting the use of these processes, that school boards forbade administrators (particularly superintendents) from participation in such processes. Administrators were their legal representatives as executives.

Another illustration arises in the following incident from the late 1960s, when the movement toward collaboration of the total teaching profession in the use of professional negotiations and sanctions was adopted as policy by the NEA. This was done to avoid the established and legally sanctioned processes used by the labor unions. A professional association of administrators, affiliated with and housed in the NEA building in Washington, sent its membership an explanation of the two NEA processes. This memorandum explained in detail that these processes were designed as professional ones, to avoid the use of more militant or extreme processes of organized labor. Necessarily, the explanation used the phrases "consult with teachers" and "talk with teachers."

Only a handful of negative comments were received from the membership. But the superintendent in one of the nation's largest cities wrote: "Throughout this document you refer to 'Talking with Teachers.' Hell, I don't talk with teachers; I tell them."

That is, of course, regal sounding, and was so meant. But it is one of the root causes of the development of the alleged militancy of teachers, and of the steadily widening schism between teachers and administrators in some school districts.

A key indication of the gulf between schoolteachers and administrators is that, since the late 1960s, virtually all of the professional associations of administrators have withdrawn from affiliation with the National Education Association and have moved out of the NEA building. Ultimately, if this trend continues, this will mean that the NEA will become an organization largely representing classroom teachers in the public schools. This is unfortunate for all segments of teaching, from preschool through the university.

Causes of Alienation

A crisp summary of the causes of the presently existing breach between administrators and classroom teachers has been suggested by John R. Hoyle:

1. Collective bargaining (negotiations, unionism, labor vs. management)
2. Teacher evaluation (supervision vs. evaluation)
3. Lack of mutual trust (between administrators and teachers)
4. Lack of accurate and current information (poor communications)
5. Sound administrators and teachers' attitudes toward life and work.[8]

---

[8] John R. Hoyle, "Teachers vs. Administrators," *Education Digest*, May, 1979, pp. 20–22.

The Matter of Pyramids

The relationships of hierarchical authority patterned upon the pyramid should be and are becoming, to a marked degree, obsolete. The pyramid inevitably must be inverted. The apex of the differentiated staffing model is of this type. It is disturbing to teachers.

Moreover, because the status factor is implied in the upper peak of the pyramid, it tends to beckon invitingly to teachers to move out of teaching to a status category.

The present status factor in such an arrangement appears to denigrate the value of teaching, thus creating among teachers a feeling of frustration and resentment. This same hierarchical status seems to permeate the several levels of teaching, making successive steps or positions from grade one through grade eight. Also, gradations according to subject matter in the high school fields appear to be sequential and successive in terms of status. And, of course, these status positions exist in higher education. There is status by rank: instructor, assistant professor, associate professor, and professor. There is another prestige ladder to climb, from untenured to tenured, and sometimes prerequisites such as professional categories accompany these gradations. Also there are directorships in certain special areas.

Growing demands, especially at the elementary and secondary levels, indicate that these pyramids must be upturned or inverted so there can grow in our educational structure the values and the prestige of all those who serve faithfully and well their particular clienteles—whether those clienteles be at the kindergarten, primary, intermediate, junior high school, high school, or college levels.[9]

COMMUNITY EDUCATION AND/OR SCHOOLS

Some basic attributes of what has come to be called community schools and/or community education originated in the colonial period. This trend became pronounced with the establishment of public schools supported by taxation. There were relatively large numbers of parochial or church schools in the early years of the nation. These, of course, held to the no-

---

[9] Phillip T. West and T. M. Stinnett, "Schools and Pyramids," *Elementary School Journal*, Nov., 1975, pp. 63–69.

tion that the church and the schools were inseparable. As the public schools proliferated, the concept grew that the publicly supported schools should become an integral part of the community. An adult evening school was founded in 1810; Kentucky and New York founded community schools in the 1830s. The first state law authorizing such schools was passed in Ohio during the 1840s, and evening schools began operating in Cincinnati in 1841.[10] These evening schools were chiefly schools for adults. There were evening lectures in the schoolhouse on subjects of popular interest, and some extension work by state universities. Public funds for the support of evening school for adults were first provided in 1865, by the board of education in Chicago. By the beginning of the 1890s, use of school facilities by the community had become more popular. In fact, a few years earlier, laws in several states were enacted providing for the use of school buildings by others for purposes in addition to regular school.

By 1900, the community school concept was beginning to reach full flowering. In 1915–16 it was reported that the school was being used as a community center in 518 cities. Playgrounds were for the use of the public; buildings provided space for lectures for adults on common problems, entertainment, social meetings, public meetings, dramatics, social dancing, reading and study. It was estimated that school buildings were open on 60,000 evenings during the year, with some 4,500,000 persons in attendance.

Of course, the real meaning of this movement was to make the schoolhouse the center for the life of the community where every citizen could participate. Particularly was this true in the one-room rural schools, where often the school was the center for church services (for all denominations), public meetings, civic discussions, and so forth—for the compelling reason that there was no other place for such meetings. Alternative centers were available only in towns and cities. And since there were no highways and the only transportation was the horse and buggy or wagon, such meetings had to be near people's homes.

The Morrill Act, passed in 1862, established the land-grant colleges, largely financed with federal funds to permit offerings in science in agriculture. By 1919, revisions of the law provided that courses for untrained adults in farming and industry could be offered. This law required that

[10] E. Cubberly, *Public Education in the United States* (Boston: Houghton Mifflin, 1919), p. 418.

these courses be given in the public schools. The Smith-Lever Act of 1913 and the Smith-Hughes Act of 1917 further encouraged the development of these fields.

As the Great Depression of the 1930s developed, the acute need of the community school concept flowered. The Flint, Michigan, community school program originated in 1935. Credit for the Flint development is attributed to Frank Manley, who was successful in soliciting the support of Charles S. Mott, of General Motors, in making the school facilities readily available for community use. With financial aid from the Mott Foundation, facilities were made available after regular school hours.

Also, during the early years of the Depression, many schools in agricultural areas, especially in the South, were able to employ two agriculture and two home economics teachers. One of each of the teachers spent full-time out in the community helping individual farmers to improve the productivity of the soil by teaching them better methods of farming, terracing of the land, better crop selection, and orchard improvement. The roving home economics teacher held community meetings of farm wives in strategically located homes, as well as at the school building, teaching improved techniques of canning vegetables and meats, and so forth. The teacher of agriculture also held meetings of all the community farmers on some nights at the schoolhouse. The community school began to improve from the experiences of teachers and others who had firsthand experience with such work.

In the meantime, the Alfred P. Sloan Foundation, the Kellogg Foundation, the General Education Board, and others began to provide additional support for school systems to extend their influence and assistance in efforts to improve the quality of living in the school community.

From 1950 to the early 1960s, the (Flint model) program was restricted to Michigan. But the movement extended greatly during the 1960s and 1970s. Here are some of the developments. In Michigan in 1963, the Mott Foundation established a community education center at Northern Michigan State University. This, in time, became a regional center for the spread of the community school education concept and procedures. By the early 1970s, a national center was established at Flint, as the central focus for the movement. Regional centers expanded rapidly as the program broadened. This expansion led to the establishment of the National Community Education Association. The basic idea, as has been detailed, goes back to the colonial period; as society becomes more complex, the needs for this basic program will increase. This is the "human equation" in education, involving every person in the school district in the process.

Some Contents of Community School Programs

Of course, as the community-school idea spread and more communities became involved, the tasks which the schools undertook broadened. Naturally, the variety of subjects offered in the schools will vary according to the size of the community involved.

One school system, in a university city of about 80,000, offers a total of 114 courses during a regular school term, in the high school, middle school, and two elementary schools. Classes are scheduled mostly in the evenings, with some being offered on Saturdays as well. The school system is able to recruit many local citizens, well qualified in specialized fields, to teach some courses at little cost. There are a few courses dealing with extremely important needs: rape prevention seminars, resuscitation seminars, crime prevention seminars, and energy seminars. For these especially urgent subjects relating to the general welfare, the schools can enlist the aid of state- or city-supported special agencies, such as the local police department or the State Energy Commission.

There are courses in cake decorating, advanced sewing, conversational Spanish, German, Japanese, typing, shorthand, woodshop, food preparation, home decoration, sewing, guitar, puppeteering, furniture repairing, house plants, auto mechanics (for ladies), square dancing, ballet, disco dancing, and tap dancing. Courses are offered in almost every activity in which people engage or would like to engage. The courses offered will vary from community to community, depending upon occupational activities, educational level, minority interests, and needs.

Such courses serve a dual need. The first is to serve adults, and children in a few instances where their needs are not met in the regular school program. This tends to help education to become a lifelong process. Second, the citizens—as many as can be attracted to participate—become increasingly involved in community interests; they contribute to the planning of the content and extension of the schools' usefulness to the entire community. This may never reach the ideal of total involvement of all adults, but a rapidly increasing proportion can be attracted to become involved.

A Community School in a Ghetto

One who wants to learn of a real life-giving community school that was built and flourished in one of the most unlikely settings should read the account in *The Heart Is the Teacher*, by Leonard Covello (with Guido D'Agostino).[11] Covello himself was a boy immigrant from Italy. He wrote in his introduction:

> In this long lifetime of teaching (45 years plus continuing years after retirement as a consultant), I have learned much about the ways of immigrant people and their American-born children. I was an immigrant boy myself. I know what the American school can do to maintain family unity. I also know how the school can function as the integrating force in our democracy and in the molding of young citizens. . . . As a consultant, I am trying to give to the latest of our immigrants—the Puerto Ricans—what I tried to give to the Italians and Negroes, to the Irish and Germans, to the rest of the nationalities and races that make up that human mixture known as East Harlem: my time, affection and above all, my understanding. For only he who has suffered—the degrading insults of *Wop* or *Nigger* or *Spick* or *Mick* or *Kike*—can readily understand.[12]

Covello's portion of the ghetto was Italian. With all the babble of tongues, the vicious infighting among different racial groups, he somehow managed to mold a high school—the Benjamin Franklin High School—into a model ghetto school by his understanding, sympathy, and love for his job and the people he served. One of the almost unbelievable things he did was turn this high school into a community education center, by mobilizing the parents and nonparents and the youth in school into a giant effort to create a program that was the dynamo of true Americanism—a true community school in every constructive sense of the phrase.

Number of Community School Programs in the United States

There were, in 1978, a total of 14,467 school districts in the United States, of which 1,525 had community school programs (10.5% of the total).

---

[11] Leonard Covello and Guido D'Agostino, *The Heart Is the Teacher* (New York: McGraw-Hill, 1958).

[12] Ibid., pp. 1–2. Reprinted by permission of the author's agent, Blassingame, McCauley & Wood.

In these 14,467 school districts, there were a total of 87,430 school buildings, and a total of 6,964 community school buildings. This means that 8 percent of the school buildings in the United States were community school buildings. In Michigan 258 districts, out of a total of 534 school districts, have community school programs, or 48.3 percent of the total districts. Alaska has 30 of 51 districts with community school programs, 58.8 percent of the total districts. Alaska is number one in the percentage of its total districts having community school programs.

Institute for Responsive Education

The Institute for Responsive Education (IRE) was created in 1973 to help citizens participate in educational decision-making. This is a right and a responsibility in any phase of a democracy such as exists in the United States. The shortcoming of this philosophy is that it does not necessarily obtain as an essential right of citizenship—the designated leadership, paid employees, tend (more by default of citizens than by philosophy) to assume unilateral responsibility for decision-making in planning and directing educational policy in a given community.

To secure the needed citizen participation, school boards and executive officers (as well as the general school staff) must consistently plan ways for involving adults of the school community in the development of policies and services. Of course, the local school board has the legal responsibility to adopt or reject the proposed policies.

Below is given the basic philosophy of the Institute for Responsive Education:

- Voting for representatives is not sufficient for a healthy, democratic society. Broad-based grass-roots participation in developing and overseeing policy is essential.
- Those affected by public agency decisions should have a voice in making those decisions.
- Those who pay for and are served by public institutions should determine institutional policies, aided but not dominated by experts and professionals.
- Equity and justice require a reallocation of power to include minorities which, legally or practically, have been excluded from decision-making and influence at all levels in the public schools.

- Over the past century, decision-making in urban public school systems has become excessively centralized. It is often bureaucratic in structure and style, controlled by educators insufficiently accountable to parents and citizens, and inflexible in the face of a changing social and economic environment.
- Educational change requires participation of those affected by the change. Top-down and outside-in models of educational reform do not work. Citizens have proven their ability to make educationally sound decisions; school systems which provide for community access and involvement fare better when faced with hard decisions than systems without such provisions.
- As the primary teachers of their children, parents have the responsibility and right to inform themselves about and require responsiveness from their children's schools.

IRE does *not* have a commitment to any particular forms or styles of citizen participation but recognizes a need for diverse structures and strategies. Neither does the organization advocate any particular substantive educational programs, that is, open education, back-to-basics, career education.

Community Education

In its essence, community education seeks to involve in the learning process not only children but also parents and the community. This means a shift from the exclusive concept of teaching children to one of identifying the needs, problems, and wants of the community and to helping to meet these needs. This effort is directed toward improvement of the entire community.

Someone has described community education as an aggressive philosophy of education, for improved community development. One of the great strengths of this movement is that it intentionally seeks the involvement of the total community of people (of all ages) in the planning of school programs. Regular meetings of citizens are scheduled for once or twice a month; meetings seek to involve citizens in identifying pressing problems of the community and suggesting how the schools can help solve them. Such a concept and philosophy would provide opportunities for citizens of a given community to identify needs which the school could aid in correcting, for example, the prevalence of specific types of violence in the community; or the weakness in the teaching of the basics; or truancy and the development of plans to stop it. In other words, the community school concept could serve to detect and help correct weaknesses in the school programs. Aided by community backing, then, the schools' tasks are made much easier to carry out and much more effective. And, in many respects, the involvement of adults who are not parents of school-age children could make a great difference in the tax support provided for schools.

Importance of Adult Support of Schools

Quite naturally, the adult who has a child or children attending the public schools is going to have more than a mild interest in those schools. Thus, at least a portion of the continuing criticisms of the schools may be attributed to the taxpayer and voter who has no children attending the schools. This is a considerable proportion of the adult population of the United States.

In 1969, when Gallup first began to survey the public concerning its attitudes about the public schools, 51 percent of the respondents were parents of school-age children, of which 44 percent were parents of children attending the public schools. In 1978, only 32 percent were parents of school-age children and only 28 percent were parents of public school children. According to the Census Bureau this trend will continue. By 1990, there will be more Americans over the age of 55 than will be enrolled in all schools grades K–12.

The Spread of the Community School Idea

As has been previously stated, the community school concept does date back, philosophically at least, to our first schools. From the beginning, the idea was an integral part of the concept of the "people's schools." Only during this century has the flow of circumstances and the developments in society—the growth of population and technology, and the resulting growth in the complexity of life—made it essential that the schools seek the means by which to become again the people's schools in every community. Thus the once-close relationship could be restored.

ESSENCE OF TEACHING AND SCHOOLS

The "Human Equation" is eloquently pictured in William Jeremiah Burke's *Not for Glory*, containing descriptions of the finalists for National Teacher of the Year over a period of seven years (1961–67). In the brief, perceptive description of the methods of teaching of each of the fifty-four finalists, superlative warmth, depth, and perceptiveness are depicted, the out-reaching search for the key to the highest and the best in every child. There are no resorts to cheap theatrics, or obviously faked shows of "sob-sister" emotionalism. But there is beautifully pictured, in simple, unpretentious, and eloquent language, the irresistible spiritual pull of the dedicated teacher.

We reproduce below two vignettes of the teachers described in that book. Helen "Missy" Adams, a kindergarten teacher from Cumberland, Wisconsin, was National Teacher of the year in 1961.

> When four-year-olds in Cumberland, Wisconsin (population 1,872) are told, "Next year, you'll go to school to Missy," . . . they know —and love—the town's only kindergarten teacher. . . . She always knew what she wanted most, to be a teacher. The youngsters gave her the name "Missy" because they had difficulty in enunciating, "Miss Helen Adams." It was a joy to watch the room and her children. The room was bright and cheerful with lots of windows and gay child-art, lots of little people's toys and picture books. There was a piano, and a phonograph and home-made drums . . . with these the children learned to keep time to the records and Missy's baton. There was nap-time on brightly colored mats. Afterwards they drank milk together, drew pictures, tried out new skills, heard records and sat entranced while Missy read a story. . . . She was a wizard at handling a small child's large problems. . . . One boy would lie down on the floor by the door and cower like a frightened animal until his parents came for him at the end of the day. Missy tried everything. Nothing worked. Then she gave him a Halloween mask to wear. The mask gave the boy security. . . .
>
> . . . Some are inclined to overlook humor in the Kindergarten. It is here and Missy found it, and enjoyed it. An example: One day the group was sitting in a square, listening to stories, etc. The kids couldn't sit still . . . it was one of those days. . . . They wiggled like worms on hot ashes. . . . So I told them how much they had disappointed me. One boy looked at his playmates and said, "Don't you know you are not supposed to disappoint Missy or God!" We

were working on vocabulary enrichment and I was trying to challenge them with new words. So I asked if anyone knew another word for big and another for little. . . . After a minute of real concentration one little boy yelled, "King size and regular."

Missy's philosophy of teaching [is that] the basis of all good teaching is a genuine love for children . . . with many, teaching is just a job . . . with some it is a profession . . . with me, it is more than just another job, more than a profession—it is a way of life. Missy went summers to college until she finished her Bachelors and Masters degrees. "Do you need a Ph.D. to teach Kindergarten in a small town?" She replied, "The children of Cumberland deserve the best I can give them."[13]

Mrs. Lawana Trout, an English teacher at Charles Page High School, Sand Springs, Oklahoma, was National Teacher of the Year in 1964.

Lawana Trout was a composite of all the good teachers I had ever met. I came to use her as a standard when I walked into a classroom. Her stamina amazed me.

But her tenderness touched me deeply. I arrived in Sand Springs, Oklahoma, late in the afternoon and Lawana's classes were over. . . . Her school day never ends. She often went to see students who couldn't attend classes. This was such a day.

We got in her car and drove to the poorer section of town. "I'm going to read to a sweet little girl who has cataracts, and hasn't been coming to school. She needs an expensive operation, but her parents can't afford it. . . ."

We stopped in front of an unpainted, sagging house. . . . The front yard overflowed with debris, we had to pick our way through it. A woman in shabby clothes and straggling hair asked us to come in. On a bed half-dressed lay her husband, recuperating from a heart attack. . . . In the next room sat little Mary. . . . "I've brought you a reading of 'The Raven' on a record, Mary. Today we are going to study Edgar Allen Poe." I have never seen such a beautiful child. She was small, soft spoken, quick minded. Lawana and I took turns reading to her and she retained every word.

"These people are proud," Lawana said when we left. "They are not defeated. They have just had a run of hard luck." . . . Most people have one of two views regarding my attempts to heal ravaged adolescent lives. . . . Some people stereotype me as a "do gooder." At the other extreme, my friends and associates preach against my

[13] William J. Burke, *Not for Glory* (New York: Cowles Education Corporation, 1967), pp. 25–30.

sacrifice of time, labor and peace of mind for a cause that one lone individual cannot perform.

. . . I touch the face of humanity each day in my classroom, for I teach the ambitious and indolent, the brilliant and the slow, the mature and the immature.

. . . As a teacher, I have an important image to paint for the public as well as for my students. An ugly act or a thoughtless word from me means a disfiguration of the image of my profession. I accept the fact that to the public I am "education" . . . I am aware that I need to grow constantly in knowledge and experience. . . . The Trout home was a cultural center for high school students. They came to play, to read, to make dates, to have parties, to find the counsel they needed. Once Lawana risked her life to help straighten out a member of a teen-age gang, even facing threats from the boy's father. . . . The evening I was there, a teenage girl joined us for dinner. "She's been living with us for weeks," Lawana said later. "Her step-father is an alcoholic and he mistreats her and her mother. The girl called me one night about around 2:30. 'Come and get me,' she cried. I hurriedly dressed and jumped in the car and drove over and rescued her from her step-father. She's been staying with us ever since. I want her to finish her term at high school, and I want to keep her from harm."[14]

At the conclusion of his book, Burke wrote: "My microscopic examination of fifty-four separate school systems encouraged me to believe that nothing in American life can match the vigor and importance of the classroom confrontation of minds. Therein lies our future. There is no turning back. The kinds of teachers I met are not content to look upon education as something finished. No teacher, no American, can afford that luxury."[15]

Of course, the above vignettes from Burke's book are exceptional cases, but there are thousands of such teachers in American public schools. It is high time that the American public recognizes this fact and acknowledges its indebtedness to the system of universal education for all American children—regardless of creed, class, or circumstance—as a major pillar in the structure of this nation's greatness.

Yes, make no mistake about it, the human equation is at the very heart of superior teaching. It is the keystone of warm, effective discipline. And, best of all, it will be remembered and cherished all the days of a person's life.

---

[14] Ibid., pp. 116–119.
[15] Ibid., p. 206.

18

New Frontiers
for the Teaching Profession

THE current controversy over the alleged weaknesses and failures of the public schools is by no means a new one. It is only one among many that have marked the existence of these schools.

As would be expected in a democracy, this controversy is an oft-recurring phenomenon. First, it is a basic right of a free society, as set forth in the First Amendment. Second, schools deal with the most cherished of all the possessions of our citizens: their children. These schools have been established and supported through the years for the basic purpose of educating those children. Third, next to the government itself, and defense of the nation militarily, the schools are one of the most expensive of all our formal public establishments. Fourth, when the people cease to quarrel about the contents and procedures of public education, that is likely to be a bad omen instead of a good one, a bad omen because it could indicate (1) a questionable belief in existing public behavior and morality; (2) a false posture of security; or (3) a fatuous belief that perfection in intellectual achievement had finally been reached.

Not only should criticism of the schools be expected as a continuing exercise of the people, but it should be encouraged—particularly by those who direct and staff the schools. As wearisome as many such criticisms may be, and as farfetched as they may at times seem, such criticisms compel those in charge of the schools constantly to reexamine their work, its successes and its failures. The very gesture of answering such criticisms compels a search for facts that often do not appear on the surface, and a digging to discover conditions as they exist in reality—not just in the imaginations of the beholders. Of course, there is inherent too in a democracy the restraint of a deep sense of balance, fairness, and justice of

255

an educated citizenry. These qualities are essential safeguards against the possibility of a wanton perversion of freedom. Too, such a search serves to underscore, as nothing else could, the need for both the public and teachers to renew constantly the quest for the means by which teaching can become an accepted and respected profession. Does this search imply that teachers need to follow the pattern or adopt the procedures of other professions which have achieved public recognition as true professions? The answer appears to be that teachers should, at least to some degree, do both. But actually they should blaze their own distinctive pathway, because professions are like individual human beings: Each is different from all others. Each is unique in a very real sense.

In a tentative sort of way, this probing effort has been underway in teaching in the United States since the formation of the National Education Association in 1857 (the first name of this association was the National Teachers Association) and the founding of the respective state education associations, some of which antedated the NEA.

In 1968, *Turmoil in Teaching* was published, a historical account of the intense conflict between the American Federation of Teachers and the National Education Association during the late 1950s and the first half of the 1960s.[1] The conflict, basically, was for the loyalties and membership, largely of teachers in the public schools, but not exclusively so. *It was also a conflict of philosophies.* One philosophy had its aegis in the labor movement; the other, in the concept that a profession is autonomous, that it is self-regulating, self-directing, and self-dependent. One philosophy sought to utilize the procedures of organized labor; the other sought independent and professional processes to gain its objectives.

The book was attacked from some quarters as "anti-labor" because of its espousal of the second philosophy described above. The author's point of view was that a profession worthy of the name solves its own problems; it does not borrow power from external sources. Teaching should not incur obligations to any one segment of the American public. This view does not imply an anti-labor bias. Any intelligent man who knows the long history of the struggle of working people to better their lot is aware of the progress that unionization has helped bring to the wage earners of this country. One thing said in *Turmoil in Teaching* has proven to be true—and that truth has been at the heart of the growing militancy of

---

[1] T. M. Stinnett, *Turmoil in Teaching* (New York: Macmillan, 1968).

teachers: "Teachers' organizations of all types have in large measure become irrelevant to the needs of teachers."[2] This is changing, but there still continues the feverish search for the processes which will bring about the conditions teachers should have in a great profession.

Turmoil in Teaching predicted the emergence of a sustained period of conflict in which teacher militancy would emerge as a way of life. This proved to be an understatement of the extent of that militancy, and the speed with which it was to come into being. The membership of the NEA has, in greater numbers than were then visualized, embraced the labor techniques of collective bargaining and the strike.[3] So have some other professions. As this is written, the medical profession is following almost precisely the same steps that teachers took in the late 1950s. First, the rising costs of malpractice insurance have grown so intolerable that some strikes by doctors have occurred, shocking the nation. A federation of physicians has been formed, with several thousand members. And, in a final step before the plunge (as was true of teachers), the American Medical Association has withdrawn its ban on strikes. Now it appears that the American people, who have generally not interfered seriously with the right of professions to regulate themselves, may insist upon some public control of the cost of medical service.

A new profession of teaching has emerged. This is what the present volume is about. While the NEA has adhered to the principles of an independent profession, many did not see or anticipate the extent to which it would rapidly come to embrace some of the procedures of the labor movement. Nor did people foresee the virtual dropping of (or the great modification of) some of the fundamentals of professional negotiations and the infusion of the basic principles of collective bargaining. Most of all, not foreseen was the gradual waning of the professional sanctions process and the widespread adoption of the strike by the teaching profession. (Perhaps as many as 1,000 teachers' strikes have occurred since 1960.) Certainly not foreseen was the almost universal use of contractual processes among the states. Some contracts exist in more than forty-five states as this is written, although no more than thirty states have enacted legislation on the subject of professional negotiation.

So far, the NEA has refused to merge with AFT, since that organization is affiliated with organized labor. One supposes that the NEA rea-

---

[2] Ibid., p. 87.
[3] Ibid., p. 406.

sons, first, that a real profession does not rely upon any power other than its own. It generates its own power, through controlling selection, preparation, and admission to practice. Second, labor has no more right to control school policies than does any other comparable segment of American society. These have been and are the viewpoints of those who visualize teachers as a great self-directing profession. It is not an anti-labor posture. It is a posture of belief in the soundness and the power of a unified, autonomous, and independent profession—more than affiliation with or adoption of labor processes. What the teaching profession needs more than these is unity. A unified group of teachers will have all the power the profession needs to secure its just and reasonable rights; all the power it can exercise with fairness to the people it serves. This unity is rapidly occurring. Of course, teaching inevitably favors, in the process, some of the processes labor found helpful.

A great new profession of teaching has come into being in the United States—largely in the course of a decade. In that decade (1965–75), the profession went through a rather complete transformation. What this development means for education, for the United States, and for the teaching profession is what this book seeks to explore. What changes may occur in the future in its attitudes toward direct approved affiliation with labor, or toward the extent of its use of labor techniques to gain its objectives, can only be surmised at present. What the teaching profession in the public schools must avoid is a hide-bound affiliation with and subservience to any other segment of our society. This is obvious in the fact that teachers represent and perform in endeavors established and supported by the entire citizenry—endeavors dedicated to furthering the welfare and interests of the nation as a whole. Teachers must beware of the dangers of becoming subservient to anyone, or any group of special interests.

STILL THERE ARE GREAT TASKS AHEAD FOR THE SCHOOLS

However great the achievement of the schools, there are yet challenging tasks ahead. Although we are the most literate and best educated people in the world, there remains room for improvement and reason for concern. Two million American adults have never attended school and 24 million others have dropped out before completing the eighth grade.[4] Most of these 26 million Americans are unable to compute simple income tax forms; read directions or safety warnings; keep up a checking account, payments, or rent; or read road signs. Most of these adults are functionally illiterate. It appears that those who do not seek to profit from universal education in their youth will never make up for their lack of foresight. This is borne out by the failure of adult education to attract more than a relative handful of undereducated adults—less than 5 percent. Anybody in the United States with less than mastery of the basics of the first four grades is classified as a functional illiterate. In many other societies such persons could get by, but not in America. Universal education in the United States must be extended to include all. The relative handful of less than 5 percent of the functional illiterates cannot be dismissed as of no consequence.

EVOLUTION OF LABOR MILITANCY
(BACKGROUND OF TEACHER MILITANCY)

The rights of organized labor are quite specifically set forth in the National Labor Relations Act and the Wagner Act of 1935, and the restrictive limits on these rights in the Taft-Hartley Act of 1947 and the Landrum-Griffin Act of 1959. Behind these acts of the federal government are almost a century of struggle (and some exploitation of labor) for legal recognition of the laboring man to a fair and equitable consideration regarding working hours, conditions, and pay scales. Until these federal laws were enacted, the laboring men were compelled to depend, to great extent, upon the sense of fairness and justice and compassion of their employers. These acts were the first which sought to spell out in law the equal rights and freedoms to which all American citizens are entitled— with certain restrictions for public employees. The teaching profession is undergoing—and has been undergoing since about 1950—the same suspended state that labor found itself in prior to passage of the National Labor Relations Act of 1935. The teaching profession is now in the process of attempting to secure some of these rights also.

---

[4] Editorial, *Houston Post*, Oct. 22, 1979.

Slow Emergence of Rights of Labor

But first, a brief description of the evolution of these rights for labor will be helpful in securing an understanding of the teachers' struggle for similar recognition. *Bear in mind, as we attempt to trace briefly the evolution of the rights of labor, that the above-named federal laws exempted all public employees (those paid from public taxation) from their benefits. This, it may be assumed, arises from the long-held convictions of the majority of the American people that public employees are basically a separate class of citizens, those depending upon public taxation for financial support.*

But to be fair to those who do hold this concept, most are motivated by the conviction that government—with its assigned functions of protection of the people and the enforcement of the laws—could be jeopardized if its own employees have the legal right to strike whatever the severity or pettiness of the provocation. Reduced to its essential meaning, this concept can be stated as follows: If public employees can strike, then the public couldn't benefit from police protection; or the military might refuse to defend the nation against invading enemies.

But Abraham Flexner, generally considered the great figure in spearheading the drive for professionalization of medicine, comments on this very point as follows: "There are, of course, always dangers that the interests of an organization may conflict with those of the body politic. Organizations of physicians, lawyers, and teachers may find the personal interests of the individuals of whom they are composed arrayed against those of society at large. But under such conditions, organized groups are apt to be more responsive to public interest than are unorganized and isolated individuals."[5]

Labor Rights as They Were

Before the passage of the Wagner Act in 1935, labor was subject to mistreatment, unfairness, and often brutality, as, for example, that visited upon the strikers in the Pueblo (Colorado) strike and the Pullman Strike (in Chicago), to cite but two among many.

Of course, it must be said at this point that collective bargaining and

---

[5] Abraham Flexner, "What Are the Earmarks of a Profession?" as quoted in *Readings in the Social Aspects of Education* (Danville, Ill.: Interstate, 1951), p. 556.

the strike are not perfect instruments in the labor field; they too have had their excesses. But they had to be invoked to get just treatment for workers. And, perhaps, they may serve as only interim procedures, until a fairer, more effective and productive plan can come into being. Certainly teachers should seek professional processes that will strengthen their bargaining power.

In the professional field, what may appear to be a more productive instrument has been developed. This, stated in the simplest possible terms, is the regulation of the supply of personnel for the respective professions, so that there are not huge surpluses produced annually. An oversupply will, in time, force the workers in the field to accept substandard salary scales or actually engage in competitive bidding for jobs. The basic instruments for achieving this balance rest on two essential points: accreditation of preparing institutions, and legal certification. (These two are, of course, not exclusive weapons of professions.) A third ingredient could be added—that of thorough, rigorous, scholarly programs for preparing the profession's members.

The medical profession was the first in America to use the accrediting process for institutions preparing its practitioners. The story that developed is an interesting one which we shall sketch here.

A brief analogy at this point may be helpful. Flexner at the outset of his study of medical education (circa 1910) wrote:

> The American medical school began soundly as a supplement to the apprenticeship system, still in vogue in the seventeenth and eighteenth centuries. The likely youth of that period, destined to a medical career, was at an early age indentured to serve reputable practitioners, to whom his service was successively menial . . . he ran his master's errands, washed the bottles, mixed the drugs, spread the plasters, and finally, as the stipulated term drew towards its close, actually took part in the daily procedure and sought a more inspired and inspiring discipline of his preceptor. . . . In time some of the brighter of those interns visited the medical centers in Europe.[6]

Flexner thus has summarized the early days of the medical profession in this country. This may serve as a rough appraisal of the early period of the organization of teachers in the United States. And Flexner was most

---

[6] Abraham Flexner, *Medical Education in the United States and Canada*, Bulletin no. 4 (New York: Carnegie Corporation, 1911), p. 346. Account also given in idem, *I Remember* (New York: Simon & Schuster, 1940), p. 115.

influential in the drastic overhaul of medical education in this country. In his studies he visited every one of the 155 so-called medical schools in this country and Canada and found that more than half of these institutions were no more than what we now would term "diploma mills," taking in a class in October—the members of which did not have to be high school graduates—and graduating them the following April as full-fledged doctors.

One has only to review the exposed scandals of collegiate football in recent years to find similarities of the "mess" in medicine, via forged transcripts and credits from nonexistent correspondence schools, to find a similarity.

As a result of Flexner's study and recommendations, the American Medical Association rescued from its files a study on proposed standards for the accreditation of medical schools prepared in 1907, but never adopted, and set itself up in the accrediting business in 1912. The results are now well known, giving great incentive to making medicine in this country one of the most (if not *the* most) highly respected professions in America. But, for teaching, this step was considered by many, especially many in higher education, as sheer effrontery. Frankly, that development is in the past; now about 90 percent of the newly graduated teachers in the United States each year are graduating from colleges and universities which have been accredited by NCATE (National Council for the Accreditation of Teacher Education). NCATE was established by the teaching profession in 1952, and began actual accrediting in 1955. In 1979 some 550 of the more than 1,200 colleges and universities preparing teachers in the United States were accredited by NCATE. These 550 institutions prepared almost 90 percent of the newly graduated teachers that year. In time, every institution preparing teachers will be required by all states to be accredited by NCATE. There will then be no back-door routes into teaching, because states will soon require this for legal certification of graduates.

So presently the major problem confronting the teaching profession is the pressing and very real one of refining and improving the curriculum for the preparation of teachers. And to most observers who have studied the problem, the great task is to strengthen the offerings in both the general, or liberal arts area and the requirements in the teaching field areas; and to improve, both in content and in internship preparation, the professional area. The second great problem facing the teaching profession is to elevate the minimum standard of preparation for beginning teachers to the master's degree level. This, of course, also must be accomplished through the legal process of elevating standards for certification by the respecting states.

A Labor Leader Warns Teachers

One of the events that gave great momentum to developments which many of the public now categorize as teacher militancy was the speech made before the annual convention of the NEA at Denver in 1962 by the vice-president of the International Brotherhood of Electrical Workers.

> If I sound shocked because the Charwomen in some high schools get a higher rate of pay than the high school teachers . . . And if the Charwomen . . . have more tenure in their jobs and more security than the high school teachers, to me it is a shocking disclosure of the method by which we pay our rewards. . . . *if the Charwomen in the schools have sense enough to band together and organize and negotiate contracts and teachers do not, I wonder sometimes who should have the degrees.*[7]

EVOLUTION OF TEACHER MILITANCY

By the middle of September, 1979, 105 teacher strikes were reported in 17 states. Michigan reported the largest number, with a total of 42; Pennsylvania reported 16; Illinois, 17; Ohio, 9; New Jersey, 5. These strikes involved both NEA and AFT affiliates, with NEA affiliates being in the majority because that organization's membership (about 1,800,000) included about 75 percent of the public school teachers in the United States. An unusual aspect of that year was the noticeable unrest of teachers; this, it appears, is growing. Of course, the impact of inflation is a great influence in the rise of strikes. One other noticeable aspect was the number of strikes in large cities—Detroit, San Francisco, Indianapolis, Cleveland, and Chicago. Unlike the strikes in the previous year, when the chief issue was money and class size, the chief motivation in 1978–79 was the lack of correction of the class-size situation and the frustration of the extended struggle to win a new contract before resorting to the strike.

The slow evolution of the trend toward teacher strikes presumably

---

[7] Quoted in Stinnett, *Turmoil in Teaching,* p .5.

caused the widespread popular hope in this country that teachers could, with steady pressure and the invoking of influences of powerful forces upon the media, especially the newspapers, bring a halt to this upsurge of militancy among the teachers.

But this does not appear likely to be successful—this effort to turn back this tide of militancy. The great majority of teachers would prefer to avoid the strike. If they could thereby secure decent consideration, they would gladly choose the peaceful and quiet process.

As a prelude to discussing this possibility, it seems desirable at this point to review the steps that led to the ultimate revolt of labor in the face of the continued mistreatment, in lieu of the law being silent or stacked against them.

Turmoil on the Labor Front Is Eased

In the first chapter of his book *The Labor Wars*, Sidney Lens graphically depicts the twilight of the running war between business firms and laboring men to achieve a balance of power in the bargaining process. Indeed, this was a war labor had been fighting for a century (or more), for equal rights in bargaining with employing firms over working conditions and pay scales. It is a brief description of the route on which teaching has gone only a little way toward a similar achievement. For teachers, the great push toward realization of the true powers of a profession still lies largely in the future.

The review of the turmoil of the labor fight will not, of course, duplicate in detail the rugged, dangerous road that labor had to follow to gain its rights, the essence of which was won in 1935 by the passage of the Wagner Act legalizing collective bargaining and the strike as a means of enforcement. Teaching has now gained some of these rights in some thirty states. But, in general, this group is still struggling to secure similar rights by the processes used by most recognized professions.

The fight that labor endured was a long, bitter, and hard one.

> For ten weeks in 1970, the largest industrial corporation in the United States—General Motors—confronted the largest industrial Union in the United States, the United Auto Workers. The firm, with resources larger than the gross national product of many countries, was shut tight as 400,000 card-carrying members of the UAW "hit the

brakes" . . . four or five decades ago . . . the company would have prepared itself with a small army of "guards" and Pinkerton spies; would have stock-piled guns and tear gas; and sponsored a citizens' committee to prepare a "back to work" agreement. Its personnel department would have combed the hinterlands for strike breakers . . . its lawyers would have drafted pliable judges. . . . In union offices throughout the country the pulse would have been equally rapid. Flying squadrons would have been formed to guard against an influx of strike breakers at railroad stations . . . plans would have been made for mass picketing . . . calls would have been made to other unions . . . to alert them to the possible need for help on the picket lines . . . and on the first day of the walkout—September 14—there would have been an air of tension . . . some of the workers would remember the sit-down strikes against GM in 1936–37 . . . when the company shut off the heat, and when the police prevented food from being sent in . . . strikers on the outside pushed through the small wall of police to carry bread and coffee to their beleaguered comrades within . . . a battle ensued in which the men in blue used tear gas, clubs, and guns; the unionists [used] metal pipes, bolts, sticks, bottles, coffee mugs, etc. . . . "We wanted peace," said strike leaders on the loud speaker, "General Motors chose war, give it to them" . . . at midnight the fight came to a halt. Fourteen strikers had been taken to the hospital with bullet wounds.

. . . But in 1970 the strike situation evoked very different responses. The company did not try to keep its plants open . . . there were no large-scale back-to-work movement, or citizens committees. There were no shootings, tear gassings, clubbings. . . . There was no fear of attack by the police or National Guard and small likelihood that management would seek injunctions in the courts. The most lethal weapon used by the UAW this time was a strike fund, upwards of a hundred million dollars, collected from dues and assessments, out of which weekly benefits were paid to those on the picket line (to feed their families.[8]

This was now the pattern of non-violent confrontation between big labor and big business.

This is neither the place nor the time to review in detail the many, many stresses and violences that Americans have had to undergo to find peace in settling disputes between competing groups. One who doubts the efficacy of peaceful means—such as collective bargaining and the

---

[8] Sidney Lens, *The Labor Wars* (Garden City, N.Y.: Doubleday, 1973), pp. 1–8. Used by permission of Doubleday & Company and Blassingame, McCauley & Wood.

strike, means specified under existing laws—should reread the history of vigorous differences among various groups in American life, to be vastly impressed with the power of what we call the "democratic process."

In that review, he will read of the horrible violence used to put down demands of workers, demands which now seem so reasonable but which at the time could be twisted and sold to the majority of Americans as radicalism, outlawry, tyranny. In recent years, they were denounced as "communism," "redism," "pinkism," and so forth. Labor even had to fight to attain the eight-hour working day, reducing the pattern of the twelve-hour day first to ten hours; then, after years of violent and cruel treatment of the workers, to the present eight-hour day, with paid vacations and retirement and medical benefits. Many living today can remember when the standard pay of common labor in certain industries was 10 cents an hour for a ten-hour day. Finally, it became an eight-hour day. Total earnings for each work day respectively were $1.20 and $1.00 per day. Of course, the inflationary trends were such that they had great influence on demands for higher wages.

These are the roughly similar goals which teaching seeks. With beginnings in some instances just as lowly as those which some workers endured in earlier times, teachers were compelled to seek better conditions. The imposition of rules of conduct, habits, customs, practices, and beliefs was even harsher (if that is possible) for teachers than for workers, because the mores for teachers were generally based upon religious beliefs or evolved from former religious practices. Surely a new day lies ahead for teachers in the United States, as members of the largest profession in this country and in the world.

END OF AN ERA

The death of George Meany, who had served as president of the AFL-CIO, in January, 1980, marked the end of an era. Meany served in the period in which organized labor came into its own, in terms of legal recognition of the organizational and procedural rights for which labor had been striving for almost a century. (And to be blunt about it—many believed that labor came into more than its own.) This new era of the rights of labor came into being, as previously stated herein, with the upsurge of a new period under the aegis of legislation sponsored by President Franklin D. Roosevelt.

Meany's death, according to some observers, marked the end of the great growth and predominance of the craft unions. These observers predicted that now the long and continuing struggle of the public employees will gain momentum, and that these workers eventually will earn rights similar to those of the craft unions.

The pontifical words of Calvin Coolidge as governor of Massachusetts in 1918 during the "wildcat strike" of the Boston police, to the effect that "there is no right to strike against the public interest, welfare and safety at any time or any place," are becoming outmoded. This high-flown verbiage was instrumental in elevating Coolidge to the presidency of the United States. But the categorical prophecy he enunciated has eroded in application, as a verbalization of the fixed, immutable position for those who are paid from public funds. Basically, this did apply then with great force to those entrusted with the safety of the public. But time has ameliorated the limitations. Already police in many places, teachers, and so forth, have earned and been granted the legal right to use collective bargaining and the strike under spelled-out conditions, or reasonably similar processes.

FREEDOM TO TEACH

There were other statutes enacted to "control" what teachers thought and said, such as the anti-evolution law prohibiting the teaching of, or about, Darwin's thesis. Then there came into being a rash of such legislation, which has been declared unconstitutional by virtue of the First Amendment. Many of the laws requiring oaths of allegiance applied not only to elementary and high school teachers but to college and university teachers as well. In five states the law applied to nonprofessional employees in private schools and colleges. As late as 1974, a total of thirteen states still had oaths of allegiance on their statute books, but they are no longer of any real validity due to the fact that they have been struck down by so many court decisions.

In fact, insofar as the threat of enforcement is concerned, nobody pays attention to these oaths anymore. But another period of national hysteria could engulf the public to the point that such noxious laws could be revitalized. Such laws are a special threat to teachers, so both teachers and the public need to be alert to any such threats in the future. Why? Simply because the danger of infringement of the right—and even the obligation—to teach about anything that is germane to freedom of speech in a democracy must be kept open always. Censorship carried to extremes is the greatest of threats to all citizens—not just to one group, such as teachers.

An editorial writer of a large city newspaper demonstrated the failure of society to provide effective remedies for securing justice and fair treatment for teachers. His column, entitled "For Teachers, Strikes Are Regrettable," goes as follows:

> Throughout the year . . . thousands of public school teachers have been on strikes which idled more than 500,000 students. Their complaints and apprehensions are understandable. For most of them, financial futures are dowdy. They are forced to forego material pleasures that others, less worthy, take for granted. Racial mixtures have subjected them to threats and physical abuse . . . mean spirited mothers react with misunderstanding and rage when their darlings are disciplined . . . yet a teachers' strike seems so out of place. . . . First and foremost a teacher is paid with tax money and is a public official the same as a policeman or an Air Force pilot. If a teacher can strike against the public, so can a policeman—the soldier guarding a military reservation or a pilot defending his country against the onslaught of an enemy.

The column continues:

> They thumbed their noses (a euphemism) at the judge who had ordered them back to the classroom. "You must remember," said Chancellor D. J. Alissandratos in a 15 minute lecture, "that you are an example for the children of this community. Stop making it a bad one."[9]

Of course, this is a mild, somewhat understanding statement. But it offers only a handslapping such as a child would get for misbehavior. No solution is offered, except Suffer some more! Be dedicated! That is reward enough.

---

[9] Dick West, "For Teachers, Strikes Are Regrettable," *Dallas Morning News*. Used by permission of the author.

THE REASON FOR THE INCREASE
IN TEACHERS' STRIKES

The foregoing has described the development of teachers' increasing militancy, necessitated by what has appeared to them as contemptuous dismissal of their pleas for fair treatment. This eventuated in the steadily increasing adoption of labor tactics, which appear to them as their only hope of securing justice in terms of economic and civil rights. It must be borne in mind that this viewpoint has not been embraced unanimously by teachers. There are yet hopes among most teachers that some other way may be found by which these goals—which they believe are embraced by the vast majority of American citizens—may be achieved. But if the history of the origin and evolution of militancy in the labor movement in the United States—from the rise of industrial development to the passage of the Wagner Act in 1935—has any relevancy for other demeaned groups, then teachers may be forced to embrace action after the labor pattern.

There is substantial evidence that the majority of America's teachers would prefer an alternative approach. They especially favor the route of being permitted to seek the further professionalization of their occupation, from the kindergarten level through the graduate school of the university.

MEDICINE: A PROFESSION ONLY FOR THE RICH

At this point, it would appear to be appropriate to review briefly the several steps medicine has pursued in acquiring its present status. This status arises, basically, because of the supreme importance of the service of its practitioners to the preservation of human life. But beyond this indispensable element are the processes used to elevate its members to such eminence.

How did the profession of medicine achieve this eminence?

1. By developing over the years a strong, vigorous, and viable professional national association, the AMA (American Medical Association), to represent its interests nationally.

2. By developing corresponding state, county, and local organizations of the profession.

3. By striving vigorously to build such a strong, alert, dedicated program that practitioners felt that membership was essential, not only to them, but to the well being of the public (i.e., membership became more or less mandatory by the effectiveness of organization in essential controls of its allocated concerns, rather than by a specified law requiring memberships).

4. By setting and enforcing such high standards of preparation that only those who could demonstrate intelligence could be admitted to medical schools.

5. By developing an accrediting process of such high caliber that any graduate recommended for certification and practice by a medical school accepted by AMA would be well qualified.

6. The profession itself so controlled, or recommended to the designated legal authorities, the types and contents of certification (or licensing) as to preclude the incompetent or the fraudulent from receiving such credentials.

7. The process, in itself, controlled or recommended to the designated issuing authority the means of developing procedures for reciprocity in certification of medical practitioners among the states.

8. Such a strict and comprehensive code of ethics governing practice was developed as to eliminate incompetent or immoral practitioners.

9. The profession established at the national, state, city, and county levels a vigorous, alert, balanced, and fair process for disciplining members who are accused of malpractice or immoral or unprofessional conduct, with the power to recommend the degree of punishment prescribed by the profession. This would include expulsion from membership, rescinding or revoking certification and disbarring from practice, and finally recommending to law enforcement officials the indictment and trial of such disbarred members.

There are other steps, but these are the basic ones followed by medicine. And these are basic to any group that aspires to be recognized as worthy of the high calling of service to the general public, whether that service be a private or a public one.

Abuse of Professional Rights

Of course, it is possible for a profession which embraces all of the above suggested practices to become so successful and so affluent as to invite efforts at revision and refinement by the designated public legal agency. Medicine has become so powerful in its controls, and in the processes it employs, as to attract constant surveillance, as the following will attest.

Surveys by the Association of American Medical Colleges reflect that in the years 1974 to 1977, the number of entering students from families with annual incomes of $10,000–$16,999 dropped from 20.9 percent to 14.9 percent; and those from the $17,000–$20,000 level dropped from 13.4 percent to 11.3 percent. Students from families of lower-middle incomes— the children of farmers, craftsmen, salesclerks and others in the $10,000 to $20,000 a year range in income—are tending to disappear from the nation's medical schools. Similar reports are being made for dental schools by the American Association of Dental Schools. Apparently because the escalating costs of medical and dental educations are surpassing the reach of families with annual incomes below $20,000, the number of applications for admission to these professional schools is declining. And there is concern that medicine is tending to become a profession of and for the rich. The median yearly income in 1977 of families of new medical students was $26,000.

What are the reasons for this clearly evident switch? One part of the problem is that medical and dental schools are rapidly shifting scholarship aid to the economically deprived students, while coincidentally the federal government is shifting aid in the form of scholarships to loans. Here again, generally, only the families of the rich can undertake to underwrite the loans or provide major help in repaying such loans. Thus the students from lower-income families must rely almost entirely on their own resources, an impossible burden for low-income families.

This situation is bound to dissuade many would-be doctors. Those who do undertake this seemingly back-breaking burden are compelled, therefore, to practice "where the money is"—in large cities, not in rural areas. Not only does this situation foreclose the possibility of thousands of youths aspiring for a career in medicine, but it lowers the numbers of qualified medical graduates who come into the profession with a deep-seated empathy for the feeling and thinking of the lower-income group. Again inflation has hit medical schools, and the cost of tuition has risen to as high as $13,000–$14,000 a year in some of them. And the differences in cost per year as between private and public medical schools are of course increasing, with total costs in private schools averaging $10,459, and $5,012 in the state schools (plus about $2,000 for out-of-state students).[10]

The prospects of medicine and dentistry becoming the "professions of the rich" are quite real. This cannot be allowed to happen in teaching. Thus there must be developed means by which teachers can secure economic justice.

PROFESSIONALIZATION OF TEACHING: PROBLEMS, RESPONSES, AND OUTLOOK

Previously, we have discussed both the problems involved in the professionalization of teaching and the responses that would make the process complete. We will now elaborate on the subject.

Extent of Teacher Burnout

Elsewhere we have dealt with the extent of physical attacks upon teachers. These have been on the increase for several years, and this increase is likely to accelerate if the speculation concerning the growing sale of marijuana and other drugs to schoolchildren proves to be true. The reports are that in the large cities students are a fruitful market for illegal drug peddlers. This is another of those vicious aspects of conditions in society which inevitably find their way into the public schools. This is a condition which by no stretch of the imagination of the most violent critic of the public schools and their teachers can fairly be attributed to either. This bitter evidence of the depths to which some members of society will descend for the sake of profits is appalling. Equally astounding is the willingness of so many people to blame the schools for the existence of this "racket" in society.

This, coupled with the extent of violence in the schools, is understandably reaching unbelievable and unbearable proportions for teachers who have to watch helplessly the horrible results flowing into the schools from society. These are conditions they have not caused, and they are helpless to remedy them. The effects upon teachers are horrendous.

---

[10] Gene I. Maeroff, "Medicine: A Profession Only for the Rich," *Houston Post*, Oct. 2, 1979.

Teachers are leaving teaching in hordes each year; 70,000 are physically and violently attacked each year. (Incidentally, this exceeds the number of armed policemen assaulted. And this number is probably grossly underestimated; some estimates run as high as 110,000 violent attacks annually upon teachers.)

This situation has reached emergency proportions. There are presently 20,000 fewer teachers in the United States who have had twenty years or more experience than in many years. Unless this situation is checked and reversed, "burned out" teachers will eventually either destroy the public schools, or their flight will so deplete the schools of quality that these institutions will sink to such low levels as to destroy the very idea of their existence.

Cases of Burnout

Emmitt Williams almost quit teaching in the spring of 1979 after twenty-three years of service. Why continue, he asked himself, when your house is ransacked and set on fire by a student you have struggled to help? Add to incidents like this the mounting criticisms of teachers about why Johnny can't read; why they can't control discipline. Constantly fearful of violence, many teachers are fed up with the persisting griping from the public—accusing them of gross ignorance, and complaining of excessive school costs. As a result thousands of well-educated, experienced, skilled teachers are leaving the public schools for more peaceful and better-paying work.

Williams was not one of these. He decided to tough it out. But he added: "To be honest, I must admit that I am looking forward to retirement."

Another teacher at the 1979 NEA convention reported: "I've heard more teachers say in the last year that if they were old enough, they'd pack it in. I've never heard that before. The enthusiasm, the joy we all have had for teaching seems to be diminishing."

A poll of 1,777 teachers at the NEA meeting said they probably would not become teachers if they could go back to college and start over.[11]

---

[11] Associated Press release, June, 1979. Used by permission.

An NEA study conducted during the 1978–79 school year and released at the Detroit meeting revealed that 5 percent of the teachers polled nationwide reported that they had been physically attacked during the preceding school year. Based on this sample, some 110,000 teachers in the country were physically assaulted. Of the total attacked, it was estimated that some 11,000 teachers required medical attention for physical injury; another 8 percent (or 9,000) received medical attention for emotional trauma.

This is definitely related to what is being commonly called by teachers "burnout." The cost of these forced absences is significant. In Detroit the budget allots $6 million per year, and from 600 to 900 substitutes are used each day. In Los Angeles, the schools spent $13.9 million. Minneapolis spent $900,000 last year for substitute teachers. Obviously, not all absences of teachers are due to these reasons, but many are. Sadder still is the rating performance of the substitute teachers. The New York Metropolitan School Study Council reported that teacher effectiveness, as measured by student achievement, consistently dropped with substitute teachers. With 7 as the highest, regular teachers were rated at 5.01; student teachers at 2.76; and substitute teachers at 0.27. The Pennsylvania School Board Association study of this problem recommended the use of retired teachers, honor students, and community volunteers to staff the classrooms in the absence of regular classroom teachers; thus there could be a substantial reduction in the amount of funding spent on substitute teachers.

Incidentally, the above study found that teacher absenteeism can be reduced by changing the methods by which teachers report that they will be absent. A system where the teacher is required to report directly to the principal has the lowest absentee rate. Where the teacher can report to a secretary, the rate jumps; the further the reporting is from the immediate supervisor, the higher the rate.

The skyrocketing stress rate and the burn-out rate are causing such acceleration in teacher absenteeism that some authorities are now suggesting (perhaps as an incentive) that at the end of the year teachers be given the amount of money budgeted for each teacher leave, whether it is used or not. The belief is that this will significantly reduce the cost of substitute teachers. Of course, this proposal overlooks several possible unfavorable aspects.

Teacher Strikes—1979 Style

The boiling anger of teachers over public indifference and mistreatment, beginning in the early 1960s, impelled many of them to embrace at long last the ultimate in militancy and revolt—*collective bargaining and the strike*. After repeated pleading for economic justice and equality of citizenship rights, from the depths of the Great Depression in the 1930s to the failure of school boards to respond, they decided they could take it no longer. Presumably with the acquiescence of the public, many school boards refused to accept the good-faith approach of the "Professional Negotiations" and "Professional Sanctions" adopted in 1962 by the NEA.

During the early years of the existence of these two milder processes, school boards (and major portions of the public) continued to ignore these so-called gimmicks of the teachers as "radicalism gone wild." What triggered the explosions of teachers in 1961 and 1962 was the quick and easy victories of the United Federation of Teachers in New York, as an arm of the AFL-CIO.

The first strike ended in one day with a victory for the teachers' union (with the overt cooperation of certain elected officials closely allied with the labor unions). The second strike in New York City occurred in April, 1962. This strike apparently was actually lost by the United Federation of Teachers. But following the established tactics of the union, the outcome was trumpeted as an "overwhelming victory" by the UFT. The education editor of the *Saturday Review* wrote:

> But the strike was only a symptom. When teachers have confidence in the administration, they work hard for higher salaries but do not walk out on their students. The decision to strike revealed that teachers' low morale of long standing, sprang from deep seated maladies in the school system and in the body politic. On the surface the strike was for more money; . . . in a deeper sense, the strike was a protest against ineffective administration, public apathy, a bumbling city government which places education low on its list of priorities. . . . Teachers cannot have it both ways. They cannot expect professional status and the respect and security that goes with it, and at the same time demand the right to exercise the ultimate economic weapon of a labor union.[12]

---

[12] Paul Woodring, "The New York Teachers' Strike," *Saturday Review*, May 19, 1962, pp. 54–56.

Granted. But what can one expect when teachers have pursued faith-fully this philosophy for nearly two hundred years, and have still been the repeated recipients of mistreatment (much of which has been in violation of our own constitutional provisions)? Their status and public respect still lag far behind that of other professions. Some exceedingly powerful seg-ments of the public even sneer contemptuously, and vigorously deny that teachers have any valid right to claim to be a profession. The past nearly three decades of deteriorating teacher-public relationships is the answer, but not the final answer.

Teachers, by an overwhelming majority, earnestly seek and continue to seek professional status. We believe they will continue that seeking. But with the continuing vigorous rebuffs from the public, that posture becomes increasingly replaced by the use of more militant processes.

In a penetrating article, Ralph Tyler responds to wholesale denigra-tion of American public schools by presenting a thoughtful defense of them. He writes:

> Disillusionment and cynicism characterize much of the current writ-ing on our schools. Why? In part, the cynicism is a reaction to the over-optimistic expectations of the 1950's and 60's. A similar mood followed the affluent period of the 1920's. . . . In part due to a lack of understanding of the impact of social changes in the schools. In the past, the school was a sorting agency as well as an educational one. Children receiving low marks in the primary grades often became dis-couraged and left school. In 1910, less than half of the population finished the eighth grade. Now the demand for unskilled labor is low, and the child who cannot read or write, compute, and understand the social system of today has little chance to work and is likely to present a serious problem to society. Hence today, the school is ex-pected to educate practically all children. . . . In fact American schools have been amazingly successful in meeting new demands as our nation developed during the 200 years since its founding. We have assimilated millions of newcomers from a variety of other na-tions without destroying our own society. Social mobility is far higher in the United States than it is in any other country in the world and much of that mobility has been attained through education. . . . Conflicts over mass education commonly occur between the existing elite and the peasants and working classes. The leaders of the latter groups perceive mass education as a means of freeing the lower strata of society from ignorance and poverty. The elite on the other hand, fearing the power that education might give the lower classes, profess

the view that only a small percentage proportion of the people are capable of acquiring an education.[13]

It is not extravagant language to assert that American democracy and freedom are in a real sense dependent upon a universal education, made vital and vigorous by free, competent, and proud teachers.

---

[13] Ralph W. Tyler, "Education American Style," *National Elementary Principal,* Nov.–Dec., 1976, pp. 38–42. Copyright 1976, National Association of Elementary School Principals. All rights reserved. Used by permission.

19

That No Talent Be Lost

WITH the preceding chapters devoted to the trials and tribulations of teachers, and often to the public's loss of confidence in its schools; with recordings of the vigorous and often vitriolic criticisms aimed at both teachers and schools, it seems appropriate in this final chapter to present some aspects of an optimistic nature. There are, of course, happier, brighter evidences of some of the magnificent contributions America is receiving from its public schools.

Ostensibly, much of the evidence cited herein is in denigration of the schools, some of it being associated with children and families who in most (if indeed not all) other kinds of society would have had little opportunity to climb above the conditions into which they were born. To George Santayana, former professor at Harvard (1880–1912), is ascribed this statement: "The essence of religion is the tender concern of God that no soul be lost." This may be paraphrased to assert that *universal education is a free nation's tender concern that no talent be lost.*

It took a revolt against the mother country, the cruel Civil War, the abolition of generations of slavery, and the integration of its schools for this nation to learn a priceless lesson. That lesson is that there is in every human being significant portions of the bottomless pools of talent that exist in all nations—talent that the tender and enlightened concepts of education can discover and develop. This is the very essence of the meaning of the public schools, open to all, free to all, for the benefit of all. To repeat, this constitutes the tender concern of a free nation that no talent be lost.

Following are some case examples which illustrate the magnificent powers and the limitless promise of ordinary human beings, wisely guided and nurtured by universal education. Some of the witnesses are people who, without the beneficent ministry of the public schools, would have

278

risen little above the status into which they were born. A few, of course, doubtless possessed such native gifts and drives that they would have achieved distinction whatever the kind of education to which they had access. And some are of such achievements as to be above partisan considerations, and thus are able to judge impartially the promise of free education, universally extended by society to every child.

In Chapters 1 and 3 we depicted how successive crises—at home and abroad—inevitably give birth to a national soul-searching for the causes of such threatening developments. But upon reflection, the use of the phraseology of "soul-searching" is perhaps too self-flattering. Because it is rare indeed when this search results in self-analysis or self-accusation of the denouncing individuals or groups. Almost without exception, such national questioning tends to wind up as a search—a seeming soul-rending becomes automatic finger-pointing at someone else. Or it evolves into accusing some agency or organization or group of people which depends upon the general public (or a powerful section of that public) for support, financial or political. This tendency seems in periods of stress to be almost universal. But it is, perhaps, most evident in the so-called free nations; that is, where the people have self-government, in form and in fact.

Why is this? Well, first of all, in a nation that is not free, the great mass of citizens have no powers except those the ruling individuals or groups see fit to give them. Thus the masses can disclaim responsibility for whatever unfortunate, debilitating conditions come into being.

But in a nation of free people, in a democracy such as the United States, where the people have their lawful rights spelled out, and a judicial system to interpret those rights, and a government elected to enforce the declarations of the courts, the escapist hatches are closed. The responsibility for whatever goes wrong in such a society cannot be passed on to some dictator, or some elite group which has appropriated the powers of government for its own selfish aggrandizement. Thus, in the United States, the free public schools will always be a whipping boy for some portions of the populace. *And this is as it should be; and it should continue to be, except that such circumstances depend upon and deserve an appropriate sense of and practice of fairness.*

While the order of the day presently is severe denunciation of the public schools and their teachers, it is extremely doubtful that the situation is as bad as it is often pictured as being. Of course, the public schools have weaknesses. In the eyes of many they always will have. By the very nature of the basic appeal of "Come all, admit all, serve all," there will continue to be spotty progress, gaps, and evident weaknesses. Any agency that has as its task and its goal the adequate education of some fifty million children will likely always be under the gun.

Again, this is to be expected. But criticism ought not to be thoughtless, and it ought not to be destructive. The public in such a nation should always be searching for answers and remedies as fervently as it searches for criticisms.

It is easy for taxpaying citizens to berate teachers when they fail to enforce the old-fashioned concept of discipline, as was once the mark of the isolated one-room rural school. But the scene has shifted, often to ghetto schools or crowded city schools, large, small, or medium-sized. Here is a graphic picture of the education process in a large city more than a quarter of a century ago.

> More than a million children of every station and every national background are living in that enormous arena, the metropolis of New York City. The city, which stifles thousands of them in jammed tenements and garbage-littered lots, also attempts with genuine compassion and real hope to educate them and fit them for useful, decent, even happy lives. It is not a simple or idyllic process. The classroom struggle for the minds and hearts of New York's young is as complex, as baffling and painful as the struggle for gain and survival which goes on in the perpendicular samples of masonary outside. . . . For more than a century and a half, as the catalyst in the greatest U.S. melting pot, New York has been assaulted by wave upon wave of immigrants from abroad; and the schools have been forced to spread their light amidst squalor, machine politics, and fogs of apathy, racial prejudice, and ignorance.[1]

Here is a description of the sad plight of a young, idealistic teacher in such a situation:

> Nobody warned me about a thing before I went to a near-slum district in Brooklyn. I was full of ideals . . . I learned a lot of things about teaching that aren't in the books. In a high school like ours you have a few tough ones and a few vicious ones in almost every class. They sit watching you like snakes, waiting for the first sign of weakness. It's frightening when you know that some of the boys carry switch-blade

---

[1] "Boys and Girls Together," *Time*, Oct. 19, 1953, p. 72. Copyright 1953 Time Inc. All rights reserved. Reprinted by permission from TIME.

knives. There's always a first test. One of them will start yelling, or singing or jumping over chairs. . . . You must remember that none of these children want to be in school. They do not want to learn. They already belong to the streets. They know you cannot punish them physically or expel them. You must never raise your voice to them. You must never stand near them or touch them. Hate for the teachers is part of their code.[2]

EDUCATION AND NOBEL PRIZES

In the forefront of most criticisms of the American education system, especially those aimed at the public schools, is the old, old charge that Russia is outstripping the United States in virtually all the areas that count, at least in the building of war machines and in studies related to that end, such as mathematics and the sciences. The Defense Education Act, passed by the Congress in 1958, was largely motivated by the notion that the Soviet Union was far surpassing the United States in teaching the sciences and math. And, of course, our own citizens, as critics of the public schools, charged that the United States was being left behind in the number of Nobel Prizes won by Russia.

That accusation turned out to be far from the facts and is still far from the truth. Between 1901, when the annual awards of Nobel prizes began, and 1980 a total of 455 Nobel Prizes were awarded. Citizens of the United States have won more such prizes, by a large margin, than have those of any other nation in the world. The total awarded to citizens of the United States has reached in excess of 150—about one-third of the total—while Russia's number of prizes has been about two dozen. Yet a relatively large number of distinguished Americans continue to carp about our schools doing a poor job in producing experts in math and science.

The following is a list of the major countries in the world, and the number of Nobel Prizes won by each through 1980.[3]

United States–166	Switzerland–14
Great Britain–79	Netherlands–11
Germany–57	Denmark–11
France–44	Italy–10
USSR–24	Austria–9

---

[2] Ibid.

[3] *The World Book Encyclopedia*, 1982 ed., s.v. "Nobel Prizes."

BUT THERE ARE DISSENTERS

Elsewhere in the world, there is vehement dissent about the value of education, especially education for all and at public expense. There are dissenters in America, too.

Here is a sample of that philosophy as reported by Lewis Shayon, who set out twenty years ago to find out for himself whether all the vilification of the public schools in the nation's press was justified.

> The professor and I sat in his narrow high ceilinged office in a large state university and talked about education. . . . The professor is in the vanguard of critics claiming that our public schools fail to devote themselves exclusively to serious intellectual training. . . . The professor spelled out for me the socially desirable consequences which would flow from a tough, one-track system, one that early weeded out the intellectually unfit and shunted them to some vaguely defined side-spur. I asked him what would become of the non-verbal achievers and he smiled, shrugged his shoulders and said, "Let them dig ditches."
>
> . . .
>
> It is one thing to theorize in words about the inadequacies of your fellow man. It is a shock in the flesh to make him a hewer of wood and drawer of water. . . . now after my trip . . . I have undergone a change of heart. I am convinced that our common public school system with its promise of maximum development for the individual capacities of all, need not be scrapped. . . . I am persuaded that it would be dangerous to do so. I suggest that the professional education leadership in the nation has both the wisdom and the capacity to do that school modernization that needs to be done. Proudly our citizens support them.[4]

AMERICA'S PUBLIC SCHOOLS—KEY TO THEIR GREATNESS

What about the credit side of the ledger for the public schools? There is the impressive story of a Chicano family with fourteen children, all of whom graduated from high school in San Antonio, and one of whom graduated from a state university, largely because of the dream of their

---

[4] Lewis Shayon, "Report from the Grass Roots," *Saturday Review*, Sept. 13, 1958, pp. 15–17.

parents, migrant farm laborers. The parents had vowed that their children would have high school diplomas, not bloody fingers from picking cotton or aching backs from digging beets, as they had experienced. After their first child graduated from high school, they didn't have any doubts that all the children would make it. It was a painful struggle, but fourteen diplomas are displayed in the family home. Few examples could so superbly illustrate the "lifted lamp beside the golden door."

Reading this glorious story of the dream of these impoverished Mexican-American parents reminds one to search the records again for that touching story of Billie Davis the Gypsy Girl, who wrote so beautifully that "everywhere we went there was a school and a desk waiting just for me . . . there were laws that said so."[5]

An equally touching story concerns Mary Antin, the child of European immigrants, who started public school in Boston without then being able to speak English. She wrote:

> Education was free . . . it was the only thing my father was able to promise us when he sent for us; surer, safer than bread or shelter. On our second day I was thrilled with the realization of what this freedom of education meant. A little girl from across the alley came and offered to conduct us to school. My father was out, but we five between us had a few words of English by this time. We knew the word school. *We understood this child—who had never seen us until yesterday, who could not pronounce our names, who was not much better dressed than we—was able to offer us the freedom of the schools of Boston. No application made, no questions asked, no examinations, rulings, exclusions, no machinations, no fees. The doors stood open for every one of us.*[6]

Truly these miracles could happen ONLY IN AMERICA, which leads many to think that the promise of a free school and a desk for every child is one of America's crowning glories.

THE SAGA OF CARVER

And there is the powerful, awe-inspiring story of George Washington Carver. It is an oft-told story, but it should be retold down through the

---

[5] Billie Davis, "I Was a Hobo Kid," *Saturday Evening Post*, Dec. 13, 1952.

[6] Mary Antin, *The Promised Land* (Boston: Houghton Mifflin, 1912), p. 186.

years to remind us, and the world, that greatness can be found in the most unlikely places through the powers of universal education. George Washington Carver was born in Diamond, Missouri, of slave parents in January, 1869. On January 11, 1865, Missouri had outlawed slavery "now and forever," so the baby would, after many tribulations, grow up a free man. His father was killed in an accident shortly after his birth.

When George Washington Carver was a baby, some marauders kidnapped Mary Carver and her baby, George, and took them to Arkansas. Moses Carver, their owner, hired a man to go after the kidnapped Mary and George, offering to pay him with land, for their recovery. Reaching Arkansas, the man could not find the mother, but the baby had been left with two women who gladly gave him up.

Since he failed to bring back the mother, the man gave up his claim to the land promised him; he would take only the horse furnished him for the trip. So George Washington Carver was brought back in exchange for a race horse which his owner valued at $300.

Thus, one of the great figures in the history of this nation—and of the world, for that matter—was valued at the price of an old, probably enfeebled race horse. This humble child, because he was black, had to scratch and improvise to get the rudiments of an education. This person, who became a blessing to his fellow Americans and to all mankind, returned to his native country the value of the horse for which he was traded, multiplied by the thousands. Twice because of his derivatives from peanuts and sweet potatoes, he was offered a salary of $100,000 a year and the building of a great new laboratory in which to work, by such giants as Henry Ford and Thomas Edison, to take charge of production of these derivatives in magnified quantities. But he declined, choosing to stay at Tuskegee and to continue seeking new ways to help his people. He did not seek enrichment for his discoveries but shared with any interested parties the formulas for the derivatives.

George Washington Carver, while still a boy of tender age, developed a love of and a genius for supervising the growth of certain plants. As a child, he gained a reputation among his neighbors for working magic with the young plants that attracted his attention, early earning the title "Plant Doctor." He seemed to have an innate instinct for caring for plants. He was on constant call by his neighbors to analyze plants that were not growing vigorously. He developed a secret garden where he treated ailing plants. He had no explanation for his uncanny ability; he so loved the woods and streams that as a boy his days often were spent, not in playing games, but in examining the trees and flowers in the forests.

As a matter of fact, much of his early education was self-acquired. The new Missouri Constitution provided free schools for children from ages five to twenty, but George did not go to school with white children. So he taught himself by naming flowers, shrubs, and trees in the forests. Also, an old Webster's blue-back speller was given him by a relative, and he memorized each word therein. Finally, he was sent to school in Neosho, Missouri, about eight miles from home, where he learned all that the little school had to offer.

His abiding fascination with plant life won out, and he decided to enroll at Iowa Agricultural College, at Ames. This was a hard decision to make because it involved giving up his dream of a career in art, in order to concentrate upon equipping himself to help his people. The college he chose (now Iowa State University) was one of the outstanding agricultural institutions in the United States. It produced many leaders in the field. Of course, Miss Budd, his art teacher at Simpson, and her father, who was a professor at Iowa Agricultural College, helped greatly to encourage the young man.

Booker T. Washington, who had made a national record for himself, was building in prestige a great institution for the advancement of blacks, Tuskegee Normal School and Institute in Alabama. In April, 1896, he offered Carver the position of head of the agricultural department, at a salary of $1,500. Carver accepted at once, because he saw here the opportunity for his life's work—raising the living standards of his people through improved soil and agriculture. Here he made a record to stand through the years.

Over the years, Carver influenced an almost complete about-face in the manner and type of agriculture in the Tuskegee area. Moreover, his reputation in the care of plants and new methods, developed at Tuskegee, were in demand in places such as Germany, Africa, and Australia. One of his most productive innovations was to demonstrate the value of conserving plant life after it had been used to enrich the soil. He was instrumental in increasing productivity to such an extent that once-worn-out soil began producing a handsome annual profit. Many countries, particularly Africa, sought to lure Carver away. But Tuskegee was his home, and he could not be enticed elsewhere.

In the area of the derivatives of certain well-known products, such as the peanut and the sweet potato, he worked major miracles. As the boll weevil continued to invade the fields of the South, moving northward from Mexico, Carver saw clearly that the solution was (in part, at least) to deemphasize the cultivation of cotton and to seek other and more productive crops. He started early in his career at Tuskegee to promote the growing of peanuts and sweet potatoes as vegetables that contained virtually all of man's nutritional needs. From the sweet potato he developed a syrup, tapioca, vinegar, domestic alcohol, and flour.

As Carver's innovations began to pile up, he was asked repeatedly what he was going to do with them. His reply was always, in effect, as follows: "My job is to find these things. I leave it to businessmen to manufacture and sell them." In only a few cases did he seek a patent on a new discovery. Indeed, Carver was a major force in the transformation of manufacturing, by the use of substitutes which he largely contributed. This new development was sparked by the National Farm Chemurgic Council, founded in 1935 at Dearborn, Michigan, the home of Henry Ford's automobile plant. Carver was invited to speak at a meeting of this council in 1937, on future methods of farm welfare. Carver and Henry Ford became warm friends. Ford admired Carver's works and sought several times to hire him at a huge salary to head a new research laboratory which he offered to build.

The achievements of Carver contained, among numerous others, 118 products from the sweet potato, and about 300 products from the peanut. By 1940, the peanut became among the six leading crops, and engendered an annual business of over $200 million. The year 1936–37 was marked for celebrating the fortieth anniversary of Dr. Carver's tenure at Tuskegee. The climax of this commemorative year came in the June commencement. A bronze bust was unveiled on June 2, 1937, as was an exhibit of the products Carver had contributed to man's progress. At commencement, the decision to build the George Washington Carver Museum was made by the trustees.

In 1939, Carver was a guest at a dinner in the home of Theodore Roosevelt, where he received the Roosevelt Medal for distinguished service in the field of science. In making the presentation, Mr. Roosevelt said: "I have the honor to present not a man only, but a life, transfused with passion for the enlarging and enriching of the living of his fellow man . . . a liberator to men of the white race as well as the black; a bridge from one race to the other, on which men of good will may learn of each other and rejoice together in the opportunities and the potentialities of their common country."[7]

Perhaps one more thing ought to be said about George Washington Carver, since this book deals with public education. He had an abiding faith in the power of education, especially to create racial harmony. In this connection he once said, "You can play a tune of sorts on the white keys, and you can play a tune of sorts on the black keys, but for harmony, you must use both the black and white."[8] When he was born, only 3 percent of the blacks were literate. By the time of his death, it was about 30 percent. Today, illiteracy in America is on the way to eradication.

The thought comes to mind that, at this moment in the history of the United States, there is a great need for another George Washington Carver to find a derivative from one of our annually renewable crops with which to produce gasohol. This would be the find of the century.

NEED TO INCREASE COLLEGE ATTENDANCE

It appears now that the college-going age group (18–25) will begin increasing again only in the 1990s. Higher education institutions have several alternatives. Some universities are offering remedial work for those whose high school education was inferior. In one state, tuition and aid policies are adjusted to compete with adjoining states. Efforts are suggested to recruit foreign students. Part-time enrollment of adults is another possibility. Black and Hispanic students will increase and will soon make up a larger proportion of the total population.

DECLINE IN ATTRACTIVENESS OF TEACHING

A 1979 Gallup Poll of the attractiveness of teaching as a career reported that only 13 percent of all college students made teaching their first career choice. This reflects a drastic decrease from the choice of 23 percent five years before. Those conducting the survey attribute this drop to the existing surplus of teachers, measured by the large number who have prepared

---

[7] Rackham Holt, *George Washington Carver* (Garden City, N.Y.: Doubleday, 1952), pp. 331. Used by permission.
[8] Ibid.

for teaching but cannot find acceptable jobs; and to the creation of new fields, such as computer science, which are attracting many who had planned to teach. This poll predicts a further decline in the number who will choose to prepare for teaching. Another significant fact projects even further drops in those who will seek to prepare for teaching: while 19 percent of seniors and 14 percent of juniors indicated they would like to teach, only 12 percent of sophomores and 11 percent of freshmen indicated that teaching was their first choice. Also, while 20 percent of college women indicated that teaching is their first choice as a career, only 8 percent of men expressed the same choice. Business is first among the many fields competing for those who might have chosen teaching. Medicine, too, seems to be losing some of its great appeal, as a career choice; the choice for a medical field was 14 percent five years ago, but it has dropped to 9 percent for women and 7 for men. Law appeals to 7 percent, and engineering and accounting to 6 percent.

Teacher burnout, plus inadequate salaries, plus violence and vandalism, are driving teachers out of teaching and into other work. An NEA poll showed fully one-third of the teachers sampled reported that they would not choose to enter teaching again. Only 60 percent reported that they plan to stay in teaching. The impacts of violence and vandalism, plus comparatively low salaries, were given as basic reasons. The number of teachers with twenty years of experience has dropped by half in the last fifteen years, the poll showed.

TYLER LAUDS EDUCATION ACHIEVEMENTS

Ralph Tyler, eminent scholar and respected educator, has lauded the American educational system as follows: "No other industrialized nation expects as much of its educational system as America does. And one task facing American educators is going to be increasingly more difficult."[9] He enumerated three factors involved: (1) As our society becomes more complex, it requires more education just to attain basic literacy; (2) American schools are attempting to educate a broader and broader segment of the population; and (3) with a more mobile society, children are transferred from school to school more frequently. He wrote:

---

[9] Kevin Ryan et al., "An Interview with Ralph Tyler," *Phi Delta Kappan*, Mar., 1977, p. 544. Used by permission.

At the time of the nation's independence, only 15 percent of our adult population was literate. By World War I that percentage had risen to 35 percent and by World War II, to 55 percent. In 1979, 80–82 percent of the 17 year olds who took the National Assessment of Educational Progress Tests had attained basic literacy . . . in comparison with students of 16 other industrialized nations, American students scored at or near the top in reading and mathematics. Only Finnish and Swedish students scored better than American students on these two assessments. The scores are particularly significant because in America we educate a much higher percentage of adolescents than do other industrialized nations.[10]

SCHOOLS AS WHIPPING BOYS

The public schools of the United States are, perhaps, the easiest and most inviting target of all publicly supported agencies, for finger-pointing and scapegoating.

Why is this? Well, first of all, the school system is supported by taxation, which tends to be a prime target for citizens who are disgruntled about things in general. Second, schools are near home and largely under local control. Third, at least until recent years, schools had few if any vocal and politically powerful defenders. Fourth, a large proportion of taxpaying citizens do not have children of school age, so they tend to resent paying taxes for schools they do not directly use.

Thus in the past schools have received blame for almost every national emergency. Wars and threats of war, in particular, have turned the spotlight of accusation on the schools.

At long last the teaching profession, through its organizations, has become militant in rebutting the recurring charges. Especially have these organizations been aggressive in the last two or three decades, in defending in the courts individual teachers who have been illegally mistreated. These accusations and mistreatments have finally attracted the support of many powerful public influences. It is not uncommon now for the press, in particular, to come to the defense of the schools, and to come to the defense of illegally treated individual teachers.

A prime example is a bizarre case in Florida. Prompted by the birth of his son, a Florida advertising agent ran a full-page ad in the regional

---

[10] Ibid.

edition of *Time,* criticizing the educational system in Florida. Above a picture of the man's son, a large headline read: "THIS IS MY NEWBORN SON. I Demand Florida Give Him A Decent Education."

The ad continued: "Florida is a great place to raise children. The state provides everything from beaches to ballfields for their physical growth. And nature provides the sunshine for their beautiful suntans. But Florida's educational system stinks."

The ad went on to point out the high percentage of failure of elementary and secondary children in the state literacy tests and to lament the overcrowded classrooms, double sessions, and unqualified teachers.

The irate father then stated, "I think it's time we get off our indifferent butts and do something about it." He urged his readers to write to their elected officials and ask how they feel about Florida's underfinanced educational program and what they are doing to improve the situation. His advice was to vote them out if their answers were unsatisfactory.

He concluded: "If you are as disturbed as I am about Florida's educational deficiencies, write, shout, stomp your feet, and let everyone from the teacher, to the principal, to the school board, to the legislature, to the governor hear you. Unless you think your kid can make it in this world with just a nice suntan."[11]

An editorial in the *Tampa Tribune* of January 7, 1979, carried a facsimile of the full-page ad in *Time* and read in part:

Time Fails the Responsibility Test

With portentous fanfare, *Time* magazine's film news shorts of another generation used to end with a deep voice booming, "*Time* marches on!"

But *Time* didn't march this week in a "public service" magazine advertisement attacking Florida public schools.

Time fell flat on its face.

The advertisement is full of inaccuracies, innuendoes and misleading statements, even as to its origins. None of that apparently bothers *Time,* whose spokesman blindly replied to protests from Florida officials that the magazine "does not take a position for or against the ad. . . ."

The advertisement appeared in only the 135,000 issues of the magazine circulated in Florida, but that is bad enough.

It says that the state is a great place to raise children, but that its

---

[11] See *Time,* Jan. 8, 1979, p. 75.

"educational system stinks." Detailing its criticism, it accuses Florida of being 49th in educational funding, with "overcrowded classrooms, double sessions, and too many unqualified teachers."

"We should be ashamed of the high percentage of elementary and secondary children that failed miserably in the recent State Literacy Tests," it also asserts. . . .

None of those charges is entirely accurate.

Florida is not 49th but 30th in spending for education, according to Education Commissioner Ralph Turlington. Some indices rank Florida higher than that; the World Almanac puts the state 24th in per-pupil expenditure, the best indicator. Florida usually is near the bottom in per capita expenditures for public school education for a reason that has less to do with money than with the age of the state's people. We are 50th in the ratio of public school children to total population.

Florida has overcrowded classrooms; so does every other growing state, but in per pupil spending for capital outlay (primarily new schools) Florida (according to the World Almanac) is 15th. That shows a strong effort to catch up.

As for double sessions, Commissioner Turlington says one percent of the state's more than 2,000 public schools still are on double sessions. . . .

But the most misleading statements of all deal with the literacy tests. Elementary pupils don't take them at all, for one thing. More important, the percentage of failures in the most recent tests was only 3 percent in communications and 24 percent in arithmetic. And most of those who failed the tests in 1977 passed them on the second try, which every pupil gets.[12]

Another Florida newspaper, the *St. Petersburg Times,* responded to this advertisement by addressing its author:

Time magazine gave you that free ad . . . to demonstrate the power of print. Instead, you showed us your own weakness and how indignant teachers can get when they are wronged. . . . But you blew it . . . when you didn't check your facts. . . . You should have said something like this: Florida's public schools are better than they used to be, but they are not good enough. You should have cited SAT scores. Florida's college bound students averaged 428 on their verbal SAT scores. That's good, but not good enough; also the math scores improved, but both scores were still below the national average. . . . You should have said that too many Florida schools (23)

---

[12] "*Time* Fails Responsibility Test," *Tampa Tribune,* Jan. 7, 1979. Used by permission.

are on double sessions . . . that too many kids don't have individual text books . . . but the Legislature sharply increased text book money last year. You goofed when you said Florida spends less money on schools than 49 states . . . Wrong . . . Finally, you said that if Florida's children are going to have the best schools . . . you and other parents must be willing to work for them and pay for them. That's the way to do it.[13]

WHAT IS THE PURPOSE OF EDUCATION?

These days the American people seem so inundated with sales pitches about the failings of the public schools that they often, momentarily at least, seem to vacillate about the real purposes of education. Here are some of the sophistries that they swallow (thankfully, only temporarily), most often on superficial or nonexistent evidence: "Education is an instrument of national policy." "Education is an instrument of survival." "Education is an instrument of economic growth." We must not overlook those who seem to believe in education only for the gifted, the elites—those who thrive on education reserved for the upper few, and those who inherited wealth.

Fortunately, Americans have never believed any of these for long, only as spur-of-the-moment impulses or under the influence of super salesmanship. Deep down, they know in their hearts that education exists for the cultivation of talents of the individual. And any society—be it a democracy, an autocracy, or a collectivist one—that insists upon viewing the child as a resource or a weapon or a tool or an instrument will end up by treating him as such, and no more.

COST OF SCHOOLS

The cost of the public schools has quadrupled, some say. This charge is rarely, if ever, connected to any time factor. (The CBS program "Is Anyone out There Learning?" did use the time period since 1948.) This accusation could readily be probable, if one goes back far enough in history. Compared with the cost in 1900, for example, current cost of the schools might be ten times as great. Whatever comparisons are being

---

[13] Editorial, *St. Petersburg Times.* Used by permission.

made, it is imperative that distortions caused by nationwide inflation be avoided.

But let's consider current costs compared with those of a decade or two ago. In the decade 1967–68 to 1977–78, the total cost of the public schools in the United States rose from $74.8 billion to $80.2 billion, an increase of 7.2 percent. This increase in school cost was 4 percent less than that of the increase in the Gross National Product in this same period. In expenditures per pupil for the decade, the dollar amount rose from $648 in the first year to $1,742 in the last year, or a percentage increase for the decade of 164.7 percent.[14]

As to the revenue sources of the $80.2 billion cost of the schools in 1977–78, the shares provided by the federal, state, and local governments approximated the following: federal, 9.1 percent; state, increased from 38.5 percent to 44.1 percent; and local, decreased from 52.7 percent to 47.6 percent.[15]

To present a balanced picture, it should be pointed out that the total enrollment in public schools over this period increased from 57.3 million to 60.2 million, an increase of 2.9 million or about 5 percent. Enrollments are now expected to decline annually until about the middle of the 1980s.

As to the teachers' salaries which, of course, are a major share of the total cost of schools, these salaries continue, as they always have, to lag behind those in other professions. Many citizens, indeed perhaps most, will tend to attribute the oft-cited "quadrupled cost of education" to the greedy teachers. This idea is far from reality, far from the truth. In one of the largest cities of the United States, this notion is so far out of line that the city's largest and most conservative newspaper editorially refuted this notion. One comment was that the average teacher's salary in that city ($14,380) for nine months was not competitive with private industry (see relative salaries for the United States in Table 19.1). That city lost 225 of its experienced teachers in one year because of the salary scale. Next in cause was the growing discipline problem. Many large cities have been feeling the pinch of teacher flight; highly skilled, experienced teachers are moving to other occupations, and this will continue. Of course, considering the history of teaching, it is quite natural for citizens to harbor the notion that teachers are like religious workers salary-wise—because

---

[14] *Financial Status of the Public Schools*, 1978 (Washington, D.C.: National Education Association, 1978), p. 46.

[15] Ibid.

TABLE 19.1
Comparisons of Average Starting Salaries of Teachers in the Public
Schools Compared with Those in Private Industry

Position or Subject Field	Dates	
	1970–71	1978–79
Beginning teachers	$ 6,850	$ 9,713
Engineering	10,476	14,904
Accounting	10,080	13,464
Sales-marketing	8,580	12,636
Business administration	8,124	12,048
Liberal arts	8,184	11,408
Chemistry	8,708	14,700
Mathematics-statistics	9,468	13,632
Economics-finance	8,808	12,072
Computer science	No Data	14,160
Other fields	9,264	13,848

NOTE: From *Financial Status of the Public Schools, 1978* (Washington, D.C.: National Education Association, 1978), p. 46. Used by permission of the National Education Research Services Division.

NOTE: These figures apply to individuals at the bachelor's degree level of preparation.

once most of them were. But no longer will they, or can they, work for what is offered by many communities.

In another of the nation's largest cities, the superintendent started a fund for reimbursement of teachers' property losses through vandalism by donating $200 to a fund for this purpose. Public funds in this state cannot legally be used for such reimbursements. Some cities have already established such funds, financed by general school revenues.

DIMENSION OF EDUCATION IN THE UNITED STATES

No other nation in history has exhibited such commitment to education as has the United States. This is, of course, tantamount to saying "as have the people of the United States." The magnitude of this commitment is reflected by the following. In the school year 1978–79, more than 60 million were enrolled in schools of all types, from nursery through kindergarten, elementary schools, junior high schools, high schools, junior colleges (community colleges), colleges, universities, graduate schools, professional schools, vocational trade schools, music schools, business schools, and so forth. There are public, private, religious, and individually sponsored schools. As to public support (by taxation), there are local (city, county, town or school district), state, area (several counties), and national schools. As to private support there are church (or religious) schools, sect or denomination schools; private corporation and private individual (often called proprietary or free enterprise) schools; there are schools operated for profit, as business enterprises. The array of governing bodies of the public schools supported by taxation is monumental. Presently there are 15,000 to 16,000 local school districts in the United States. (This number varies from year to year and is steadily declining due to consolidation of school districts to create school units large enough and rich enough to support schools from kindergarten through high school, and often community colleges, providing the first two years of higher education.) By virtue of a falling birth rate in the country, a decline in enrollments in the public schools is already underway and will continue until toward the middle of the 1980s.

Overloading the Schools

As evidence that many members of the general public tend to look upon the public schools as charity agencies, one columnist says, if we aren't careful, we're going to wind up doing to the schools what we have already done to the military. We're going to overload them with so much extraneous social baggage that they will be unable to carry out their primary mission.

Every time somebody comes up with a social objective that seems to make sense, we give it to the schools to implement. When we saw the need to end racial segregation, we looked to the schools to do it. Now we are complaining about the cost of busing (in one city, this cost is about $8,500 per bus per year). And more is probably to come. There are still several schools which are all white (in one city the number is 63). And it is clear now that the federal courts, for consistency's sake, will surely rule eventually that all schools must be desegregated. The schools didn't create this problem, but we Americans expect them to solve it. Ditto with the idea that there surely is no justifiable logic to the existence of hunger, a curable ill in the richest of all countries. So we turned to the schools to provide school lunches (and in some places school breakfasts), and health diagnosis and healing stations. Poor car-driving habits and accidents grew to such proportions that it became the task of the schools to wipe out bad, ignorant, and reckless driving by assuming the duties of teaching existing law on the subject and providing driver education.

Eventually the schools became so overloaded with these problems of society that the time remaining for education was limited.

So, what are we doing to the military establishment? For those unable to afford college, the military provides a remedy. Or if too many of our minorities can't find jobs—urge them to enlist in the armed services. Too, there is the serious matter of a lack of teaching of appropriate discipline— let the army or other service branches do it. We have decided that these same services shall be furnished by the military to women also. These are all accepted practices by the majority of our people. But it is hardly fair to overload the public schools *or* the military with duties that belong to society as a whole, thus robbing them of the time and the personnel to provide the basic service at quality levels expected by the public.

And, of course, many of the fervent critics of the public schools tend to forget entirely the economic returns to the public of public education. Former Vice-President Walter Mondale said:

> When I chaired the Senate Committee on Equal Educational Opportunity, the Committee found that for every dollar the United States spends on education, it returns $6 to the Gross National Product. Every $4 the country spends to get students to complete high school returns $7 to federal, state, and local governments. . . . A dollar invested in education works for every goal we have as a nation. It strengthens our democracy. It improves the economy. It increases our lives. And it provides the greatest incentive for social justice and opportunity. There is no better investment in the nation than education.[16]

The Debt Eternal

In the dreariest period of World War II, the minister of education of England reminded his fellow countrymen of their obligation to provide education for their youth, at whatever sacrifice—that after health and safety it is the first obligation of the state; it is the eternal debt. And so it

---

[16] Walter Mondale, "Leave Them Alone to Do Their Jobs," *Today's Education*, Nov.–Dec., 1979, p. 29. Used by permission.

is. But here in America, the richest nation in the history of the world, the obligation to maintain schools for every child is particularly and peculiarly a debt which, in the midst of prosperity and peace, we can only escape by inviting disaster that exceeds the imagination.

Fuss-budgeting over more or less minuscule imperfections in the instrumentalities of education is not the answer. The answer is to spot the existing weaknesses—the real ones, not the fancied ones—and fight to eliminate them.

This is the one and only route for honorable discharge by the people of the United States of this inescapable obligation—to fulfill this "debt eternal." And that obligation falls with special emphasis upon those charged with the actual conduct of those schools.

It is generally conceded that our system of universal free schools, available to every child—whether rich or poor; whether of aristocratic parents, or of hard-working ones whose energies are almost wholly spent in the essential task of earning a decent living for their families—our public schools are the magic ingredient in guaranteeing an equal chance for all, at least as equal as human beings can assure. These schools are, in the long run, the great levelers of circumstances.

It must inevitably enter the minds of thoughtful people that the public clamor against the schools is ironic, indeed. To state the matter in another way, to paraphrase Lincoln's statement in another context, "Such schools are the last best hope of man on earth."

The people of the United States have a great hope for a better life for their children. That hope rests largely at one point: the promise of a full education for every man's children. It is ironic that many of us should forget this fact of life so easily. The anomaly of this situation—with more teachers being violently attacked annually—is almost beyond comprehension. These figures are astounding, and very sad. Because these teachers are being driven to physical and mental breakdowns by the children of those who presumably are being given a new hope and a new promise by their chance at full education.

THE VALUE OF EDUCATION AND DEMOCRACY

Eric Sevareid, the noted TV newsman, spent six years of his life covering World War II all over the world and ended up covering the closing drive of the Allies in France, across the Rhine into Germany and Berlin. He awaited the night before the last great battle, at the Rhine, across from the last German bastion, a small town on the German side of the river. When it was battered down by the shells of the Allies, the way to Berlin would be clear. Sevareid, awaiting this bombardment, stood by the Rhine and thought about the impending victory:

> The last battle would be fought just across the river. . . . The Germans did not know that this was the last day when the endless war would still be a war. Tomorrow the great German raid against the human race would be all over save for the meaningless odds and ends. . . . The whole situation was selfishly satisfying, and I savored it. I, an ordinary man with a name and origin of which Caesar [Hitler] was ignorant, was standing a couple of hundred yards from his camp knowing the secret of his fate and the fate of his empire. And he didn't know. I, one of his intended slaves was so much mightier than he. I, who had never kicked a Jew, or looted a village, or burned a bank, or stolen a country, or killed anything larger than a hare, was standing with empty hands looking into his final citadel, possessed of the biggest, brightest fact in this moment of eternity—the fact that the terror and tyranny of our times would come to an end this night. . . . now that I am here, I'll represent the whole human race, all the millions of people who haven't done things Caesar [Hitler] has done.[17]

This passage by Sevareid phrases eloquently the deep-down, earnest, and generally accepted goals of universal education in America, whatever the type of school—public, private, or church sponsored; kindergarten, elementary, secondary, college, or university—and whatever the age or level of achievement. And the measure of realization of these hopes is largely based upon the quality and dedication of teachers in these schools.

The charge being peddled wholesale during the current criticisms of the public schools is that "teachers today are not as dedicated as they used to be." The closing comments of Jerry Burke in *Not for Glory*, describing the finalists for the National Teacher of the Year in the years 1961–67, from which we abstracted some vignettes in Chapter 17 herein, are appropriate:

---

[17] Eric Sevareid, *Not So Wild a Dream* (New York: Atheneum, 1976), pp. 497–98. Copyright 1946, 1974, © 1976 by Eric Sevareid. Reprinted with the permission of Atheneum Publisher and the Harold Matson Company, Inc.

I could close my eyes and re-create the sights and sounds, the words, faces and atmosphere of those adventures in friendship. My microscopic examination of fifty-four separate school systems encouraged me to believe that nothing in American life can match the vigor and importance of the classroom confrontation of minds. Therein lies our future. There is no turning back. The kinds of teachers I met are not content to look upon education as something finished. No teacher, no American, can afford that luxury.[18]

Of course, there always have been and always will be some undedicated people in the teaching profession, as there have been and always will in all professions. But they are so few as to destroy the intended sweep of the indictment.

---

[18] William J. Burke, *Not for Glory* (New York: Cowles Education Corporation, 1967), p. 206.

SUGGESTED READING

INDEX

Suggested Reading

"Accountability, Competency Testing, Back to Basics Symposium." *NAASP Bulletin*, 62 (Oct., 1978), 1–93.

Alvins, James J., and Theodore J. Gourley. "The Challenge of Our Gifted Children." *Teacher*, 95, no. 4 (Dec., 1977), 45.

Andrew, Michael D. *Teachers Should Be Human Too.* Washington, D.C.: Association of Teacher Educators, 1972.

Aquila, F. D., and J. First. "Disproportionate Suspension and the Teacher Referral Process." *Viewpoints: Teaching and Learning*, 56 (Spring, 1980), 56–64.

Armstrong, David G., et al. *Education: An Introduction.* New York: Macmillan, 1981.

Barutz, Joan C., and Jay H. Moskowitz. "Proposition 13: How and Why It Happened." *Phi Delta Kappan*, 60 (Sept., 1978), 9–11.

Baughman, M. Dale. *Baughman's Handbook of Humor in Education.* New York: Parker Publishing Company, 1974.

Bloom, Benjamin S. "The New Direction in Educational Research: Alterable Variables." *Phi Delta Kappan*, 61, no. 6 (Feb., 1980), 382–85.

Bogdan, Robert. "The Soft Side of Hard Data: Education Statistics as a Human Process." *Phi Delta Kappan*, 61 (Feb., 1980), 411–12.

Borton, Terry. *Reach, Touch, and Teach: Student Concerns and Process Education.* 2d ed. Santa Monica, Calif.: Goodyear Publishing Company, 1978.

Boyer, Ernest L. "What's Right with Our Schools?" *Ohio Schools*, 41 (Sept., 1978), 15.

Bracey, Gerald W. "The SAT, College Admissions, and the Concept of Talent: Unexamined Myths, Unexplained Perceptions, Needed Explorations." *Phi Delta Kappan*, 62, no. 3 (Nov., 1980), 197–99.

Broed, Ihy. *Alternative Schools: Why, What, Where and How Much.* Arlington, Va.: National School Public Relations Association, 1977.

Broido, L. "Rules Governing the Private Lives of Teachers." *Education Digest*, 45, no. 28 (Jan., 1980), 3.

Browne, James. "Power Politics for Teachers, Modern Style." *Phi Delta Kappan*, 58 (Oct., 1976), 158–64.

Butts, Freeman R. "The Search for Purposes in American Education." *The College Board Review* (Winter, 1975–76), pp. 3–19.

Campbell, Jack K. *Colonel Francis Parker: The Children's Crusader*. New York: Teachers College Press, 1967.

Campbell, Margaret H. "Testimony of a Battered Teacher." *Phi Delta Kappan*, 60, no. 6 (Feb., 1979), 441–42.

Cheyney, Arnold B. *Teaching Children of Different Cultures in the Classroom*. 2d ed. Columbus, Ohio: Charles E. Merrill Publishing Company, 1976.

Coles, Robert. *Uprooted Children*. New York: Harper and Row Publishers, 1970.

Combs, Arthur W., ed. *Perceiving, Behavior, Becoming*. Washington, D.C.: Association for Supervision and Curriculum Development, 1962.

Commager, Henry Steele. "The School as Surrogate Conscience." *Saturday Review*, 2, no. 8 (Jan. 11, 1975), 54–57.

Conroy, Pat. *The Water Is Wide*. New York: Penguin Books, 1972.

Coombs, J. R. "Can Minimum Competency Testing Be Justified?" *High School Journal*, 62 (Jan., 1979), 175–80.

Corwin, T. M. "Assessing the Impact of Mandatory Retirement at Age 70." *Junior College and University Personnel Association*, 29 (Winter, 1978), 63–68.

Cremin, Lawrence A. *The Genius of American Education*. New York: Vintage Books, 1966.

———. *Public Education*. New York: Basic Books, 1976.

Cronin, Joseph M., and Sally B. Pancrazio. "Women as Educational Leaders." *Phi Delta Kappan*, 60, no. 8 (Apr., 1979), 583–84.

Deane, B., and J. A. Walker. "Florida's Basic Skills Test, and Why Everybody Likes It." *American School Board*, 165 (May, 1978), 28–30.

Denton, Jon J., and Kenneth T. Henson, "Mastery Learning and Grade Inflation." *Educational Leadership*, 37 (Dec., 1979), 150–52.

Dolgin, A. B. "Supervisory Process: An Important Trend in Administrative Hearings for Teachers." *American Secondary Education*, 10 (June, 1980), 56–62.

Donley, Marshall O., Jr. *Power to the Teacher: How America's Educators Became Militant*. Bloomington, Ind.: Indiana University Press, 1976.

Drummond, William H., and Theodore E. Andrews. "The Influence of Federal and State Governments on Teacher Education." *Phi Delta Kappan*, 62, no. 2 (Oct., 1980), 97–100.

Eisner, E. "You Have Political Clout: Are You Using It?" *Instructor*, 88 (April, 1979), 28ff.

Ellett, Chad D.; William Capie; and Charles E. Johnson. "Assessing Teaching Performance." *Phi Delta Kappan*, 62, no. 5 (Jan., 1981), 219–21.

Erikson, Erik H. *Identity: Youth and Crisis*. New York: Norton, 1978.

Fantini, Mario. *The People and Their Schools: Community Participation*. Bloomington, Ind.: Phi Delta Kappa Foundation, 1975.

Flygare, T. J. "Free Speech Rights of Teachers." *Phi Delta Kappan*, 60 (Nov., 1978), 242–43.

———. "Teacher's Private Expression: Constitutionally Protected, But With a Limitation." *Phi Delta Kappan*, 60 (April, 1979), 602–3.

Frazier, Clavin M. "State/Federal Role in Curriculum Development." *Educational Leadership*, 35 (Feb., 1978), 339–41.

Friendenberg, Edgar. *Coming of Age in America*. New York: Vintage, 1965.

Frymier, Jack. "On the Way to the Forum—It's a Very Standard Error." *Educational Forum*, 36 (May, 1979), 388–91.

Fuhrman, Susan. "School Finance Reform in the 1980's." *Educational Leadership*, 38, no. 2 (Nov., 1980), 122–24.

Gallagher, J. J. *Teaching the Gifted Child*. Boston: Allyn and Bacon, Inc., 1975.

Gallup, George. "The Eleventh Annual Gallup Poll of the Public's Attitudes Toward the Public Schools." *Phi Delta Kappan*, 62 (Sept., 1980), 33–45.

Gilman, David A. "Logic of Minimal Competency Testing." *NASSP Bulletin*, 62 (Sept., 1978), 56–63.

Glatthorn, Allan. *Alternatives in Education: Schools and Programs*. New York: Harper and Row, 1975.

Glazer, Nathan. "Ethnicity and Education: Some Hard Questions." *Phi Delta Kappan*, 62, no. 5 (Jan., 1981), 386–89.

Gold, Milton J.; Carl A. Grant; and Harry N. Rivlin, eds. *In Praise of Diversity: A Resource Book for Multicultural Education*. Washington, D.C.: Teacher Corps, Association of Teacher Education, 1977.

Goldhammer, Keith. "The Proper Federal Role in Education Today." *Educational Leadership*, 35 (Feb., 1978), 350–53.

Good, Thomas L. *Teachers Make a Difference*. New York: Holt, Rinehart, and Winston, 1975.

Goodill, C. *The Changing Classroom*. New York: Ballantine, 1973.

Goodlad, John I. "Can Our Schools Get Better?" *Phi Delta Kappan*, 60 (Jan., 1979), 43.

———. *The Dynamics of Educational Change*. New York: McGraw-Hill, 1975.

———. *What Schools Are For*. Bloomington, Ind.: Phi Delta Kappa Foundation, 1976.

Greene, Maxine. *The Public School and Private Vision*. New York: Random House, 1965.

Greer, Mary, and Bonnie Rubinstein. *Will the Real Teacher Please Stand Up?* Santa Monica, Calif.: Goodyear Publishing Company, 1978.

Gross, Beatrice. *Teaching Under Pressure*. Santa Monica, Calif.: Goodyear Publishing Company, 1979.

Haney, W., and G. F. Madaus. "Making Sense of the Minimum Competency Movement." *Harvard Educational Review*, 48 (Nov., 1978), 462–82.

Haringhurst, Robert J., and Bernice L. Newgarten. *Society and Education*. 5th ed. Boston: Allyn and Bacon, 1979.

Hechinger, Fred M. "Growing Up in America." In *This We Believe*. Washington, D.C.: National Association of Secondary School Principals, 1976.

Heinemann, Alison. "Module 6: Underachievers Among the Gifted/Talented." In *STAR Power: Providing for the Gifted*. Austin, Tex.: Educational Service Center, Region XIII, 1977.

Henson, Kenneth T. "Emerging Student Rights." *Journal of Teacher Education*, 30 (July–Aug., 1979), 33–34.

————. "Humanizing the Classroom." *The High School Journal*, 59 (Dec., 1975), 144–47.

————. "A New Concept of Discipline." *The Clearing House*, 41 (Oct., 1977), 89–91.

————. *Secondary Teaching Methods*. Lexington, Mass.: D. C. Heath and Company, 1981.

Henson, Kenneth T., and James E. Higgins. *Personalizing Teaching in the Elementary School*. Columbus, Ohio: Charles E. Merrill Publishing Company, 1978.

Herndon, James. *The Way It Spozed to Be*. New York: Simon and Schuster, 1975.

Hodgkinson, Harold. "What's Right with Education." *Phi Delta Kappan*, 61 (Nov., 1979), 159–62.

Holt, John. *Freedom and Beyond*. New York: Dutton, 1974.

————. *How Children Fail*. New York: Pitman, 1975.

Jackson, Phillip W. *Life in Classrooms*. New York: Holt, Rinehart and Winston, 1968.

Johnson, H. C., Jr. "Some Reflections on Educational Reform," *The Educational Forum*, 38 (Nov., 1973), 85–92.

Johnson, S. M. "Performance Based Staff Layoffs in the Public Schools: Implementation and Outcomes." *Harvard Educational Review*, 50 (May, 1980), 214–33.

Jones, Alan. *Students Don't Push the Teachers Down the Stairs on Friday*. Baltimore: Penguin Books, Inc., 1973.

Jose, N. L., and G. E. Richardson. "Ageism: Need We Discriminate?" *Journal of School Health*, 50 (Sept., 1980), 419–21.

Kamber, V. S. "Protecting Workers' Rights." *USA Today*, 109 (Sept., 1980), 49–50.

Keyes, Ralph. *Is There Life After High School?* Boston: Little, Brown, 1976.

King, Edmund J. *Other Schools and Ours*. New York: Holt, Rinehart, and Winston, 1979.

Kirst, Michael. "The New Politics of State Education Finance." *Phi Delta Kappan*, 60 (Feb., 1979), 427–32.

Knoblock, Peter, and Arnold P. Goldstein. *The Lonely Teachers*. Boston: Allyn and Bacon, 1971.

Koerner, J. D. *Who Controls American Education?* Boston: Beacon Press, 1968.

Kohl, Herbert R. "Developing and Sustaining New Schools." In *Innovations in Education: Reformers and Their Critics,* edited by John M. Rich. 3rd ed. Boston: Allyn and Bacon, Inc., 1981.

————. *Thirty-Six Children.* New York: Norton, 1968.

Kozol, Jonathan. *Death at an Early Age.* Boston: Houghton Mifflin, 1967.

L'Abata, L., and L. T. Curtis. *Teaching the Exceptional Child.* Philadelphia: W. B. Saunders Company, 1975.

Laurie, E. *How to Change the Schools: A Parent's Handbook on How to Fight the System.* New York: Random House, 1970.

Lembo, T. *Why Teachers Fail.* Columbus, Ohio: Charles E. Merrill, 1971.

Lewis, J. B. "Freedom of Speech and Expression in the Public School: A Closer Look at Teachers' Rights." *High School Journal,* 63 (Jan., 1980), 137–45.

Loeb, J. W. "Effectiveness of Affirmative Action for Women." *Journal of Higher Education,* 49 (May–June, 1978), 218–30.

Long, James D., and Virginia H. Frye. *Making It till Friday.* Princeton, N.J.: Princeton Book Company, 1977.

Love, Harold D. *Educating Exceptional Children in a Changing Society.* Springfield, Ill.: Charles C. Thomas Publishers, 1974.

Mace, Jane. "Teaching May Be Hazardous to Your Health." *Phi Delta Kappan,* 60 (Mar. 1979), 512–13.

Mahon, J. P. "Giving Reasons for Terminating Employees: Principal Explains Why." *NASSP Bulletin,* 63 (Dec., 1979), 35–42.

Middleton, R. T. "Recent Mississippi Decision Affects Education and Women's Rights." *Negro Education Review,* 30 (Jan., 1979), 47–52.

Mitzman, B. "Is Minimum Competency Flunking Its Test?" *Learning,* 7 (Nov., 1978), 98–101.

Nagi, Mostafah, and Meredith D. Pugh. "Status Inconsistency and Professional Militancy in the Teaching Profession." *Education and Urban Society,* 5, no. 4 (Aug., 1973), 385–404.

National Center for Education Statistics. *The Condition of Education.* 1976 Edition. Washington, D.C.: Government Printing Office, 1978.

————. *Projections of Education Statistics to 1981–1987.* Washington, D.C.: Government Printing Office, 1978.

————. *Students and Schools.* Washington, D.C.: Government Printing Office, 1979.

NEA Reporter, 18, no. 4 (May–June, 1979), 4–5.

NEA Research. "School Violence." *Today's Education,* 67, no. 1 (Feb.–Mar., 1978), 16.

————. *Status of the American Public School Teacher, 1970–1971.* Washington, D.C.: National Education Association, 1972.

"L. A. Schools Set Goals to End Sex Bias" (Newsfront). *Phi Delta Kappan,* 62, no. 2 (Oct., 1980), 83–84.

Nolte, M. C. "Thinking of Firing a Teacher? Before You Act, Carefully Read This." *American School Board Journal,* 166 (Nov., 1979), 45.

Olivia, Peter F., and Kenneth T. Henson. "What Are the Essential Generic Teaching Competencies?" *Theory Into Practice,* 19, no. 2 (Spring, 1980), 117–21.

Parker, Franklin. *The Battle of the Schools: Kanawa County.* Bloomington, Ind.: Phi Delta Kappa Foundation, 1975.

Passow, A. Harry, ed. *The Gifted and the Talented: Their Education and Development.* 78th yearbook, part I. Chicago: National Society for the Study of Education, 1979.

Perkinson, Henry J., ed. *Two Hundred Years of American Educational Thought.* New York: David McKay, 1976.

Peseau, Bruce, and Paul Orr. "The Outrageous Underfunding of Teacher Education." *Phi Delta Kappan,* 62, no. 2 (Oct., 1980), 100–02.

Reynolds, Mary C., and Jack W. Birch. *Teaching Exceptional Children in All America's Schools.* Reston, Va.: The Council for Exceptional Children, 1977.

Rich, John Martin. *Innovations in Education: Reformers and Their Critics.* 3rd ed. Boston: Allyn and Bacon, Inc., 1981.

Rodger, Frederick A. "Past and Future of Teaching: You've Come a Long Way." *Educational Leadership,* 33 (Jan., 1976), 282–86.

Rubin, Louis J., ed. *Facts and Feelings in the Classroom.* New York: Walker and Company, 1973.

Ryans, D. G. *Characteristics of Teachers.* Washington, D.C.: American Council on Education, 1960.

Safer, D. "Socioeconomic Factors Influencing the Rate of Non-Promotion in Elementary Schools." *Peabody Journal of Education,* 54 (July, 1977), 275–81.

Schimmel, David. "To Speak Out Freely: Do Teachers Have the Right?" *Phi Delta Kappan,* 54, no. 8 (Dec., 1972), 258–60.

Shane, Harold G. *Curriculum Change Toward the 21st Century?* Washington, D.C.: National Education Association, 1977.

———. "A Curriculum for the New Century." *Phi Delta Kappan,* 62, no. 5 (Jan., 1981), 351–55.

Sharp, D. Louise. *Why Teach?* New York: Holt, Rinehart, and Winston, 1957.

Silberman, Charles E. *Crisis in the Classroom.* New York: Random House, 1970.

Smith, Vernon; Robert Barr; and Daniel Burke. *Alternatives in Education: Freedom to Choose.* Bloomington, Ind.: Phi Delta Kappa, 1976.

Stanley, Julian C.; William C. George; and H. Cicilia. *The Gifted and the Creative: Fifty Year Perspective.* Baltimore: Johns Hopkins University Press, 1977.

Stinnett, T. M. *Professional Problems of Teachers.* New York: Macmillan, 1968.

———, ed. *The Teacher Drop-Out.* Itasca, Ill.: F. E. Peacock Publishers, 1970.

Stinnett, T. M.; William H. Drummond; and Alice W. Garry. *Introduction to Teaching*. Worthington, Ohio: Charles A. Jones Publishing Company, 1975.

Stuart, Jesse. *To Teach, to Love*. New York: Penguin Books, 1973.

Tanner, Laurel N. *Classroom Discipline for Effective Teaching and Learning*. New York: Holt, Rinehart, and Winston, 1978.

Taylor, B. L. "Effects of Minimum Competencies on Promotion Standards." *Educational Leadership*, 36 (Oct., 1978), 23–26.

"Tests on Trial in Florida." *Time* 114, no. 5 (July 30, 1979), 66.

Thompson, M. "Because Schools are Burying Social Promotion, Kids Must Perform to Pass." *American School Board Journal*, 166 (Jan., 1979), 30–32.

Travers, Robert M. W., and Jacqueline Dillon. *The Making of a Teacher*. New York: Holt, Rinehart, and Winston, 1975.

Turlington, Ralph D. "Good News from Florida: Our Minimum Competency Program Is Working." *Phi Delta Kappan*, 60 (May, 1979), 649–56.

Tyack, David G., ed. *Turning Points in American Educational History*. Waltham, Mass.: Blaisdell, 1967.

Tyler, Ralph W., et al. "Impact of Minimum Competency Testing in Florida: Panel Report." *Today's Education*, 67 (Sept.–Oct., 1978), 30–36.

Valverde, Leonard A., ed. *Bilingual Education for Latinos*. Washington, D.C.: Association for Supervision and Curriculum Development, 1978.

Weil, Marsha; Bruce Joyce; and Bridget Kluwin. *Personal Models of Teaching*. Englewood Cliffs, N.J.: Prentice-Hall, 1978.

Whitehead, Alfred North. *Aims of Education*. New York: Mentor, 1949.

Whiteside, Marilyn. "School Discipline: The Ongoing Crisis." *The Clearing House*, 49 (Dec., 1975), 160–62.

Wilson, Charles H. *A Teacher Is a Person*. New York: Holt, Rinehart and Winston, 1956.

Wilson, Elizabeth C. *Needed: A New Kind of Teacher*. Bloomington, Ind.: Phi Delta Kappa Foundation, 1973.

Yarbrough, E. G. "Affirmative Action: One Nation Under God . . ." *Man Society Technology*, 39 (May–June, 1980), 9.

Subject Index

Name Index

317